Kiss Daddy
Goodnight

Kiss Daddy Goodnight

A SPEAK-OUT ON INCEST

Louise Armstrong

HAWTHORN BOOKS, INC.
Publishers/New York
A Howard & Wyndham Company

Contents

Acknowledgments

For their patience, their willingness to share their views and experience with me, I would very much like to thank:

Lucy Berliner, social worker, Sexual Assault Center, Harborview Medical Center, Seattle, Washington.

Dr. Diane Browning, Department of Psychiatry, University of Oregon Health Sciences Center, Eugene, Oregon.

James Cameron, Director, Child Protective Services for New York State, Dept. of Social Services, Albany, N.Y.

Peter Coleman, coordinator of Child Protective Services Incest Program, Tacoma, Washington.

Michael K. Corey, Assistant Director, Child Protection, American Humane Association, Englewood, Colorado.

Raylene DeVine, Children's Hospital National Medical Center, Child Protection Center, Washington, D.C.

David Finkelhor, graduate student in social work, University of New Hampshire.

Henry Giaretto, Director, and Bill Munday, counselor, Child Sexual Abuse Treatment Program/Parents United, San Jose, California.

Kee Hall, Program Director, National Center on Child Abuse and Neglect, Washington, D.C.

Ruth Humphrey, Executive Director, Task Force for Child Protection, Inc., Poughkeepsie, New York.

C. Henry Kempe, M.D., Director, and Pat Beezley, Assistant Director, National Center for Prevention and Treatment of Child Abuse and Neglect, Denver, Colorado.

Dr. Ira S. Lourie, Deputy Chief, Center for Studies of Child and Family Mental Health, National Institute of Mental Health, Rockville, Maryland.

Mike Nunno, Family Life Development Center, Cornell University, Ithaca, New York.

Florence Rush, author and social worker.

Frank Schneiger, Executive Director, Protective Services Resource Institute, Rutgers Medical School, Piscataway, New Jersey.

Maddi-Jane Stern, Director of Social Services, Center for Rape Concern, Philadelphia, Pennsylvania.

Bennie Stoval, coordinator of Child Sexual Abuse Division, Children's Aid Society, Detroit, Michigan.

Roland Summit, M.D., psychiatrist, founding member of Parents' Anonymous Board of Directors, and ongoing consultant to children's service units, Los Angeles, California.

James Walsh and Janet Geller, Victims' Information Bureau of Suffolk (VIBS), Hauppaugue, New York.

Mary Wells, Co-Executive Director, Family Services of Burlington County, Mt. Holly, New Jersey.

Dr. Alexander G. Zaphiris, professor, Graduate School of Social Work, University of Denver.

Kiss Daddy
Goodnight

My Father. Me

During my early school years, I held an almost belligerent belief in the magical powers of fathers—all direct personal evidence to the contrary.

Other girls' fathers were shadowy figures. When they returned home for dinner, I'd have to leave off trading comics and go. But I knew those fathers lay behind some marvelous main events. It was fathers, I knew, who made Christmas happen in the way that no single, working mother—committed to galoshes and sensible sweaters, struggling to meet the rent, buy and cook the food—ever could. I knew, it's true, that fathers held an awesome power of approval over report cards. But my report card was good. I was ready anytime.

No. Direct personal evidence was beside the point. The fact that *my* father—remembered by me at six, at eight, as large, mercurial, dramatic, erratic—was absent was surely explainable. Must be correctable.

Most of my friends were uneasy at my incomplete condition and, with the bits and pieces of information I'd gathered, I construed different stories to relieve their disquiet.

"Don't you *have* a daddy?"
"Oh yes I do."

"Well, where is he?"
"He's a famous newspaper correspondent."
"Well, why isn't he here?"
"Well, because he can't be. He's very busy."

I was eleven when my father reentered my life. My mother had already scrounged enough to put me in boarding school where, at least, I would not be a latchkey kid after three o'clock. The word came by phone that he was back, that they were driving up to see me. They had something to tell me.

I knew, standing and waiting that Saturday on the vast, fresh school lawn, what it was. They were going to get married again. That was thrilling. Tall, though not quite as tall as I'd remembered, he stretched out of the car with a great grin, arms wide, inviting.

"We're going to have a real home," he said. "All four of us!"

The unwelcome fourth was a nine-month-old baby whose mother, his last wife, had died.

That winter, at boarding school, I got pneumonia twice, once by sitting in a large snowdrift for a long time. With pneumonia you got to go home. And check up on things.

I'd figured it right, though. That kid was getting a lot of attention.

I turned twelve. All the other girls had what they called the curse.

His summer plans were to drive to New Mexico. He was to do publicity work for a summer theater there. I was invited along. I was actually invited along. Of course I was also being invited to leave my mother home minding that kid. But she did think I should go—and get out of the city—and get to know my father better. If she wanted me to go and I was invited. . . .

"As long as you act adult. I don't want a kid hanging on me all day. I won't have time for that."

Of course, act adult. What else?

He had a Chevy coupe. Watching the road going by, the world going by, I fell into a trance. I came to believe I could tell the exact spot where one state turned into another without looking at signs. Pennsylvania. Snap. Ohio.

We lunched at roadside inns. The juke boxes were playing "On

Top of Old Smokey." In the car, he lit Lucky Strikes and talked about a play he was writing. A romantic comedy about his last wife—this beautiful, waiflike, delicate person who. . . . I was on stage. He talked the plot, the scenes. I was sure of it. I could bring off every one of those scenes brilliantly. In my mind, I brought down the house.

In an Oklahoma motel, we shared a double bed. I woke restless, crampy. In the bathroom, I discovered I'd started to bleed. Acting adult, I waited till morning in the bathroom. Then, wadding up lots of toilet paper and praying it would stay in place, I emerged and, very adultly, indicated it might be best if we found a drugstore. Oh. And then a gas station.

In Santa Fe, some days I tagged after him: to the theater; on jeep trips with one of his friends—the cripple who smelled bad and was writing a book, or the alcoholic painter whose work featured faces on stems in jars. Other days he snapped at me to act adult, to go off on my own. Then I would follow dried-out arroyos to see where they went and fret about getting lost.

Eventually though, acting adult made me cranky. Obviously, it made him cranky too. He could not decide which of the two rooms he preferred for his. The living room, which one entered straightaway from outside, had only a daybed. The bedroom beyond that, however, had a nice cushy double bed—and the only bathroom, attached. If he kept the living room, he could conveniently have his new girl friend over at night (and save himself having to deal with her wild, half-breed children and alcoholic mother). On the other hand, there was no denying the comforts of the double bed. Invoking his right, as a grown-up, to choose, he chose one and then the other and then back again.

One morning, while the bedroom was his, I unthinkingly started through, to use the bathroom. My mind's eye photographed him naked, just stepping into his shorts as I quickly backed out. How long after that was it that he climbed into the daybed with me and began fondling my breasts? In completely unformulated discomfort, I wriggled away and feigned sleep.

I wanted my mother. I flew home alone.

One year later, I was still in boarding school when I learned he had taken that kid—claiming my mother was alienating him as she'd alienated me—and he'd left.

But not for long. We were installed in a midtown apartment. I was in high school in the city. He and the kid were back, living in a hotel, just two blocks away.

Now, truly, came a good opportunity for me to get to know my father better. ("I really think it would be *nice* for you to get to know him better," my mother would say.) A publicity job required him to go to Pennsylvania for the weekend. It was spring. The weather was fine and, once again, what a good idea that I go. At this time, I must say, I did not remember the New Mexico trip in its particulars. I simply didn't.

I was by now a committed sophisticate. A dedicated cynic. Hours had been spent swallowing the words of *The Threepenny Opera* and spitting them out again.

I saw my father now as a glamorous figure who got free theater tickets and would sometimes invite me along. (In the theater, he'd sit, fingertips touching supporting his chin, a man who *knew*.) A ·man with a marvelous sense of mischief, who appeared to play tricks on the world. A man who would sometimes take me to very grown-up places—like Toots Shors. Someone who recognized, and was recognized by, people one had *heard* of.

Saturday. An early drive to Lancaster. There, he took me to a store and bought me some clothes. Older-woman clothes. He shopped with command, getting quick attention, making rapid selections, not looking at price tags. Later in the day, I was used as a glamorous model in the amorous publicity photos which were part of the assignment.

At dinner we talked *a deux* (I was taking French)—like grown-ups. And, like a grown-up, I told him carelessly that, since he asked, yes, I had slept with a fellow recently for the first time. (I carefully did not tell him that "slept with" had, in this case, been a technically accurate description. I don't think I really knew that then.)

("All women," he wrote to me in one of his later letters, "are either old maids or whores." Was that the moment when I fell into my proper category?)

Once again that night I discovered we were to share a room. This time there were separate beds.

As he put stuff away, settled us in (he was a hotel person; he unpacked the few overnight things we'd brought and put them carefully in drawers as though we faced a week's stay), he told tales of bisexuality among the theatrically famous, which I supposed to be droll, so I laughed.

I was nervous. I'd have laughed at anything.

I knew what was in the air. A will-he, won't-he charge. But did I know what was in my mind? What I wanted? No. Or at least I didn't know then the important thing in my mind, which was that (at fourteen) I wanted to be held—by my daddy. The way six-year-olds are.

Nevertheless, what I got in the end, just as I was finally, definitely, decidedly in my own bed and drifting off to sleep, was oral rape.

But surely, at fourteen, I should have been capable of escaping, of preventing that. Of screaming, perhaps? Or, as one psychiatrist put it, of *biting*? Damn right.

And I would have been, too, you bet, if I hadn't so carefully preserved a portion of my kid-self, wrapped nicely in tissue paper. That portion which held as tightly to a belief in the magical powers of fathers as to a stuffed animal.

It was time.

More than ten years had passed since my father's death. I'd come a long distance; had long lost the dailiness of my sense of trust violated; had scrapped the flashbacks, the gross physical memory.

Even I, raised by a liberal mother, without notions of "tainted," without the virgin/whore burden, had found the attack, the betrayal, a horror to deal with. What about others?

If I'd never been particularly ashamed of myself—what of those who, on top of the sexual insult, bought the societal assumption of shame? The incest "dread?"

Even I—who had friends to whom I felt I could say anything. When I said, "My father chased me around a hotel room," I found them uncomfortable, blank. No one ever asked, "Did he catch you?" Rather, the room shifted, recrossed its legs, tapped its fingers on the table and—changed the subject.

Now wait a minute, folks. Why?
Because you don't talk about it.
Why?
Because it's taboo.
Why?

R. E. L. Masters effectively pokes holes in the many theories that have been proposed in the incest taboo–origin parlor game over the years. He says,

> Of all the arguments to be presented against incest (where no coercion or exploitation is present), this one seems the most forceful: The family would be disrupted, and in some cases, destroyed, were its members permitted sexual access to one another.
>
> Sexual rivalries, with consequent hatreds, would spring up in some cases. Incentives to exploitation would be maximal, deterrents minimal. Roles within the family would be confused and discipline would be difficult or impossible to impose. The always-precarious harmony of the family unit could not survive the tension.*

Let's leave aside the "where no coercion or exploitation is present," for a moment. Let's ask again, why "taboo?"

Nothing else is taboo except cannibalism—and that seems more like an aesthetic taboo. I think we don't believe we'd taste very good.

Most things that seriously threaten us are called wrong, against the law. What's the bogey-bogey business about incest—about specifically, sexual abuse of a child by a needed and trusted parent? (Consanguinity—sexual relations or marriage between related, consenting adults—can go find itself another word to live under.) It's a moral issue? So is murder.

It certainly *happens*. What people now call stats say so. The National Center on Child Abuse estimates that in 1976, 12 percent of the over one million reported child abuse cases were cases of sexual abuse. Most of the children abused were girls.

---

*R. E. L. Masters, *Patterns of Incest*, p. 60.

Most were abused by members of their own family, by fathers and stepfathers.

The consensus is that these figures, based only on *reported* instances, are way, way low. (Some estimates suggest that there are twenty-five million women in this country who have been sexually abused by their fathers.)

What kind of a working taboo has such a high incidence of violation? It is in the nature of a real, serious, taboo that it carries the full weight of a truly believed superstition: the dread certainty of discovery and horrendous punishment. A true taboo is a true deterrent.

Sexual abuse of child by parent, it would seem, then, is not a taboo.

Talking about it is the taboo. Why?

You just don't say such things.

Phooey. If you can say diarrhea, you can *say* incest. (It's sure easier to spell.)

I found two opposite and violent reactions when I spoke of incest to people.

1. Horror—fear, really.

2. So? What's so bad about it? It's a form of affection.

Both of those reactions certainly foster the continuation of incest. If you can't talk about it, you can't tell. If you don't tell, it won't stop. (And, obviously, if it's OK, it's OK.)

It's almost as though, if we do talk about it, someone's game will be in jeopardy. Almost as though a commonsense, listening-based awareness might blow the whole thing. When people understand that incest isn't *incest*, it's daddy diddling Susie under the covers, isn't daddy going to feel a little sheepish?

It was time to take a journey among other women who'd had an incest experience. It was time to talk.

After I'd dealt with one small problem.

First I'd have to tell my mother.

On the phone, between the details of a lunch with a friend and complaints about the weather, I slipped in the fact that there was news.

"Good?"

"Well, and bad. No, I'll tell you in person."

By the time she arrived, my mind was locked, frazzled. (Even mothers who become good friends retain the power to make us feel miserable children again.) Imagination, dread, had gained hold in me. And in her as well.

"What's the bad news?"

First thing. Before the coat came off.

"The story can't be told that way. I have to give you the good news first." Book. Contract. Good, good, wonderful . . . impatience.

"What's it about?"

That's the bad news. See, there's something I neglected to mention to you awhile back when I was and so forth and so on. . . .

Slowly, slyly, she looked relieved. No terminal diseases were being reported. Nothing in the present, in the immediate future, was changed, threatened. A glint. A thoughtful listening. Then:

"You know, dear—I never did trust that man."

Two days later, she phoned.

"Dear? I've been thinking about it."

I'd been worrying she'd do that. Flak now, perhaps?

"You know, after all—when you get right down to it I suppose it goes on fairly often. I suppose, really, it's a matter of control. And—I guess—some men just have more control than others."

No tears. No screams.

Still, I was uneasy. As it turned out, I was right to be.

It's Natural

Why did he do it? That's what my mind threw up to me for a long time. Not why did he want to. What turned the impulse to act? "It's natural," he kept saying. "It's perfectly natural." And, indeed, if *natural* means a common human impulse commonly acted upon, I suppose he might have been right.

But if the adage holds that all little girls try out their charms on their daddies, are all daddies tempted to respond?

I first ran into Pete at a party nearly two years ago. His daughter had just turned twelve. He was tremendously proud of her and eager to talk. His manner was immediate, candid. So, after a short hesitation, I ventured to ask whether his feelings toward her had changed recently, as she became adolescent.

A sudden, surprised look was followed by interest, a nod.

"Yeah. Well, you know, we were always very physical," he said. "Kidding around and wrestling. See I'm very into sports. My daughter's a terrific pitcher—I worry she's going to throw her shoulder out sometime. Always very open, we talk about everything.

"And I'm not the kind who has the television set in the living room. We have it in the bedroom. So always my daughter would be on the bed with me. And during the commercials we'd wrestle.

Kidding. She'd jump on me. I'd jump on her. She's built just like my wife. When my daughter is lying on her stomach, you can't tell the difference.

"Fun. But a year or so ago I realized—she wasn't a kid anymore. She's mature. I mean we'd be wrestling and I'd grab her breast. The first time I did that and I was enjoying it—I was getting aroused—I got, not frightened, confused. I think she noticed it. Yeah. I think she did.

"And you know, she's doing sit-ups and I'm holding her. Or I'm doing sit-ups, she's holding me. There's a lot of contact, physical contact. But that first time I fully realized—this isn't a little girl, this is a woman. And I got aroused. And I didn't know what was going down.

"You can see sometimes my daughter gets jealous. There's competition between her and my wife. If I'm paying a lot of attention to my wife, she'll come in and snuggle, kind of play. She's tremendously feminine. Very tough but not tough at all—very feminine really.

"But I can control myself. We've been married thirteen years. I've never had another woman, had any interest. There've been opportunities. Some guys prove themselves that way.

"Sure I think my daughter's testing me. She's testing me to see if she's really a woman. And she's finding out that she is.

"She wants my approval. I think that's why she's such a good pitcher. She knows I'm into sports."

When we talked recently, Pete had this to say:

"We still kid around, yeah. Only I'm a bit more careful. But not cold. I don't think it would be fair to her to suddenly completely change the relationship. That would be a rejection. But I'm just more aware that I'm the adult. I'm in charge of whether I control myself, control the situation."

Pete, I found, was not unique. I talked with Bob, a psychology professor at a small university. He has two daughters—one thirteen, one eight.

"I see my adolescent daughter in many ways as an uncanny replica of my wife, and I find myself playing out affections toward her as I do toward my wife. And I feel that if my wife were rejecting me at this time, I would be very vulnerable to the strong support my daughter gives. If my wife were punishing Annie for what she is doing, I would be defending Annie and alienating my wife further. Then we would have a war going in which Annie would be the best person in the world to console me. See, it's clear that she is separating from her mother at this point by finding ways to demean and discredit her, to feel more independent and grown-up herself.

"Now my eight-year-old, Pat, crawls around on me and rubs her body against me. She is still doing that as a continuation of what she has done since infancy. She would hold and cuddle and rub around on you as much as you would let her. She is sensually insatiable. If I had a pedophilic kind of response, if I saw her need for touching as sexual, there would be no trick at all in indulging that. I would be responding to her. I wouldn't be initiating anything with her.

"But I am the parent Annie flirts with. I'm just a prototype male for her at this point, besides being a nice guy and the source of good times for all. But to act on her openness would be the ultimate betrayal. I only say that at this moment she is very vulnerable to being led into a more physical relationship than would be good for her. She is not in a position to see the long-range effects of that. And I think it would be damaging or competitive with the growth that she has got to make toward peers and toward developing a more honest reflection of who she is and what her attraction is.

"I guess one way of thinking about it is that my associations are less based on my experience with little kids, with my children, and more reminiscent of my experiences with girl friends as an adolescent. Now that's a key.

"She feels like my clear, tactile memory of adolescent girls. And I haven't had access to an adolescent girl since I was an adolescent.

"And the physical side then was very exciting, partly within a context of newness and discovery. Doing things for the first time. And that's something you can never recapture again, except by trying to replay it with someone symbolically in the same place.

"I'm certainly aware that there are people who believe that a level of modesty is really kind of sick. And you ought to share with your kids a much more open, natural feeling. But I run into a problem with that. It is simply too important that we hold the dividing line between parents and children.

"You see, we are all so close. We have all long ago developed our endorsement of one another. And it is very easy to make that feeling more intimate. But it's that very endorsement it seems to me that we very much need in a complex world. We very much need good friends, a feeling that there are people we can trust. And when every good friendship—when every relationship that feels reliable to us—turns quickly into a sexual exploitation, that's very embittering."

An old friend, a psychiatrist, was in town to attend a conference. We had lunch. Having caught up on events, I broached the question. His girls were now grown. How had he responded to them as they'd entered adolescence? Had there been any sexual attraction?

"No," he said. "No." He paused a moment as we emerged onto the street. "I completely repressed it. I would never have allowed myself to think anything like that." He was quiet as we walked to the corner, and I sensed I'd raised something awkward. I was sorry.

"You know," he said just before we parted, "as a matter of fact, my wife used to say, 'Sally's getting to that age when she needs some special attention from you. Why don't you take her out alone to the movies or for a soda?'

"And I wouldn't. I never would."

Still the question lay inert, lumpen. Why did my father *do* it?
Hey, dad, why?
Oh, for godsake. What a fuss about nothing. You were fourteen. You're not going to tell me teenagers aren't sexual.
Is it tacky to say—you were my father?
Oh, look. I told you at the time it was perfectly natural. Besides, look it up. Use your brain. You'll find it's perfectly natural in nature. And some native cultures certainly encourage it.

Since when do we emulate animals and savages?

You know, for someone with a sense of humor you're being awfully gloomy. The trouble with most of you women is you just won't admit that at fourteen you enjoyed it.

The funny thing about it, daddy, is many, many of us weren't fourteen when it happened.

Our Brazen Poise

I am a woman writer doing a first-person, documentary book on incest. I am looking for others who have had an actual or near-actual incest experience to participate in my "forum.". . .

Others. How many other women were there? What did we share besides our silence, our secret? What were our feelings at the time? Later? Did we have common stages of recovery? How many of us had managed to seal the experience off in a tomb? Could anyone do that forever? Or did it always breed enough noxious gas to explode? Was it, ever, a neutral experience? Was the effect related to the degree of assault?

I worried a morbid thought: I was going to find that, after all, I was the only one in the world this had happened to.

"Dear Louise:

"I feel my letter is proof that there is help and at least partial recovery for incest victims. I am thirty-four years old and could not until this year have lifted a pen (or struck a key) to write about a subject that has always been painful for me, let alone 'admit' my experience.

"My first recalled incestual assault was at age three with my father and continued until age six when my mother finally left and took us one thousand miles away, much to my relief. When I was seven, she remarried. Although this marriage lasted only three months, I remember being used by my stepfather much of that time.

"I kept the memory of these experiences inside for the first twenty years of my life. I prayed day and night that by the time I was a teenager the memory would be gone from me and I could finally have freedom through amnesia. But once a teenager, I realized I would have to live with the memory—it would never leave.

"I think I intuitively knew it was not a natural experience that had happened to me. And because such subjects were still in the closet in those days, there was nothing for me to read in order to get information. But I knew somehow that I was different from other kids, felt I was tainted, and that something was wrong with me forever. It was like invisible scars from a childhood disease. . . ."

"Dear Louise:
"Don't like to talk about it—think about it—although I am now a grandmother. I was only five. My mother caught my father in the act . . . she had hysterics and threw him out of the house. They were separated after that. . . . During the years that I grew up I saw my father only briefly off and on. . . . She never left me alone with him until I was about fifteen. And then it nearly happened again. Only this time I avoided the encounter by quickly moving out of the room. In both instances I was terrified. I remember the feelings much more than the *act*. It was so horrendous and frightening that I had a hard time telling my analyst about it thirty years later. He wasn't much good, being a Freudian from the ground up, and I had the feeling that he really sympathized with my father and thought I made it up. Do you want further comments? Like how I hated my father? How I was glad when he died? How I felt as though a burden of unbelievable *guilt* was lifted from me when he died? Now, I thought to myself, no one will *ever* know. Perhaps this will help someone else."

"Dear Louise:

"I can't remember the exact age I was when things started to happen, but it was somewhere around four or five. . . ."

Age three. Age four. Age five. So.

A great, great many of these sexual insults were directed at little kids, not at plump and juicy (if poorly adjusted) sex objects like I was. At little, little kids.

Knowing this, as I began to talk to psychiatrists and to poke around in the literature on incest, I began to feel like a witness at the tribunal called by the Red Queen. With a few reassuring exceptions, "they" seemed to feel that our survival was proof that we got what we wanted. And our failure to survive was proof that we were defective merchandise to begin with.

Everywhere I turned I ran into quotes from a paper, "The Reaction of Children to Sexual Relations with Adults," written in the 1930s.

> The most remarkable feature presented by these children who have experienced sexual relations with adults was that they showed less evidence of fear, anxiety, guilt or psychic trauma than might be expected. . . .
>
> The probation reports from the court frequently remarked about their brazen poise, which was interpreted as an especially inexcusable and deplorable attitude and one indicating their fundamental incorrigibility. . . .
>
> The few studies that have been made of this subject have been contented to consider it an example of adult sex perversion from which innocent children must be protected by proper legal measures. Although this attitude may be correct in some cases, certain features in our material would indicate that the children may not resist and often play an active or even initiating role.*

Not only that, but we "do not deserve completely the cloak of innocence with which [we] have been endowed by moralists,

*L. Bender and A. Blau, "The Reaction of Children to Sexual Relations with Adults," pp. 500–518.

social reformers and legislators." If we say daddy threatened to
break both our legs if we didn't do it, or if we told, Bender and
Blau observe, "the child often rationalized with excuses of fear of
physical harm or the enticement of gifts, but these were obviously
secondary reasons. Even in the cases in which physical force may
have been applied by the adult, this did not wholly account for the
frequent repetition of the practice." No ma'am. The only possible
accounting is that we tried it, we liked it.

Not only that but you can tell it was nontraumatic because
some of us survived. They quote the findings of Rasmussen on the
aftereffects: "Forty-six of the [fifty-four] victims seemed none the
worse for the experience; many of them at the time of the survey
were married and had children, and several were stolid and com-
mendable members of the community."*

> I told you you were making a big fuss over nothing.
> Oh, daddy. Shut up.

The other prevalent professional attitude toward us, of course,
has been that it was all a fantasy. We just wished incest would
happen. And we imagined the lurid details.

The late Dr. Joseph J. Peters was director of the Sex Offender
and Rape Victim Center of Philadelphia General Hospital and
associate clinical professor of psychiatry at the University of
Pennsylvania. He prefaced a paper he presented to the Association for the Advancement of Psychotherapy in 1975** with:

> Psychiatrists and others have too often discounted reports of
> sexual attacks upon children and ascribed the incident to fan-
> tasy. The author's experience in private psychoanalytic prac-
> tice and in Philadelphia's rape victim clinics indicates that
> these assaults occur frequently. If the sexual attack is dealt
> with improperly or repressed it may cause serious psycho-
> logic problems for the victim as an adult.

He placed part of the blame for professionals' disbelief of
women reporting early sexual abuse by fathers on the Vienna

---

*Ibid.
**J. J. Peters, "Children Who Are Victims of Sexual Assault and the Psychology
of Offenders," pp. 398–421.

doorstep of Sigmund Freud. Freud and Breuer's *Studies on Hysteria** was the first work to connect hysterical symptoms with actual childhood sexual trauma—a thesis received with considerable lack of enthusiasm by their professional colleagues. As Dr. Peters put it: "Even Freud . . . was having difficulty accepting the full impact of the discoveries concerning childhood sexual trauma, particularly when it was a question of incest."**

Freud himself, after all, had a daughter. And by 1924 he had managed to replace actual childhood sexual trauma with "infantile fantasies." The Oedipus/Electra complex.

Dr. Peters sums up:

> Both cultural and personal factors combined to cause everyone, including Freud himself at times, to welcome the idea that reports of childhood sexual victimization could be regarded as fantasies. This position relieved the guilt of adults . . . both Freud and his followers oversubscribed to the theory of childhood fantasy and overlooked incidents of the actual sexual victimization in childhood.
>
> In their aversion to what are often repulsive details, psychotherapists allowed and continue to allow their patients to repress emotionally significant, pathogenic facts. . . . In addition . . . because the reported offender was frequently the patient's own father, in order to avoid the fact of incest, our colleagues seized upon the easier assumption that the occurrences were oedipal fantasies.†

And went off, as Dr. Peters puts it, on "oedipal wild goose chases."

In quest of more average shrink-on-the-street testimony, I called an ex-psychiatrist of mine.

"No," he said. "Can't help. Never had a case."

"Except me?"

"Oh," he said. "Yeah."

I called another psychiatrist.

---

*J. Breuer and S. Freud, "Studies on Hysteria (1893–1895)."
**Peters, "Children Who Are Victims," pp. 398–421.
†Ibid.

"Incest," he said, "occurs at the onset of puberty."

"But," I said, "so many of the women I'm hearing from—for them it began at four, five, six."

"Did you call me as an expert?" he said. "Or did you call me to argue?"

I tried again, this time a psychotherapist.

"It's completely individual in effect," said Dr. Wilbert Sykes. "It's what each individual does with it. The meaning the experience has to that person."

And that's what I was to begin looking for.

Incest. Victim. Harsh, apocalyptic words. What really happened between homework and cookies? How did we each feel, deal, cope?

The Grisly Details, Part One

Jenny and I were to talk often. Charming and attractive she certainly is (whatever one wants to make of that), but shy on coming out with the grisly details.

"Look, Jenny," I'd say. "I don't want to push you."

"No, really," she'd say. "I just have to make myself do it. It'll just take a little time."

"Well. Maybe you'll find it's not so bad as you think. Words don't bite."

"No. They just nibble a little."

"I seem to be having trouble getting this letter under way [she first wrote], so, after several false starts I have decided to just plow ahead. I hope what results will be useful.

"Early childhood by most standards was pretty ideal. Raised in the midst of an old established family, we had a fairly traditional upbringing. It was very clearly child-centered, and our world was protected to the point of being sheltered. We all had our own childhood battles to fight, but it was safe, and we never doubted that we'd win.

"Basic background stuff included prominent lawyer father, a college professor mother, and three younger brothers. We all did the private day school, summer camp, and boarding school number. I have just finished my third year at a small, liberal arts, women's college.

"The times are hazy. But Daddy had always come by to kiss us good-night. At some point I woke up and realized he was sitting on the side of my bed and had pushed my nightgown up and was just touching me, more or less all over. I foxed sleeping and after a while he left. These visits grew more frequent and longer. He always came in long after I was supposed to be asleep and never spoke. I was always awake when he arrived although I was pretending to be asleep (I wonder now if he knew). These encounters were obviously clandestine, and there were a whole other set of visits, right at bedtime, that were less actively physical, but in some ways more pressured. At these points, Daddy would ask me to do something for him and would be displeased if I balked. In some ways they bothered me more than the other visits, because I was awake and he knew it and I felt therefore responsible.

"During this time, Daddy and I were fighting like cats and dogs—tooth and nail, which at the time I did not connect at all with our evening encounters. By the time I left for boarding school, I couldn't wait to go. Until that time I was deadly afraid of becoming pregnant, because then everybody would know. I never told anybody, but fought with the world—my grades dropped for the first time in my life; I hated my teacher (although that was legitimate in and of itself); I hated school, friends—everything. It took me years to connect all this stuff with Daddy with the time period Mom says I arrived home from school every day in tears (and that she dreaded it).

"Until about a year ago I had no awareness that any of it had happened. I had completely removed it from any form of consciousness. Until that point I had not come near to having a relationship even as close as a best friend. Two years ago I began seeing the college psychologist (generalized dissatisfaction with the way I was leading my life). A year later I came perilously near being close with somebody and was greeted with a rush of memories—flashes of scenes, disconnected and disconcerting. Because so much had happened when I was asleep or half asleep, I had never been sure that all of it had happened, much less how or what or anything else. After almost a year of working at piecing it all together, I'm still blocking most of the sense of it.

"As far as remaining effects, I am just discovering them. I have finally figured out, for example, why, even when I am literally falling asleep at my desk, as soon as I lie down I wake up to the point of being aware of everything going on around me, and stay that way for at least a half hour.

"Or why, coming from a very physical family and enjoying touch as much as I do, I recoil from some sorts of touch (and how surprisingly contingent that is on the sex of the individual). I don't by any means 'hate all men'—I'm just a little leery about them in general and tend to be careful in particular. Learning to accept it, and spend time with my father, knowing it. Dealing with him regardless of it. Learning to let myself enjoy my body, under my own control and choice. Trying to find a place to put the feelings I sense are there and don't want to face. Not throwing it in his face.

"I really want for this to be helpful—I guess because it seems that sharing my experience might have some redeeming value. In a week I leave for California, so further talking must be done before then."

"Hey, Jenny."

"Hi."

"When do you leave?"

"Day after tomorrow."

"You going alone?"

"Nope. Going with a friend. I don't know for how long. I just told Mom and Dad that I'm taking this year off from school. They don't like any of it."

"Your letter was great but—not really clear on the grisly details."

"Um, OK. That is not the easiest part. As far as that goes—I'm not very good at this kind of thing. It takes a little bit for me to get to the point of being able to make myself say those things."

"You never told your mother, though?"

"That was something I just couldn't do. See, I waited a long time because I wasn't positive. I needed time to make sure I wasn't dreaming or exaggerating or anything. It's a very legal-minded family. Everything was done in contracts around the house. We'd make deals about the chores around the house and have to put them in writing. Sometimes it led to hassles because we all learned to catch each other on semantics. So that really taught us how to write a contract and to cover ourselves on all possibilities and anything that might come up. So I had to be sure.

"And then I knew if I told her, she would, for sure, tell him. Because we already knew that she always told him everything. That's the pattern around here. It's always been that way and it stays that way. He comes first—then we come.

"She's a neat lady, though. Very benign. Both she and Daddy spent a lot of time with us, a lot of constructive time. They put a lot of emphasis on doing things with us. We were very clearly a big part of the house. Saturdays, Daddy would take one of us into the office with him. And we'd get to have lunch with him and we'd get to pick something to do after. That was always a big deal. And then Sundays, holidays, we'd all be together. We went to the beach every summer."

"Your parents were happy together?"

"Yeah. There was a lot of vocal dissent in the house, but it was just vocal. Our family's pretty vocal when they're mad, but it blows over quickly. But Mom's happy. She likes living with Daddy and all that good stuff."

"Was your father ever violent, out of control?"

"Un-unh. No. He does not believe in losing control of himself. Neither of my parents does and that's something they emphasized a whole lot. No matter what the circumstances are, we should be able to maintain control of ourselves."

"Do you remember how you dealt with it all at the time?"

"It was not part of my waking day at all. I would remember it when I got in bed and I'd lie down to go to sleep. I would realize that something might happen. And I learned to stay awake for long periods of time—in case. But it was on an irregular basis. Sometimes it would be several nights in a row and sometimes it would be weeks apart. But—on the nights in between, I would decide that I was just making it all up and that it wasn't really happening.

"See, half of it is—if you are sure, then it's your own fault. It may not really be. But that's what I decided at that point. That was a big part of my not saying anything. Because if anything was going on—it was my own fault."

"Could we leap into the *it*?"

"I—I'll tell you what. I'll write it out for you. I'll mail it to you. Promise."

Later that night, Jenny called back.
"There's something I didn't tell you," she said. "And that's not fair. The person I'm going away with? It's a woman."

The Family Album

Sometimes, as with Jenny, the repressed memories appeared to have the effect of a time bomb—ticking quietly, but apparently harmlessly, throughout the dailiness of growing up—then exploding viciously as the girl began her emotional getaway from home.

Other times the memories were buried more deeply. Like a series of land mines, they remained long dormant. Until something, sometimes something apparently neutral, tripped one. And later, even much later, boom. Another went off.

Anna came to me at her daughter's suggestion. Her daughter had recently gone into therapy following a rape by a stranger; a rape that, when Anna learned of it, brought back her own never-talked-about early experience with impact.

"Perhaps," she wrote me, "it would help both of us to talk."

Each object in the small living room of Anna's suburban house has significance, is cared for. The metal sculpture of a bird her son did. ("Isn't that good? It's my Tony's. He's always been artistic.") The dried flowers. ("Aren't they nice? They're from our twenty-fifth wedding anniversary.")

There is force behind her initial cheerfulness and a not-unnatural nervousness. As she said to me later, "I feel like 'This is Your Life.' "

"Let me show you around. See, since the kids have moved out all we need is this small icebox. Here, we're planning to get wall-to-wall carpeting. I like wood floors myself, I always have. They say you shouldn't wash them, but how else are you going to keep them clean? And then they warp. Here, let me show you the den. *Isn't* that nice? That's where we just relax in the evening and watch TV. Here, let me show you the basement. We *finally* finished, we've had such good times down here."

"What a beautiful bar!"

"You like it? I did a lot of the work on it myself."

She turns on the light behind the bar. It says "bar."

"I love the pool table."

"Oh, we have good times with that. We have a couple of friends over. Have a couple of drinks. Play pool. Talk. Sometimes till three, four in the morning. Such good times."

Over ham sandwiches, Anna tells me of their travels, their vacations. She's a trim, smiling woman. And she very, very much wants me to know that she is, now, perfectly happy. She loves her life.

"What are your days like, Anna, now that the kids are grown?"

"Oh, I'm always doing something. A year or two ago, I started doing sewing for people. So if you weren't here today, I'd be sewing. Usually what I try to do is get my sewing out of the way in the daytime. I don't do anything past four o'clock. Then I start my dinner. But I have a lot of good friends and we do things. Play cards. We're all going to see a play soon. Because we put a dollar a week into that. And I fill in as a waitress in the local restaurant. So tomorrow I'll be going in because one waitress has the day off. My Andy, my youngest, said, 'Mom, when your sewing gets in full swing, maybe you can stop doing that.' I said, 'I don't think I would. I like dealing with the public.'

"I have always worked so that I'd never become a recluse and just sit down here and sew. I come down here after I get my house straightened out, about ten, eleven, bring my TV down. I listen to that and do my sewing and then at four o'clock I go up whether it's finished or not. Start my dinner. Read the paper. And I don't see customers nights. If they work, I'd rather have them come on a

Sunday morning because I let my husband, Sam, sleep till twelve or so. And I'm not a sleeper. I'm up early in the morning all of the time. Seven days a week."

"What's Sam like?"

"Sam's a pussycat. That's the only way I can describe him. He's an easygoing guy. He's a good Joe. What else can I say? If I wanted anything, he'd get it for me. He's that kind of a man.

"He's a good egg. And the kids—you know, the relationship they have with him is so great. My kids never answer us back, really. And I don't mean we won't get into heated discussions. That's not what I'm saying. But they have a great deal of respect for us. If there is a special day or if they're going away anywhere or we've returned, they always hug us, kiss us, and I think that's fantastic. I just love it.

"Oh, you know, one thing I was going to do was take out the albums. I want to show you my father, too. And my mother. She was in the hospital more than she was home. She was tubercular. There. That's her—outside a hospital."

We are looking at a sepia photograph of a frail woman, gray haired, with a noncommital expression.

"She would go into the hospital for a year or so at a time. And this is me. I don't want to bore you. And here—I adored my father. I thought there was nobody like him and it's hard to explain. Like I was his favorite. My brother—he didn't do well with my brother. My brother is still affected by this whole childhood experience that he had with my father. I can remember my brother not being able to make the letter *F*. And my father throwing him against the wall. And I'm standing between them and saying, 'Don't hit him any more. If you hit him, you're going to have to hit me.' And he would say, 'Get out of the way or I'm going to hit you.' But he couldn't hit me."

The picture is of a slim-faced man with gray shadowing around suspicious eyes.

"But he was a good-looking man, and he was the kind of a man that I can remember sitting at a sewing machine and making me a skirt for Easter Sunday. You know what I mean—I have tried to rationalize myself why something like this could have happened. Because I know he liked me. He taught me how to dance. He was a very good dancer.

"I don't know what he did years ago when I was young. I do

know that he was in jail. He went to Sing Sing. I was very young then. We lived in the city. I remember a big round-top desk. And my mother used to go out to the store and we used to sit on the table because there were rats in the house. I was maybe four or five years old.

"And we had a railroad apartment. And I remember—it's funny, it's so long ago, but I remember vividly the windows outside. Because we used to sleep on the fire escape when the weather was hot and the living room was there. And I remember the bedroom was behind this air shaft. And I remember too that we had a battery-operated radio. Isn't it funny that you remember such things? I remember for Christmas having a lead cannon that shot little things out of it. Made out of lead. I remember that."

"Was it ever warm, ever happy?"

"No, never, never. Because—my mother always adored my father. But—my father is the kind of a man that was neat about himself and clean, and my mother was the other extreme. She was thirty when they married. He was only twenty or twenty-one. Her mother had died and left her one thousand dollars—so maybe that's why he married her, I don't know. She was nine years older but she couldn't boil water. She was not a housekeeper. She really had nothing going for her at all. Yet I loved her. I mean she was the sweetest woman in the world. She was an Edith Bunker type. Sweet. Never talked about anybody.

"But she never did anything. I can remember most of my life being very annoyed with my mother. I think that's why I have the hang-ups about sleeping. My mother always slept. She used to sleep late in the mornings. And it annoyed me that every time I would come into the house, she was just sleeping. I guess it was her illness—now that I'm older and realize she was a sick woman. But, that—or she'd be playing solitaire. That's how I remember her spending her life—because my father was always out. Always out.

"I remember a woman staying—her name was Florence—I'll never forget that. When we moved again we had this Florence staying with us. And naive the way we were—it never occurred to me to say to my father, 'Why have you got a woman in the house?' Today's children would say that. But not then you didn't.

Your father was your father and your mother was your mother, and he was too radical. too violent.

"I remember I belonged to a club, a teenagers' club, and we used to do the lindy up there. We would have a meeting every Saturday night and all of the boys and girls, like brothers and sisters. There was no hanky-panky going on at all. But there was mistletoe up. And we were dancing and this fellow had a crush on me, and as we danced past the mistletoe, he kissed me and that was it. No big deal. But at that second, the only time my father ever came up there—he came up the stairs. And he punched the fellow all over that place. This is when I was about sixteen, seventeen.

"And here, here I am with Sally, a friend of mine."

Two girls, pretty, giggling self-consciously, sharing some joke, looking sidewise at the camera.

"Now there. That says 1936. I was born in 1922—so I was fourteen.

"But here. The reason I'm looking at my friend Sally's picture is that Sally was petrified of my father. I had borrowed a dress to go out one time because those days you couldn't afford anything. I had borrowed the dress from Sally and he was going to rip it to shreds, and I pleaded with him. 'Please!'—because it was Sally's dress. He was a very tyrannical man, he really was.

"Here. I have a later picture of my father I brought down to show you. This is a few years ago, before he died."

A white-haired, frail man, seeing space. No trace of menace any longer in the eyes.

"My mother did absolutely nothing. She was petrified of him. As I said, like Edith Bunker. Only Edith Bunker talks. Mama didn't. And yet I could see his side. He came home and did the housecleaning. I do know that he liked living in a nice, clean place and taking care. And I do remember her confiding in me much later in life that she never had any feelings when she had relations. So all of these things, I'm saying, drove him to other women. So I never blamed him in that area. He would come home and do the cooking and the cleaning and as I said that Easter Sunday he was up until the wee hours making me a skirt to wear. I'll never forget. It was a white wool. And he had lined it with an off-white silk, and there were suspenders."

"Was there affection?"

"My mother—that's the one thing that she gave us was love. She loved us. She lived for us. She lived for my kids. My other children don't remember her, but Andy still says, 'Ma, I wish Nanny was still here.'

"And we were always kissed hello and good-bye. My family does too. Always. Because my father used to say, 'You never know when you walk out the door, it might be the last time you see somebody.'

"Then during the Depression, I was about nine, we were sent to a Catholic home for a time. My mother was sick. My father wasn't working. The nuns were rotten there. That's why I don't go to church on Sundays anymore.

"And then he sent us to another home because he couldn't work and take care of us. So it was one of those things we never blamed him for. But unknowingly—the place he sent us—we couldn't come out. It was for orphans. And he had to go through a lot of red tape to get us out."

"At what age did he start the sex stuff with you?"

"Seven. About seven. Because I know I was going to St. Peter's School. And I remember my father was on this side of the bed and my mother was on the other side where the air shaft was. And I just stood up in the bed to go to the bathroom, to walk off the bed. And it was almost like I had a dream. Suddenly my pajama bottoms 'fell' down. That first time, it was a fleeting thing. But that's my first recollection.

"Then, through the years, it would always be after I was asleep and he would wake me up. How can I say it? He was always on top of me, and that would wake me up, but he was trying not to wake me up. He would lay on top of me but keep his weight off me, only his penis touching me.

"I guess it was like a mutual masturbation thing, now that I'm older and can try to realize it. You know, I've spent years trying to wipe it out of my mind so it's hard to bring it all back. But I think it's the last incident that I remember that's most vivid in my mind. When he made me look at him and—I was so upset.

"It was in a brown metal bed, and we had the lamps, the old bed lamps. And he was lying on it this way. Spread-eagle. His pants were open. And he made me go down on him. And I was crying. And I kept crying. I was about thirteen.

"And he said, 'Sweetheart, I want you to look at something.' And I started to cry. And he said, 'Come on, now. I don't want anything to happen to you. And if anybody ever bothers you, you'll know what it looks like.' And I kept crying. And I was so frightened. I was really frightened. And I said something about having a baby. And he says, 'You know I would never do that to you.' But I really feel—it had always happened when I was asleep so that I would wake up and pretend to be asleep because I just didn't know what to do. I just did not know what to do. And he was a very violent man, extremely violent. And I guess I was afraid of what eventually happened when I confronted him. Did I tell you I had confronted him?

"Well when my son was six months old and I had gone to visit him—he had by then remarried. And my husband was in the service and I had just gone out there. It was just laying on my mind, and I thought, 'I'm going to let him know what my feelings are. Because now that I'm married and I have a child I know all of those years what he did was wrong.'

"And he owned a bar. There was nobody in the place. I was sitting here and he was sitting there. I don't know how I approached the subject, but I said, 'Now I know that what you did to me all those years was wrong.'

"And he just hauled off and punched me. He punched me from one end of that place to the other. I went home almost in a stupor.

"He really beat me, and I never saw him again for twenty-four years. I would never go to see him. That's why I was so upset when he died. My stepmother thought I was feeling bad because I hadn't seen him. I wasn't feeling bad for that. I wanted him to tell me he was sorry. And give me some reason for what he had done. And it just never happened. And I felt cheated. I felt so cheated. You have no idea.

"And my poor husband. I went through a period where I just couldn't have anything to do with him. Because he was reminiscent of my father at that stage of his life. And the poor man didn't know. I just used to stay up late. I didn't want to go to bed at all. It was the gray at the temples or whatever. Something there was a reminder. But all I can remember is that I used to always be waked up, and steeling myself. Not knowing what to do. Being afraid to run away from home. Just not knowing what to do. And when I finally realized that I should do something, I was so old that I can't believe it. It's hard to believe that I was thirteen when this happened. To me, it seems so old. Could I have been that stupid at that age?

"As to if he had an orgasm, I wouldn't have known what it was. I wouldn't have known one if I fell over it. I kept my eyes closed and my fists clenched all of the time. I started my married life out like that, which is sad to say. In fact my husband didn't bother me until we were married a week.

"The first night I cried and he said, 'Look, honey, go to sleep. Don't worry about it.' Then I got my period the next day. But I was petrified.

"When the week was up I went out and—I didn't drink beer at all—but I poured beers. I was determined to have a couple of beers because—he was so good and so—I think if it took a year to have intercourse with me he would have waited.

"But I was nineteen when I got married. I didn't know how I was ever going to tell my husband something like that. I had only mentioned it to my mother when I was seventeen and they were divorced. And she used to cry. I told her because I was trying to tell her he wasn't worth crying over. I said, 'Ma, he's not worth it. You should make a life for yourself.' And, 'He wasn't a good man.' But she just wanted to blot it out."

"But you didn't tell her in time for her to do anything about it?"

"No. Because I felt she would not believe me. She wouldn't have believed me. Not only that. I think in my mind I knew she would do nothing about it and that would hurt me even more. Do you follow what I mean? If I told her and she did nothing, it would kill me.

"So then I buried it—and that didn't really work. Because there were those flashbacks. And I'd get all unresponsive and not knowing what to do and not wanting to be bothered. Not wanting to be bothered at all.

"And panicking in a different way because now my husband is there. He doesn't deserve to be treated like that. In fact, I only found out a few weeks ago that he was going to leave me once. He had rented a room, in fact. And I never—you know, as you get older, you can open up to each other more, and this came up. And I said, 'Sam, you rented a room, and you were going to leave me?' I couldn't believe it. But then when I thought back, I thought, 'I can't really blame him.' He thought I didn't love him anymore.

"But you see when I married Sam I didn't know if I was a virgin or not. I really didn't. I don't think my father ever penetrated. I really don't think so. But then I don't know. All I could remember was feeling him there. And steeling myself. Never said a word. I would just stay there. And pray that he would just go away. I mean a seven-, eight-year-old—and a man with a very short fuse. He would put us through walls with anger. If dinner was at six o'clock, you were there at six o'clock. And if you were told to stay at the door, you stayed at the door. You just didn't do anything to rub him the wrong way at all.

"So those feelings came back. They would last for days. Sometimes I would be out in the car and I would think, 'When is this going to stop?' You know, 'I just don't want to think about it.' And the more you don't think of pink elephants, you know, the more you do. And the more I would try to get it out of my mind, the more it would last. Days. Thinking about the first time, all the incidents. Flashbacks. Like subliminal advertising. I could almost feel it happening. Just remembering his erection coming between my legs, him trying to keep his weight off me. It was like trying to take a tooth out from under a child's pillow while he's asleep to put the money in the bed. That was what it was like.

"And did I show you pictures of me when I was little? I was ugly. Here I am at nine. Now do I look like a seductive child to you? That's when we were in the home.

"And one movie I can think of that really moved me—*A Tree Grows in Brooklyn*—did you see that? The father/daughter relationship was so nice there. Do you remember? And that still moves me to tears, that picture."

"Was Sam the good daddy in your life, do you think?"

"Oh, no. No. He is my husband. All the way. No way. I have—my husband has never stopped me from doing anything. I mean, of course, I'm not stupid enough to do things that would be crazy. What I mean to say is—like he never wanted me to work. But I said, 'Honey, I can't stay home.' First of all, he wanted to get two jobs when the kids were little because things were rough. And I said, 'It's no marriage then. If you're going to be out all night and all day too. It's crazy.' I said, 'I would rather get a part-time job.'

"But oh, no. In no way. I'm not the clinging vine type that he could be representative of my father. There is no way in this world."

"And did you enjoy a kind of vicarious, happy childhood through your kids?"

"Oh, I enjoyed all their childhoods. I really did. In fact, I went to a shower. This good friend of mine, she said, 'Anna.' They were talking about one of the women's little granddaughters. And she says, 'Anna, tell them about Penny, Andy, and Tony—a couple of things they did when they were kids.' And I did. And they said, 'You must have killed them.' And I said, 'No. They were cute as hell.' I said, 'But when they did it again the next week, then I fanned their behinds.' But I enjoyed them. And Sam—well here, if you ever—you can tell the kind of father he is from these pictures. Really, he's such a good egg. He really is. This is Tony. And here's Sam and I. Penny must have been about three at the time, I think.

"And here's my brother. He's happily married now. He often says, 'I wish mom was alive to see how everything worked out.' Because we have worked for everything we have got. He and I. And we're very proud of it. We had nothing at all when she was alive. She would be so pleased. Like I say, she couldn't cook, she couldn't clean. But she was a loving, loving woman. She was on welfare before she died, but she never came without bringing the kids a box of crayons or a coloring book and she just loved them all and she kissed them.

"But you know—during those bad times I just did not want Sam touching me. I just did not want to be touched. I got to the point where he would walk in the door and I would just give him a dirty look. I can't begin to explain how I treated him those years.

"It was just so big. Like I never felt I could trust any man. My husband was the only one. And at that time he was in that category too. I don't know what started it. Don't know what made it stop.

"During the days I would cry over the way I was treating him. But unable to help myself. And I just couldn't bring myself to talk about it. I tried burying it in the background and just forgetting it ever happened. But it doesn't work out that way. There is something that comes to the surface every now and then. And there is nothing you can do about it."

"But you think that's done with now?"

"I do. I really believe so. Otherwise, you wouldn't be sitting here today, honey. You really wouldn't. I cried with Penny talking about it on the phone. And a little when I talked with you on the phone. And it's getting a little easier to talk about it as time goes on."

"You feel the talking about it is part of the getting over it?"

"I hope the hell it is because I would like to get finished with it. Done with. Once and for all.

"Look here. This—I was a den mother. And this was my den. And this is Sam and I when we were married and—this is the cruise we went on and—.

"I thoroughly enjoy my life. I really do.

"Of course we've had our problems through the years with the kids and that. That's par for the course. But that's water under the bridge. Thank God the good things have outweighed the bad. I think I've been very, very lucky and—do you know?—I didn't think I would even be able to look you in the eyes today.

"Isn't that strange?"

Being Faithful

Rape by a stranger is quick and brutal. It allows for a straight-forward reaction—anger, hate. But the seduction or coercion of a child by a needed and trusted parent is far more complex.

It's not amazing that some run away, that some turn to drugs, that some, having been called slut by their fathers, become promiscuous, prostitutes. What's amazing is that many (no one knows *how* many) do not.

What makes the difference? Probably all the other things in our lives that work to bolster, or to further erode, our self-esteem. And, unfortunately, what's innate. A *New York Times* article in July 1977 described studies being done on what the National Institute of Mental Health called "superkids." Children who, "defying any reasonable prediction, seem to go from strength to strength,"* who seem to flourish in spite of disaster and chaos.

But where there are good times alongside the abuse—how does it get resolved?

Maddi-Jane Stern is director of Social Services at the Philadelphia Center for Rape Concern. She says, "Those women who are functioning members of society—where the incest has gone underground—have a tremendous need to resolve it. A tremendous

*Richard Flaste, "The 'Invulnerable Children' Who Thrive Against All Odds," *The New York Times*, July 22, 1977.

need to go back and expose it to their fathers. 'Why did you do it? What was going on? Mother, why didn't you stop this?' There are feelings of guilt. A lot of our survivors come to us unable to express their anger at their fathers. They do a lot of justifying on all scores and really internalize their guilt. There is a lot of anger there, and once that starts to surface, they want to confront. It's very threatening for them to confront. But the point at which I feel they're getting well is the point at which they say, 'I want to talk to my father.' Not, 'I want to kill him.' But 'I want to talk to him. I want to find out why.' "

By that standard, Pamela is coming along just fine. She first wrote to me two years ago.

"Just as a brief introduction to my experience; I am twenty and for the first time in my life I have begun to recall and discuss my relationship, initiated and perpetuated by my father. (I thought I was so alone.) The relationship lasted about five to six years and was definitely a harrowing experience.

"I was seven when it first occurred. It was an experience that lasted until I was twelve in terms of actual encounters with my father, although the tension existed until I was out of the house and away at school.

"There was a time in my life when my father would coerce sex from me at least once a week. It is almost unnecessary to say that I gave up fighting. I would hide, I would hate, but somehow I couldn't run away from home as I so often wanted to do.

"My family is fairly large—four sons, one daughter (me, I'm also in the middle of the line)—and, of course, a father and a mother. If anything, the household was of an authoritarian nature. My father worked in factories for a good part of his life. He experienced layoffs, strikes, etc., and finally became financially secure after qualifying for a job in local government. My mother is a housewife, and as her husband didn't want her working, she never did, unless we expressly needed the money.

"My mother was raised in a very Victorian home. My grandmother came from England. And my mother saw a very unhappy marriage growing up.

"As I've never been able to speak with my father about our relationship, I don't know any of his motives aside from desire, but the pleasure principle took over very quickly and probably obliterated any other motivation. I don't know.

"There were occasional references to sex education outside of the rape incidents when my father was interested in teaching me where babies came from and how they were made.

"All I would have needed was to carry his child!

"I would enjoy helping you out as I feel information is sorely needed on this subject. My experience was real, frightening, and packed with guilt. I feel that even though I have not fully realized the extensive effect it has had on my life I will be able to provide some insights."

It was apparent during our first conversation that the pain was still fresh for Pamela. It was the first, but not the last, time I felt a tremendous impulse to leave the rock where it was, not to lift it.

"You see your parents?"

"Occasionally. I go home to visit or they'll come to the college and take me out to dinner. They live in a real small town not far from here."

"You like seeing them?"

"It depends—on what they feel like bugging me about. Sometimes I really enjoy seeing them. But it's strange. Because sometimes my mother will get on me about not being married. She got married at eighteen, and in the town where they live it's fairly common for women to get married at eighteen. And stay in the town. Never venture out."

"But you're different?"

"I don't know. I just didn't want to get married. But they do give me a lot of emotional support when I need it. My father, I think, supports me more. Because when he was young he ran away from home. And he can understand, I think, better than my mother can.

"We're not a close family. My two older brothers always used to pick on me. I was their little beating board. So I didn't get to know any of my brothers until I was in ninth grade. When they decided I was acceptable. But they are uncommunicative, as is most of my family. I think out of everyone I'm the only one that talks to my parents. And really tells them what's going on.

"I think one of the reasons is that my father can't really talk to us. He teases us—but my brothers always thought the teasing was being nasty. That was his way of showing affection, you know, by teasing us. I got used to it because I was teased all the time. But my brothers just put up a wall rather than deal with him."

"What made you decide to write to me?"

"Well, it's something that I had always wanted to talk about. Because for one thing I just didn't know if any other people had experienced it. And it's the sort of thing where no one in my family knows except for my father and myself. It wasn't a good time. Nobody I felt I could tell. Because at that time I felt everybody would condemn me. That if I told anybody, they would think I was really bad—because it was my fault and not my father's.

"And it's funny. Because I can remember when I was very young I used to want to marry my daddy. He was everything to me. I was the only daughter and I did love him a lot. I can remember him being so much more important than my mother. My daddy was always the important person.

"But then as all this went on, I remember starting to hold my body in a certain way. Trying to hide the fact that I had breasts. I started feeling ashamed.

"I remember one time. It was Christmas. I had gotten some clothes from them. And I put them on. One thing was a V-neck sweater. And I didn't want to wear it. I told my mother I hated it. And she said, 'Why?' And I said, 'Well I just don't like the way it looks.' She said, 'Oh, what are you worried about? Showing off your body or something?' I just felt really uncomfortable in it because I felt like I was showing my breasts off. And my father would see that."

"Do you and your father ever talk about it?"

"It only came up once and that was last year—when I had decided to take a leave of absence from school. I had decided to get out of nursing and I didn't know exactly what I wanted to do. So I decided to work for a while. Make some money. And he was upset. And the only thing he said to me was that he was sorry for what he had done to me—as a young girl.

"Then my mother walked into the kitchen. So nothing more was ever said.

"When I first started talking about it just this year, I did all this crying. I'd cried about it alone. But I still have all this crying to do."

Now, over a year later, we met again. Each time I'd heard from Pamela in the interim, she'd sounded a little stronger, a little farther back from the edge. But now there was something new in her voice. Energy. Now she virtually bounced into my apartment, slim, neat, and sure of herself. We sat down and picked right up on our conversation.

"Yes," she said as I remarked on her spirit, "things have been getting better and better. I mean as I'm getting older, things are getting better. A lot of shit falling away and things falling into place. I found out a couple of days before I came to New York that I've won a scholarship from the college which is great. It'll help me out. I'll still have to get a job. Don't really want one, but I'll need it in order to live while I go to school. Because I don't want any more loans. I've already taken out a couple of loans and I want to finish school without any more. When I get out, it's going to be rough paying them back.

"Other than that, I guess I just feel that I'm growing up. For the first time in my life I'm beginning to deal with people honestly. Maybe dealing with myself honestly for the first time.

"My relationships with fellows are starting to get better. I think for a long time with men I was afraid of being really dependent, like falling into being a housewife or into a passive sort of role so that if I just had a boyfriend everything was OK with my life. I didn't want that. So it was kind of hard to try to have a relationship and still be doing things for myself."

"And the thing with your parents?"

"It's improving. They've just had a flood—the last storm flooded them out—so things aren't so good with them. They're not living at home. And they won't be able to get back in for a couple of months. So things are just really tense with them. But other than that, they're doing all right.

"My father and I are starting to talk again. I forget. Did I mention to you that I did talk to my father about it?

"And it was strange. Because I told him I was coming down to talk to you and everything. And one of the things he said to me, he said, 'Tell this to your friend.' (Because he was kind of worried about it all, thinking, 'Oh, no, what is she going to ask you?' And I just said, 'Well, I don't know. Wait and see.') And he said, 'Well you tell her that I really don't see anything wrong with it.' Society condemns it, he said. But he, really, when it comes down to it, he doesn't see anything wrong with it."

"How did you feel about that?"

"I had mixed emotions. On the one hand I thought he was wrong. But on the other hand—sometimes I think that in different societies there's nothing wrong with it. You know, it's sanctioned, more or less. And so it's hard to tell. Just—I don't agree with him.

"But now this is the thing he said to me once, when I was growing up. He was reading books on sexuality and stuff in the Middle Ages, ancient history, primitive societies and things. And he said that there, there was nothing wrong with it, with the father initiating the daughter."

"Is that how he put it to you? 'Aha. Now you're seven, I'm going to initiate you?' "

"No."

"Did he more or less say, 'Hey, you know, you belong to me and you're going to do what I tell you?' "

"Yes."

"Well, suppose everybody had said—even your mother had said—'Hey, no kidding! Congratulations! Isn't that wonderful!' Do you think you would have liked what happened?"

"No. No, I don't think so. I think when it first started happening, I wasn't aware one way or the other. It was just something my father started. I did it because he wanted me to. I think most young girls idolize their fathers at a certain age and then later start looking at boys. But I don't know what it would have been like. I knew I was afraid to tell my mother."

"He said not to tell—but he still thought it was all right?"

"Well, he knew she would get angry."

"So it was sort of like, 'Us two kids can play but we don't tell mother?' "

"In a way. He thought at the time—this is something strange—it really bothered me when he said this. At the time, my mother and he were not communicating at all. But he said he had vowed never to be unfaithful to my mother. So by raping me, it wouldn't be necessarily being unfaithful to his wife. That's what he said when we started talking about it. Because I asked him why. And I said, 'But I was only seven.'

"And he really didn't have an answer for it."

"How did it all start?"

"I remember the first incident. It was strange how it happened. I only had brothers—so I used to play a lot of the time with boys. I really didn't play very much with little girls. And this one day, outside, I asked this boy to show me his penis. I was starting to be sexually curious. And—kids were doing that, you know. And he did. And then my father called me inside. He had seen us.

"And he said, 'Don't do that. If you want to see it, I'll show you mine.'

"You know, like—there's my father saying this. I was frightened. I was just frightened. But at the same time, I guess, I was curious. Obviously, I'd been curious enough to ask my friend. But I do remember being really scared, like I shouldn't be doing this. But it was your father. And you listened to your father.

"I did it at first because he wanted to do it. It was expected of me. He wanted me to do it, so I would do it. That's another thing in our family—you don't argue. No one has rights in my family until you're out of the house and self-supporting.

"And then after that first instance—it's strange because as time goes on I begin recalling more and more. I remember my mother would go out. She would go bowling. That was a big night. Wednesday night. And I would just be petrified. But he would just come to me and—I hate to say the words, it seems so childish—he would ask me if I wanted to tickle. That's what he used to call it, a euphemism. And I would say no. But he would still say, 'Well, I want to.'

"I remember like hiding behind things and him just saying, 'Pamela, come here.' And I would say, 'No. I don't want to.' And he'd say, 'Pamela, come *here*.' He'd say, 'You don't want your brothers to hear, do you?' And I used to say, 'I hate you! I want to kill you!' But for a long time he just wouldn't listen to that. So all my crying, my saying, 'I hate you,' were meaningless. It didn't matter if I hated him. It didn't stop him from pursuing me. I mean because if I wouldn't leave my room, he would do it in my room.

"He wasn't like mean, nasty, hitting. But obsessed. Like that's the only thing he saw. I mean when somebody says, 'I hate you!'—I mean if someone says to me, 'I hate you,' I want to leave them alone. But to him it obviously didn't matter. Because he knew what he wanted.

"And I couldn't run away from it.

"But what I was thinking earlier. I remember when it first started happening—and this is upsetting to remember in a way, because it's hard to realize that, yes, I was like that—when he would ask me at first, I would want to. That's upsetting to remember because now I say, 'Well, I wouldn't. How would I? My father.' But there were times when I was seven and eight when it still wasn't totally repulsive to me.

"And sometimes we'd go for a drive and take my little brothers. We'd go to a playground. He would send them out to play. And I'd sit on his lap in the car.

"Other times it would be in the bedroom and I'd be on the bed. He would be on top of me. What he would do is I would lie on my stomach on a pillow and have my pants down. And he would be on top of me. And just rub his penis back and forth. He never penetrated me. He said he always wanted to, but he would wait until I was older.

"And then he would ejaculate, but it would be onto a handkerchief or something.

"And the older I got, the more he wanted to penetrate. And then I would say no!

"But I just couldn't get away from it. There was no way I could escape it. I didn't want it. I did not want him to bother me. And after a while, it wasn't even sexual any more. I didn't feel it. It was just something my father wanted. I wouldn't allow myself to feel. He would do whatever he wanted. I would just cry during the whole time and say, 'I hate you! Leave me alone. I hate you, I hate you, I hate you!' And crying my eyes out. I would cry and scream and he would say, 'Shut up. Shut up.' And he would do it until he was satisfied.

"Then, I would go into the bathroom and wash myself. And I would keep crying. And there were times I would hide. Run away to somebody else's house for a while. Or hide in the backyard.

Eventually, he would get me because if I didn't come home on time, he would tell my mother. And then how would I say to my mother, 'Well, my father was trying to, you know, rape me.'

"I stopped thinking of myself as a kid. After a while, I guess, I never thought of myself as a kid.

"I do think possibly one of the things that compensated at the time was the power. I had these two older brothers, but I could get what I wanted from my father. That was a real strong weapon. If everything else was against me, I'd just go to my father and have him do whatever I'd tell him. And I remember when I was growing up and money was really tight, I could get it from my father. Whereas my mother would say, 'No, no, we don't have the money.' So that's weird to remember. To know that after a while I used it for my own advantage.

"I remember when I was little, after he would do it, I would say, 'Well, could I have a brownie?' Or, 'Could I have this?' You know, something I liked, could I have it? So I could get around some restrictions because my father said it was OK. And then after a while, when I started wanting money because I wanted to buy clothes or something, I'd just say, 'Could I have money?'

"Sometimes I used to think about that. I was no different than a prostitute. I guess I was just lucky in the long run that I'd learned early to rely on my brains—in school and things. Lucky that I always succeeded there even if I didn't succeed in other places. That was always a saving grace.

"But I used to think I brought it on, you know. Just—by being female. I knew it was wrong. Maybe that came from religion. We had Sunday school stuff. Protestant Sunday school. And you learned the Ten Commandments.

"And I considered it adultery. Because it was against my mother. Who was my father's wife.

"So I felt like a sinner. I don't know if you're aware of what the Protestant religion is like at all, but at the time it was really like fire and brimstone. I mean, sinners burned in hell. And I really thought they did. Little kids take that literally and say, 'Oh, no!'

"I remember before it all happened—I really loved my body. I just liked to play with it. And little girls are always fussed over. And everybody would say, 'Oh, you're so cute.' And then you believe it. And I guess adolescence is maybe when you figure out whether you are or you aren't. Whether it was true what they said.

"But there was my father then telling me how much he loved me. How beautiful he thought I was. How he couldn't *resist* me. And as a result, I used to think I was really ugly. Because I didn't want my father to be attracted to me. And so if he told me I was beautiful, I didn't want to be beautiful. 'If being beautiful attracts you, I don't want to be that way.' And for years I had a totally negative self-image.

"For a while, I got fat. So I didn't feel like I was attractive to anybody. Sometimes I think I did that on purpose. That possibly it was a defensive thing. That was something I don't think I realized for a while. But I think his finding me attractive—I wanted to be ugly.

"And then just—eventually he couldn't control me the same way. I think that's a lot of how it stopped. I just—stopped loving him. I was less ambivalent and moving more toward hate. I was getting bigger and stronger and just saying, 'If you don't leave me alone, I'm going to kill you!'

"And there'd be my mother saying, ''What's wrong with you? Why are you always so mean and rotten to your father?' "

"How do you think it affected your relationships?"

"I don't know what my relationship with boys, with men, would have been like had it not happened. The first sexual experiences were with my father, a man, not with somebody of my own age. I think what I really wanted was a normal relationship with my father like I imagine most other girls have. Because I think most of the time I did feel jealous that other girls' lives seemed normal. They loved their fathers, their fathers loved them. And I always felt different. At the same time that I knew my father loved me, I couldn't say I loved my father.

"And I remember when I was growing up, when the girls I was growing up with started kissing and everything—it was all so new to them. And there were so many things I knew about. I think I felt dirty. I think I felt sex was bad.

"I really can't understand. Because my father wasn't an alcoholic. He didn't treat my mother badly—was in no way abusive. He took it out on me. And he was attracted to me at the same time. So sometimes I wonder if I wasn't a double release for him.

He could release any frustrations he was feeling, because he didn't drink, and he could also satisfy his desires.

"He's not violent. He never hit my mother. The only time they argue is over finances.

"And I've resented it. For a long time I was really angry with him. And hated him. But my relationships were really weird. Because I never wanted to be used for sex. No. It was that I was afraid of being used for sex. And afraid of my own initiative. I used to try to deny that part. That I was attracted to someone.

"I think I do have problems relating to men sexually. I don't trust them—with my feelings. I mean all those years I spent going, 'The only way you're going to get me is if you corner me.' You know, 'I don't want to do it, but what else can I do? So the only way you're going to get me is if you force me.'

"And I think he was jealous. I remember one summer I'd gone on a diet and lost a lot of weight. I was thirteen. And I was going to a friend's cottage. And before I left, my father said, 'Don't let any of the boys feel your titties.' "

"Do you think it was that your mother was turning him down?"

"Well, I can imagine she's like that. Although she doesn't seem to be a prude—she's told me she thinks men and women should have a good sex life. But my father told me they didn't have sex for the first few years they were married. So I must believe it. Because when I was living at home, I would never hear them. And in a small house you just know when your parents are having sex. It's hard for them to hide it."

"You think your father turned to you, a seven-year-old, out of loneliness?"

"I don't know. I think probably in some ways, yes. Some ways out of loneliness. My mother was turning him down. Possibly. I knew that at that time of his life, he was having a lot of problems too. And he was laid off. And he had a health problem. I don't know whether it was my mother not giving him enough support. I don't know how much support he needed. I don't know whether he wanted a mama or what. Maybe he just needed somebody who would be very supportive. And—how could I turn him down. I would always be there. I mean, he's your father. You couldn't say no. I wouldn't let him down."

"And whether his sexual performances were good or bad, you wouldn't be critical."

"Right. How could I criticize?"

"Might he have been impotent or a premature ejaculator or had some sexual problem?"

"Yes."

"Possible?"

"Oh, I think that's very possible. I think that's very possible. Because one of the things he said when we were talking was he said he felt like he couldn't satisfy my mother."

"And you're sure your mother doesn't know?"

"Yes."

"What do you think she'd have done if you'd told her then?"

"She'd probably have left him. There was a time in their lives when I remember my mother saying to me, 'I wish I could walk out on your father.' "

"Would she have turned around and blamed it on you?"

"Probably not. But at the time, you know, I really didn't think of all these things."

"Some of the experts say mothers are collusive, they set it up. You think?"

"No. That's not—no, that was never the case. Never the case. No, my mother would have believed me. And that's probably why my father said don't tell. He knows she would have believed me.

"But you know sometimes I think in a way if it wouldn't have happened, I would have been less dissatisfied with my life. I would have been less driven to escape it. And so I would have accepted a lot more. So in a funny way—it made me hate so much, it made me hate my own life so much that I wanted to leave, to get away. And I began examining a lot more than I might have otherwise at fifteen, sixteen, seventeen. I mean it was horrible, but it was good, you know. I got out.

"And I think it made me tougher than I would have been otherwise. And because I survived, in a way it makes me believe in myself more. That I must really have some sort of strength that I'm not even aware of. Because I did survive at such an early age."

"And you never felt like just cutting him out of your life?"

"No. No. Because—he's still my father. Which is something I've had a problem dealing with. Because people will say, 'Why? How do you deal with him now? How do you feel about him now?' And I say, 'Well, he's still my father.'

"Because up until that happened, there were so many good things. And after that happened, when my mother wanted to keep me from doing things I wanted, my father would say, 'Let her do what she wants.' So it's—very ambivalent."

"Can you say why you wish it hadn't happened?"

"I think there's too much power involved. That somehow sex becomes linked with submission, domination. And you want to be able to seduce. You want to try out being a little seductive with someone your own age. And you want to feel safe knowing you can be a kid with your parents."

"When you talked with your father, was he concerned that he'd hurt you?"

"Yes. Because when I told him that when I was growing up there was just such a feeling of isolation—like I couldn't tell my mother—but it just carried over into almost everything. Like I couldn't tell anybody. And I was always very much of a loner. Never really had any close friends. And I could never deal with my feelings openly.

"And he said he was sorry, you know, that he had done this to hurt me. But what could he do now? And he cried. That he had hurt me. And he said he was sorry he ever did it. But to say you're sorry after the fact—what can you do? And what I don't know is whether it's something he doesn't see anything wrong with, defensively. Or whether he really doesn't see anything wrong with it and he sees something wrong with society."

"It seems a little tricky to condemn. adultery and then condone incest as a solution."

"That's where he does contradict himself. Because if he couldn't do it with his secretary or a woman down the street, then he really shouldn't have taken advantage of me. It's hard to know how he really feels. I don't think he knows yet either. He says he's lived with it like a burden ever since it happened."

"But when he learned you were coming here—it made him nervous?"

"Yes. I think he was afraid. He said he was afraid of me being—
used or something. 'Don't let her take advantage of you.' He asked
me if names were being used or something. And I said, 'No. Don't
worry about it.' But I think that's probably got a lot to do with it.
That he was afraid of being revealed.

"Probably he doesn't want to face up to it himself. He is,
because I'm talking about it to him. We'll never tell my mother. I
would like to. I would still like to. Just that she always used to
blame me for not getting along with my father.

"But now—I began realizing this spring that I didn't want to
look at myself as a sick person that always had problems. I didn't
want to look at myself that way anymore.

"It's past. It's over. Sure it created a problem. But I'm twenty-
two. I have to start dealing with that problem. Take control of my
life."

The Grisly Details: Not Yet

Jenny was back from California. It was less than a week after she'd left.

"Jenny. What happened?"

"I don't know. Really. She—my friend—just started in with this stony silence. I mean here was this big, beautiful house with a big, big pool. Everything seemed to be going to be beautiful. That was one day. Then the next day, a sudden freeze. And I said, 'Don't you want me here?' And she said, 'It doesn't matter what you do.' And I said, 'Now and forever?' And she said, 'Yeah.' So, here I am. I'll have to get a job. And I'll go back to school.

"But what I wanted to tell you was—I just want you to know that last night when I was sitting in bed working on the grisly details for you, my paranoia—when I start getting upset, I get paranoid—if I ever went crazy I'd go paranoid—and my paranoia started in, 'Are you sure you know what the reasons for writing this are?' "

"That's not paranoia. I ask myself that every day. You mean, what will this strange person do with all this ugly material?"

"Yep."

Mother's Fault

Suddenly, I noticed, authorities were springing up full-blown to pronounce on us; to explain the dynamics of each member of a family involved in the mischief of incest. And to lay it all on mom.

Here we are, world, five minutes into a conversation you've refused to have for a million-odd years, and we've already developed bromides and buzzwords. Things to recite in the dark.

Sexual relations "deteriorate."

Communications "break down."

Mothers are "inadequate." (Also, "passive," "cowardly," "domineering," and "manipulative.")

Fathers have "nurturing needs."

A story appeared in the newspaper about a pioneer program working with incest families.* The story described a couple— he, robust, energetic, abloom with psychological jargon garnered from eight months of counseling. Expansive about, almost kind of proud sounding about, his psychosexual problems and dependency needs. Like some new part of his anatomy he'd discovered

*Georgia Dullea, "Pioneer Therapy Deals With Incest by Treating the Entire Family," *The New York Times*, October 3, 1977.

he could play with that gave him pleasure—and got him approval.

She, on the other hand, was described as pale.

" 'If they put him away, I'd be in a lot of trouble,' she confided, almost in a whisper. 'I don't work and I don't drive.' "

Now the story says that he confessed to her that he'd been diddling their daughters, aged ten and six. (They had five children. She was twenty-nine years old.) He'd obviously gotten tired of hiding in the coal cellar waiting for her to catch him, to come tag him "it."

Then, the story says, she "just sat down on the floor and began ripping up magazines."

The story says that now he was afraid she was losing her mind.

I don't think he should have been afraid. I don't think she was losing her mind.

Undoubtedly, those were *family* magazines. Everything they had promised her, everything they'd reinforced in her, everything they'd told her about how to behave to make her family life appear to conform to a mythic happiness had just exploded in a million little pieces. She was just making little pieces match little pieces.

Am I making her up? No more than the experts who are now about to explain her to herself.

I think she'd been trying to be what everything around her told her to be. Agreeable. Accepting. Deferent to his decisions. Accommodating.

They call her names: passive, dependent.

They want her to understand where she went wrong. To say she was sorry. ("If you say you're sorry, I'm sure he'll say he's sorry, too.")

Now, for conforming to everything we've taught her, she's going to be helped to understand that she got it wrong. She should never have listened.

Should she have stood up to him? Done battle? Ah, then she'd be called domineering.

Pale? I would be too. She's in a double bind. It's no-win. As usual, she's paying for what he did. In the office of the Pioneer Program, I think she's being astonishingly patient. But then, she's been there before. Remember the principal's office?

"Uh—I'm afraid your son, Steven, is doing poorly in his work."

"I—I've been trying. I've been helping him every night."

"Well." A glance out the window. "He's a bright boy. I know he'd do well with the *right* help from you."

I once walked into a plant store. I had a tree—I didn't know its name, I never had to address it directly—it had skinny "finger" leaves, which were looking grungy. I pointed to what looked like its sister in the store and said to the owner, "Mine isn't doing well. It's looking brownish and sad."

Immediately, helpful, expert, he said, "You're not watering it enough."

"I water it when it seems dry."

"You're watering it too much."

Question: Who will save us from those who would help us? (It's been asked before but no one ever answered.)

As I talked with social workers all over the country who were working with incest families, I discovered it was now axiomatic among most that "the mothers always know—*on some level.*" That they were collusive in the incest. That they were sexually rejecting. That, if mother didn't positively shove Susie in as her replacement, she at least *allowed* that replacement. And so our lives would seem to be mapped out for us—to go from seductive children to fat, cold, manipulative mothers.

Lucy Berliner, social worker at the Sexual Assault Center of Harborview Medical Center in Seattle, Washington, says: "Frankly, it's the same old thing. The mothers are always blamed for everything. Ultimately. If you can't find anybody else to blame. It just doesn't bear up from our clinical experience. We have had one hundred-odd cases in the last couple of years. And it just doesn't hold true that the mothers knew about it. Most of the kids tell us they have tried to keep the mothers from finding out.

"When I give a presentation, I usually go through what I consider to be the main myths related to incest. First, that the child lies in bed and fantasizes about it. Second, that the children provoke it or participate actively in it. And third, that the mothers know or they collude in the relationship. Again, most of the children say, and the mothers say, that the mothers didn't know about it.

"In hindsight, many women can look back and see some signs.

Signs that at the time didn't mean anything or weren't significant. But the kinds of signs they are talking about are things like being asked to go to the store all the time. Or the husband getting out of bed to see if everything is OK in the house. If those kinds of things happened in my house, I would not immediately assume that my husband is diddling my kid."

Some wives, some mothers, in incest families, in nonincest families, are less than admirable. But, simply, to have father-daughter incest, *whatever* mommy's behavior is, it's *daddy* who must decide to sexually abuse his kid.

Some mothers do find out and do nothing. Because they're rotten? Or because they're helpless? Some, when they find out are jealous. (But that is not causative.)

Consider one much-offered explanation: "She's been sexually rejecting." Implicit here, of course, is the idea that *he* has no sexual problem, and that she *owes* him constant sexual acceptance— or else. But even beyond that, it simply does not always hold. One family I spoke with who had been through an incest treatment program in Tacoma, Washington, run by Peter Coleman for the Child Protective Services there, said their sex lives had been just fine. Peachy. Then what was the problem?

"He was a very authoritarian person," she said. "He's really dealing with that now. But he didn't see our daughter as a person. She was *his*. He didn't see it as incest."

"Dear Louise:

"I can't remember the exact age I was when things started to happen, but it was somewhere around four or five. The first big incident was one night when my mother went to my grandmother's for the night. It was always a big kick for my brother (he's one year older) and me to get to sleep in mom and dad's bed, so of course we wanted to sleep with daddy that night. He told my brother to sleep on one side to 'keep his back warm,' and me to sleep on the other to 'keep his front warm.' He was lying on his side. He put his hand up my nightgown and down my underpants in front. He asked me why I wore underpants to bed because mommy never did. He put his penis between my thighs and began pushing it back and forth and told me that 'Mommy likes it when I do this.' I just lay there. I didn't have any idea about what it was that he was doing. I remember trying to figure out what the thing was between my legs. It didn't seem like anybody could have something like that as a part of their body. I had seen little boys' penises when us kids would play show and tell but those were nothing like this. He didn't put his penis into my vagina, and I don't know if he ejaculated or not. I knew that what he had done was not right, I guess, because of the sneaky way he was acting.

"I didn't tell anybody about it. The way I interpreted the above occurrences was just that I had a vague idea it was something bad. I didn't know what sex was. I only knew that the way he acted was something I didn't want to be part of. I would try to avoid getting into those situations, but once there I just sort of passively avoided—i.e., I would just sit there, I wouldn't talk to him, and when he let me go I would get out of there as quickly as possible. I never told anybody what he was doing, probably because I didn't know myself.

"Well, I guess I've written about all I can stand for one day. This is a lot more difficult than I thought it would be. My father finally raped me when I was nine or ten, but I will tell you about that at a later date.

Sandy"

"OK, then," Sandy said. "So where shall I begin?"

"Well, you told me some of the early stuff and I gathered it wasn't all that easy to get on with. So why don't you just start in the middle. Or tell me what you're doing these days. Start at the end."

"OK. That was one thing I wanted to ask you, to talk to you about. You asked me how it affects my relationships now. Well I'm gay and I'm really, really concerned about how you're going to present that—if you are."

"So am I. I've talked with some gay women, who do make that connection. But more often, women say there is no connection."

"I hate to see it treated as a disease. That you have to find reasons for it and that sort of thing. I try to be as proud as possible, and I hate to see it treated that way."

"I'm just trying to get people to listen. Incest is a subject that scares people."

"Oh, I'm sure. It scares me too. But being gay—I live at home with my parents. And that sometimes has its tensions. They don't know I'm gay. I have decided I'm going to tell them as soon as I leave the house. Because I don't want to be living there while there'll be a lot of friction."

"How old are you?"

"Twenty-one."

"And you've been gay for—?"

"Oh, I've always been gay. I didn't accept it until about a year ago. I went out with quite a few guys between my last year in high school and my freshman year in college. I was practically a whore for a while. It was really strange. When I look back on it, I think I understand why it never worked. I always thought that if I kept trying it would turn out right. But it never did. I'm happy the way I am now."

"What're your parents like?"

"Well, my father's something straight out of Archie Bunker and my mother—she's an Edith on the road to liberation. She's— through my pushing and prodding—she's going to college and she's really getting her act together. I have never seen one person grow so much as my mother has in the past four years or so."

"Under your auspices?"

"Yeah. It's great. Great to see it. And I've made the first steps to get her some counseling. I went in for the initial interview because I'm really concerned. See, I took my father to court—I'll tell you about that. But when I took my father to court, the social worker that my mother and father had, told my mother that it was her . fault because she didn't put out often enough. Now it could have been that my mother was saying no. But I don't think that's any excuse for what he did. I think I'm certain he could have handled his sex drive in some other manner."

"How did he treat you when you were little?"

"He treated me and my brother fairly equally. We went on a lot of trips. We'd always go fishing with my dad. We had a pretty good family relationship when I was little. My mother was always very religious. My father was always more of a hedonist. My mother would have us confessing our sins and my father would have us out fishing and stuff.

"We were a pretty typical family. Where he went off to work every day. And my mother was home with us all the time. So I'm sure I was closer to my mother then, as I think probably any child is. As for my brother—we were a typical brother and sister, fighting and hollering. We grew to be very, very close when we were teenagers. And we are still real close.

"But the best times were at our summer house, when we'd all go. That was my favorite thing.

"And then when he started acting strange, at first it was just something I didn't understand. I just knew that there was something wrong. I mean, there was my brother lying right there and my father acting just super-sneaky and me trying to figure out what it was that he put between my legs. I felt it was—you know, flesh. But I couldn't see how it could be part of anybody's body. It was really, really strange. And as I got a little older, I started realizing what was going on. He started bouncing me on his lap and stuff like that. He would bounce me right there and then he'd get up and try to adjust his hard-on. And I started putting it together, what it was. Usually it was little things like that. And trying to put his tongue in when he kissed me good night. And trying to give me screwdrivers, vodka and orange juice, and telling me it was orange juice, and trying to come into bed with me. Usually when he did that, I would just lie there. Just pretend I was asleep through the whole thing.

"I thought if I pretended I was asleep he would go away. And I really didn't want to acknowledge that it was happening.

"Well, I would avoid my father as far as getting kissed good-night. And hugs. But when I was in about fifth grade he started getting super-strange. He'd start bouncing me on his lap and feeling my breasts, which, of course, were a fifth grader's. And asking, you know, 'You can't wait until you get a bra, can you?' And I said, 'Whaaaat?' I never even thought about a bra. And that was when—he raped me.

"My mother had a woman friend she was very close to. We owned this candy store where my brother and I used to work every Sunday—and we'd split Saturday in half. It was my weekend to work so my mother decided to take my brother and this friend up to the country because she'd never seen our house there, you know.

"And oh—I fought. I knew it was going to happen. I mean I screamed, I cried, I ranted, I raved. But they didn't take me with them because I had to work in the store. With my father.

"See, we lived over the store. And I knew it was going to happen because he had been acting really strange. My mother used to go to church group on Thursday nights and that's when he'd always—have his fun or whatever. Trying to hop into bed with me. Trying to get me drunk. Saying, 'Do you like this? Your mother likes this.'

"And I never said anything. I just kind of lay there. But this one night when my mother went off with my brother, I went to bed. He had been trying to give me screwdrivers, and I think I had about two sips and I told him, 'No, it has vodka in there.'

"He said, 'Oh, no no no. Drink it. The orange juice will make you sleep better.'

"And he was drinking pretty heavy around that time. He said, 'Why don't you come sleep in my bed with me?'

"And I said, 'No, I don't want to. Because the dog, Harry, isn't allowed to sleep in your bed.'

"And he said, 'Oh, well, he can sleep in there tonight.'

"And I said, 'Oh, no. Ma wouldn't like that.' You know, 'Harry can sleep with me in my bed.'

"And then he said, 'Well, then I'll sleep with you in your bed.'

"And I said, 'Oh, no. No. I want to sleep alone. There's not enough room for more than me and Harry.'

"And I got in bed and then he came in and went through the same things and—except this time he went all the way.

"He just—uh—got on top and—before, he would always lie on his side and—I think that's the first time I ever remember seeing him erect."

"You were—hurt? Angry? Curious?"

"I was very hurt. I mean it hurt physically. And I pretty much pretended I was asleep the whole time and—isn't that strange?

"But then he got off and went back to his bed. And then I had to spend the rest of the weekend with him. And you know I still really didn't know the facts of life at this time. This was the age when we started wondering. My best friend and I—we'd always have these strange ideas about just what sex was. But I didn't know that that was what had happened to me. That was 'sex.' "

"And did you tell your friend?"

"I did when we finally figured out what it was. It was a big thing, you know. There were three of us actually, and we always did everything together. Nobody thought—they didn't think it was anything bad. They just thought it was, 'Wow!'—you know.

"And I remember one time when one of my friends said, 'Oh, is that your father, the one that you-know-what?' And I just turned terribly red and told her to shut up. I realized then that it was kind of stupid of me to have said anything. Because I realized that I didn't want my father to know that I knew. And I didn't want my mother to know. I just could never—I mean to admit it to him would be to admit that he had done something not too good."

"You didn't want your mother to know?"

"Well, my mother had all these very Victorian attitudes toward sex. To the extent that my sex education, verbally at least, from my parents, was when my mother—I think I was nine or ten—she handed me a Kotex book on menstruation. That was it. And then she asked me if I had any questions.

"That was that. I was a typical kid. My parents never did that kind of thing. Let alone my telling her what he did to me. But he left me alone after that. He started going around with another friend of mine. She used to come over and help out in the store. And he'd take her in the back room and she was developing at a faster rate than I was, and he'd give her ten dollars for a quick feel. And she was a typical American kid. Money was money. And we'd talk about it. She'd tell me everything. And I'd say, 'How much did you get?' And we thought that was pretty cool. Here was my dumb father giving her money just to feel her boobs, you know."

"Did it give you any sense of power over your mother?"

"No. I felt it was more like a secret that I really had to guard, because I knew that it would just kill my mother to find out. I wasn't glad to have the secret I had. I was very much concerned about protecting her."

"You liked her?"

"Oh, yeah. And I felt guilty with relationship to her because I had a terrible secret that I couldn't tell her. But yet I was suffering for not telling her.

"And, see, I'm sure that at the time she didn't know. I've heard people say, 'How could a mother not know?' But my mother is— or was, well, she still is—so uptight about sex that I don't think it would ever have crossed her mind that somebody would even think of doing that sort of thing.

"I mean now at least she tells him what she thinks. Sometimes it's a hot situation between the two of them, with her refusing to be dominated and him refusing to let her refuse. And she's getting a lot more vocal and sometimes to the point of screaming and yelling. I don't know if that's good or bad. I want her to be happy. I do think it's good to get things out. But sometimes I don't think she gets them out in the right way. She gets pretty mean about things. That's one of the reasons I want her to go for counseling. So that she can decide what she wants. She told me just this summer that she was going to get a divorce just as soon as my father makes some repairs on the country house. But that was the last time she mentioned it. I'm not going to bring it up because I don't want to push her that way. I want her to get some help and figure out what she wants to do."

"But you can live with your father today without—any of these memories?"

"My father? No! Are you kidding! Last night we were waiting for my mother to come home and eat dinner. And my father was having a long talk with me about—what do gay people do in bed? And telling me about his sexual fantasies. And I really, really felt so uncomfortable. He always has to talk about sex. Whenever we get alone, he has to talk about sex. And I don't feel comfortable with it at all. And yet I'm not assertive enough to say, 'Hey, dad, you really bug me when you talk this way.' He doesn't kiss me or hug me or anything now because I told him I didn't want him to. I told him that about a month ago. So now he kisses my mother good-night and shakes my hand. Ha, ha.

"But we pretty much lead separate lives. I come home and I eat with them. Then I'll go in my room and read. On weekends they're out of town or I'm out of town, staying with some friends. They pretty much respect my freedom to do what I want. They don't always agree with me, but they pretty much let me do what I want. It's not that bad. It really isn't. But I do want to get out.

"Right now I've got a car that's falling apart. I've got a job. I'm going to graduate school in the fall. I'm wondering if I can patch up my car while I'm out to get an apartment or if I'll have to stay home longer to get a new car."

"Does the rape ever come up any more? How about with your brother?"

"Well, he knew at the time. When I took my dad to court when I was fifteen, everybody knew.

"As I said, my father had been fooling around with my girl friend. But then we sold the store so she wasn't always around. Then one Saturday afternoon, my mother and brother were out. And my father started chasing me around the house, telling me he wanted a kiss. And he kept grabbing me. And I mean I was running around the house. And he grabbed me and threw me down on the lounge chair—this sofa chair. And started humping on me. We had our clothes on. And I mean I just freaked out and ran upstairs to my room and shut the door and sat there and just trembled, and I was so afraid he was going to come up and finish off what he'd started. But he didn't come up. And by that time—you know, my brother and I, both, we were independent kids, rebellious kids. And I decided that I was going to run away.

"So I spent all the next day in my room. I got everything ready. And Monday morning I woke up and I had about six pairs of pants on and ten pairs of socks. And my father would drive my brother and me to school at seven, and we wouldn't get home until four.

"So I just took off.

"And I went over to my boyfriend's apartment. I had a boyfriend. And he drove me out to a friend of mine's house in the suburbs and I spent the night there. I was trying to figure out just what I was going to do. I knew I couldn't tell my mother. And the only thing I was concerned about was my own safety.

"My girl friend took me over to this woman's house. She was maybe about thirty, and she liked talking to all the kids. They'd come over and tell her about their love lives and stuff. She was a pretty cool lady. So I told her the whole story, and she said, 'Well, my god, if you told the police this, I'm sure they'd get you in a foster home.'

"And I said, 'Well—.' I realized I certainly wasn't going to make it on my own at the age of fifteen. So I decided to do that. So she took me down to the police station. And I told the police the whole story.

"And that was really a terrible experience. I cried and cried and cried. It was—that was really traumatic. I mean, I was—'cause you know what I was doing? My god. I was destroying my parents' marriage. I was—I was—squealing on my father, whom I was supposed to love. And making him out to be a real dirty crook. And—oh, god. It was just—then they had my father down there. My father in one room. Me in another room. They were—comparing stories. This and that. And my father moved in with his brother. And my mother kept pressing me for the details."

"How did she behave?"

"Oh, she was going nuts. She was really just shook up. She was taking all kinds of tranquilizers and—I don't know. I was—really going nuts myself.

"And nobody ever mentioned getting me into a foster home.

"I mean everybody's attitude was—my mother was mad at me. For telling the police. She sat down and said, 'Sandy, you know that, now you've done this, if your father gets laid off where he's working now, he's never going to be able to get another job. Not with this on his record.'

"And she made me feel like—like I had really done the wrong thing.

"Because I didn't get into a foster home.

"And my father moved back in.

"And there I was. Except I had just made everything worse by opening up my mouth."

"What were the cops' attitudes toward this?"

"Oh, they thought it was great. Yeah. Wow. Whoopee. Let's hear that story again. They kept saying things like, 'Well, tell us that again. Tell it to these people.' And then they'd say, 'Well, you know, I think this is really a family problem, and this shouldn't be police business.'

"I'm sitting there going, 'Whaaat?' And they took him to court. And I got my girl friend involved. And she wasn't too happy about telling because she was from a really uptight Catholic family. And it was her mother and my mother pressing charges."

"Your mother did press charges."

"Yeah. And then they—what do you call it? They plea bargained. But he did plead guilty to indecent liberties with a minor. And got off on six months counseling.

"And I told you the kind of counseling they got. That's where my mother was told it was her fault.

"My father to this day doesn't think he did anything wrong.

"And the whole family knew. Nobody talked about it. But I

guess my aunts, my father's sisters, came over and told ma to take
him back. Really pleaded his case.

"She wasn't going to take him back. She'd been staying at my
uncle's. But—she felt so guilty, well not so guilty, just—she didn't
have anywhere else to go. And although he had one very big major flaw he had a lot of good qualities."

"Did he?"

"Yeah. He's a good provider. And, I mean, very handy around
the house. This is what my mother says."

"Were you disappointed that she took him back?"

"Yeah."

"Did you wish she'd taken you and run off with you or
something?"

"Yeah. I wanted her to get a divorce so bad. I mean I just kept
telling her all the details. Like how my father used to tell my
girl friend that he wished she would marry my brother, when she
got older, so that he could always be close to her. And I told my
mother that and—'Oh, I'm going to get a divorce.' And I said,
'Whoopee. Go. Go ahead. Get a divorce.' You know."

"How do they get along now?"

"Terribly. They went to the country for the weekend, and my
mother was walking out the door after my father and I said, 'Have
a good time.' And she said, 'Yeah. Right.'

"That's how they get along. It's just kind of day-to-day. Let's do
this. Let's do that. They don't seem to really share anything
besides the fact that they're living together and they cooperate."

"But he's reformed?"

"My father? He hasn't tried anything since I've been home. But
I'm still scared. I don't know. Last night I remember I heard my
father get up—and walk to the bathroom, right past my door. I
just froze. I was deathly afraid. I really was. Because I thought he
was going to come in. But he didn't. He walked on by. But I
really, really felt terrible."

"What part of it stays in your head as the most scary thing?"

"Well, like the middle of the night. I'm twenty-one years old
and I'm deathly afraid of the dark. And when my father starts
talking to me about sex, I keep waiting for him to do something.
And yet I'm about as assertive as a rock. Because I spent so many

years learning to hide it, and not to talk about it, that it's just become a reflex."

"Did he ever apologize? 'I shouldn't have done that?' "

"No. He has never admitted to actually raping me. He never did it, according to him. That's one reason I'm afraid to tell that I'm gay. Because he was talking to me, we were working on the car, my car. We were alone so we had to talk about sex. And he said that every time I do something that my mother doesn't think is too great—she blames him for it. It's all his fault because of what he did to me.

"And he said, 'I know that didn't have any effect on you, Sandy. If it had had any effect on you, Sandy, then you wouldn't want to have anything to do with men. You'd be deathly afraid of men.'

"So there I am again, protecting him.

"It's a reflex. I protected him since I was about five years old. Before, I knew *why* I was protecting him. Now it's just ingrained.

"But now at least my mom and I can talk about it. She told me how her mother gave her this big rap about, 'You're married. You've got two kids who can't support themselves. He's a good provider.' And my grandmother's very old country. Then my father's relatives came to her and told her that he's a good guy. He's really sorry. He's so miserable without you. Take him back.

"And she talks about it with anger. It's good to see it. And I try not to be too opinionated. I just kind of say, 'Wow, how are you feeling?' And listen to her more than anything else. Because I'm the only one she can talk to about it. And, god, I'm glad we can talk about it."

"Do you think she was ever jealous of you?"

"Oh, yeah. She is. Very jealous. She told me one time during one of our long talks that she saw this movie where this suburban family—they had one daughter, and the father was always doing things with the daughter: always taking her places and buying her things. And the mother was really jealous. And the daughter ran off and, you know, typical runaway, turned into a prostitute, a dope addict. And finally decided that she couldn't make it on her own.

"So she called home. And the parents were having this big party. And the mother answered the phone. And the daughter said, 'Mom, I want to come home.' And the mother said, 'No. No, you can't come home.' 'Cause I guess the father had been paying a lot of attention to the mother now the daughter was gone.

"And my mother was practically in tears. She was telling me that that's how she felt a lot of the time. Yeah. She can tell me at least."

"You said a while back you find the subject of incest scary?"

"Right. I don't know. Sometimes I have a few drinks and I'll be with a friend and I'll just start talking about it because I just have to get it out. And they'll just kind of look at me and go, 'Wow. Wow. That's really, really terrible.' When I try to put myself in somebody else's shoes, listening to them or something, as though I haven't lived through it myself, I can very easily see myself extremely grossed out. Repulsed, really. Because it is repulsive. It's really sickening. Not just a grown man molesting a child, but his daughter, yet."

"Have you run across the people who say, 'Why can't it be all right?' "

"Oh, god. Tell them to ask somebody who's been through it.

"But I do remember that my father in one of his big talks about sex with me, this was a very long time ago. He said that part of the reason he did it, went all the way, was because he had read an article in a magazine about some tribe where the father initiated the daughter before she got married and that was just what kind of pushed him over the edge. I don't think that kind of stuff around is too good."

"You're the second person who's said that. I wonder if it was the same article."

Prisms of Hate

Things were starting to get a little tough. The morning mail turned the coffee bitter. The day's interview turned the dinner bland. I added a kitten to the household. Something simple. Something cute.

Some daddies are multiply abusive. For some kids, abuse is so pervasive—sexual, emotional, physical—there is no room for compartmentalizing, for living on two levels, for the luxury of denial. Yet some of them survive too.

Wendy was seventeen when she wrote to me.

"To Whom It May Concern:

"I am a seventeen-year-old girl with several painful memories of a near-incestuous relationship with my father. (I am not sure if it was total incest in that I never had intercourse with him, although that's what he wanted—it was mainly molestation.)

"I have been considering writing a book on my life myself, though I'm not sure how to go about it.

"Therefore, I am more than willing to help you, for I feel I have a lot to tell.

"The reasons I wanted to write the book are that I want to bring this awful thing to the public's attention so that we can *do something about it. It must stop!*

"I would never wish on *any* child what I've gone through.

"I know it will be painful for me, but it's worth every painful memory if it will somehow contribute to the termination of incest.

Wendy

'Prisms of Hate'

"Through crystaled rain I ran in my fury. Through fire, through hate. Running, running, hoping never to have to return. At my destination, all hope was lost. It was empty, deserted. Now, nowhere left to go but home. Home? No! Never again! Slowly, slowly, I walked back. Fear, defeat, expanding in me until I fought back tears, crystaled tears, prisms of hate. I must remain strong. Go back and take the blows until—until what?

Wendy
(written Saturday, September 6,
by me after an attack by my father)"

"I've been looking through various diaries that I kept during the worst times when my father was really bugging me, and now, looking back on it, it's hard to believe that it all happened to me. It's like I've tried to wash all those bad memories out of my system. And in looking at that pool of memories I see reflections, not of me, but of a young, very confused, very hateful person. But I now see that I had a right to be.

"My entire childhood was a strange blend of love and hate. When I was younger, I had an older sister and brother. My brother died of leukemia when he was only eight. I was four at the time. He died at home, practically right before my eyes, and although I was so young, I'll never, never forget.

"Our house was an extremely tense place during my brother's illness. My father would shower gifts on my brother and then turn around and beat up on my older sister. I was really too young to remember any exact events. I've more or less blacked out that period from my mind. The only days I remember clearly are the day my brother died—and the funeral.

"When my parents first found out my brother was ill, my father had the 'habit' of taking *all* his frustrations out on my older sister. Though she was only about ten years old, if she did not do her homework right, he might make her kneel in the corner with her hands above her head for hours.

"If she'd come home a few minutes late, he'd beat her until my mother had to pull him off of her.

"I was only about four then and could not quite understand what was going on. However, I was scared most of the time.

"My father had a way of being cruel. He'd tease me about my flat feet, telling me I walked like a duck. And I cried hard and often.

"For all of my childhood, ours was the type of house where the only time everyone was relaxed was when daddy was gone.

"He was gone much of the time, being a perfectionist and a workaholic. But work was the only thing he was addicted to. Though he was a heavy cigarette smoker, he never touched alcohol.

"He hated and still hates priests and doctors. I think this is due to his time spent in orphanages. He once told me how the nuns would watch the boys while they showered, and if they'd do anything wrong, they'd beat them with some type of stick.

"As a child, I was afraid to admit when I was sick, because he'd blame it on me. He'd say I purposely got sick by 'hanging around with those snotty-nosed kids.'

"I was also a late walker, and when I did walk, my left foot turned in. He'd always imitate me sarcastically and say I was doing it on purpose to get attention. I didn't know how to cope with this, but at the time just figured that all fathers were that way.

"When I joined Camp Fire Girls, I learned that all fathers are not the way mine was.

"My father would never participate in father-daughter dinners or any other activity that I was involved in. So my mother would go, after fighting with him on how he took no interest in his children.

"School grades were important to him. Luckily for me, I got good grades in school. However, I was always scared to death to ask him for help, knowing how angry he'd get if I couldn't understand something.

"As a child, I used to daydream of having a different

family—one like our next-door neighbor's who had two daughters close in age. These people led an extremely active and social life. They would travel a lot and also would entertain guests almost every night. They would have outdoor barbecues, and sometimes my older sister and I would be asked over to help finish off the leftovers.

"Their family seemed so loving, and the girls were involved in music, sports, and Camp Fire Girls—their mother was a leader of their troop.

"They seemed so happy all the time that I would actually pray that I would wake up and be one of their daughters.

"I would also watch the show 'Bewitched' and wish that I could 'twitch' myself into being one of them instead of who I was—a nervous, bewildered, frightened girl.

"I believe my father began molesting my older sister when she began high school. By this time my mother had had another child—a girl.

"I'd see my father go in the bedroom I shared with my older sister at the time, then I'd start to hear her laughing—she always laughed when he'd molest her.

"The part of his molesting her that is so painful for me to write about is when he would get her down on the floor, get on top of her, pull up her shirt, and unhook her bra. He would then pull her bra up over her breasts and begin biting and gnawing on her breasts, making roaring and grunting noises like an animal. My sister would cry out then laugh and put up with it—usually because she had a date with her boyfriend that night and didn't want to blow it by getting my father angry.

"While this was happening my mother would ignore it—she was usually in her room—and after a while I tried to ignore it, too, by keeping my eyes glued to the TV set. Nevertheless, this ignore-it tactic didn't work for me. I was repulsed by what I was seeing and hearing and I wondered why *didn't she do anything to stop it? Why didn't anyone stop it?*

"Those are questions I feel I still don't have the answers to.

"The problem grew worse and more violent. My father would not even let my sister's boyfriend come up on the driveway. He'd make my sister walk home from work late at night.

"He hooked up a secret phone in our basement and listened to all her telephone calls. He went through her purse and stole money and read notes she had written or received.

"Even when she'd rip up the notes, he'd piece them back together.

"My mother during this time did very little or nothing to alleviate the problem. She went through my sister's things a few times herself.

"When my sister was sixteen, she ran away to her boyfriend's house for a few days, then came back.

"For the next two years, she had to cope (as we all did) with my father's moods. Sometimes he'd let her see her boyfriend—sometimes he wouldn't. He still molested her often.

"Looking back on it I know there was a time when my mother did stand up to my father. I was about four or five and my older sister had gone to the local swimming pool and had come home fifteen minutes late. My father met her in the kitchen door inside the house and the second she walked in he started beating her up so hard as if to kill her! My mother and I were in the bedroom and we heard my sister's screams and ran to the kitchen.

"My sister was standing in front of the door in her bathing suit trying to protect herself with a towel, but my father was beating her on her back and arms with his fists.

"My mother ran and tried to pull him off of her and was screaming, 'What in the hell are you trying to do to her?'

"He pushed her out of his way with great force—almost knocking my mother to the floor. He then went outside and did not return for a while.

"I was terrified. I remember holding onto the wall for dear life. I did not know why this was happening. My stomach felt like it was in knots—a feeling I would get hundreds of times later in life—when I myself was to be the target of my father's attacks.

"Perhaps my mother stopped trying to do anything because she was afraid of getting knocked around herself—and a few times she did get knocked around.

"One time my youngest sister was in her crib and wouldn't stop crying. It was about nine o'clock and I was lying in bed. My father kept coming in the room and slapping her in the face and telling her to shut up. She was about six months old then, so of course she didn't understand him and cried more.

"He was hitting her so hard that I could hear her body bouncing in the crib. I was scared—knots in my stomach and breaking out in a cold sweat.

"Finally my mother tried to pull him off of her and my father shoved her so hard that he knocked her into the hallway and she fell down.

"Then he stopped hitting my sister and returned to the living room.

"When my older sister had been out of high school for a year (my father had refused to go to her high school graduation), she became pregnant and got married.

"My father disowned her, called her a slut and refused to let any of us go to her wedding, which was taken care of by her new in-laws.

"When I was in seventh and eighth grades it all started. My father refused to give my mother money. He'd do the grocery shopping and pay all the bills. He was spending about twenty dollars a week. (My mother by this time had had another child—a girl.)

"The food was mainly frozen—or else hot dogs and beans. There was not much my mother could do with this food to make it taste even halfway decent.

"My father would usually begin eating and then say, 'Where'd you learn to cook, lady?'

"My mother seldom responded to this remark.

"Then my father would get up and empty his plate in the garbage and then make himself something else to eat.

"After awhile we began to eat dinner before he got home, my mother always being sure to save some for my father, which he never ate.

"He began to go to fast-food joints, bring the food home, and then eat a big juicy hamburger in front of us, who had just had beans for dinner.

"Soon my mother got up enough guts to find the receipts and take back some of the rotten cereal he'd bought and purchase some pop tarts to replace it. The next morning the pop tarts would be gone, and we would have nothing for breakfast except some more stale cereal.

"Soon after, my mother got a job in a factory, working from

five P.M. to one A.M. This meant I was left to clean up after supper and put my sisters to bed.

"I can't recall the first time I was molested, but I know once it started it became more and more often.

"I became sickened by the sight of my father—who now that my mother was not around would lay almost naked in front of the television set in the living room and masturbate.

"I remember that when I was in fifth grade and he explained the facts of life to me he insisted on showing me how the sperm came out. He lay down on the bed and put my hand on his penis and made me rub until it came out. A phone call interrupted his doing anything else.

"I remember feeling totally embarrassed about the subject of sex for a long, long time after that experience.

"Unlike my sister, I did not laugh and pretend to enjoy what he was doing to me. I told him outright I hated it and wanted it to stop—that only made the attacks much worse.

"I dreaded each night after my sisters were in bed and when I had to go to bed because I never knew what he'd pull.

"It was a tradition in our house to kiss our father good-night, and each night my stomach became knotted before I had to do this.

"Sometimes he'd pull me down on the couch and lay on top of me, rubbing his penis against me. I'd cringe beneath him and he'd call me a big baby and send me to bed.

"He'd also come into the bed after I was in it, with hardly anything on, and tell me to let him screw me and say, 'No one will have to know—it's just between you and me.'

"I would fake being asleep or say nothing or no. After a while he'd leave saying things like, 'You'll be sorry.' Or, 'I'll show you.'

"The times I was the most frightened were when like during or after dinner he'd say things to me like, 'You're gonna lose your cherry tonight.' Or, 'Kiss your cherry good-bye.' Or, 'Tonight you're gonna get it right between the legs.'

"On those nights, he'd usually get me down and put his hands inside my pants—but he'd never stick his fingers inside me.

"As I grew older, it got worse. One night we had a talk. He said he wouldn't touch me anymore providing I went along with any decisions he made whenever I asked for anything. Needless to say, he always said no to everything and for the next two years I hardly ever went out unless he was out of town.

"When I graduated from eighth grade, all types of dumb rules started appearing.

"I had to cut my hair. I couldn't wear makeup or nail polish. I could only stay on the phone so long and he was the only one who could answer it. I couldn't date. I had to ask to get something to wear. If I was outside, I had to ask and give a reason to go back inside.

"My father and mother were still not communicating. They'd write each other notes.

"One morning, I found a note saying something about how my mother wouldn't sleep with him. She had written back saying she'd only sleep with him if she was paid five dollars each time!

"Both my parents are penny pinchers, though my father always made a good salary. But this was a note I just couldn't believe. During eighth grade, he kept asking me if I'd started my period yet. I hadn't and he kept offering to put vaseline on his fingers and stretch out my vagina. He said he'd done it for my sister and that it had started for her.

"Still being naive, this scared me. I began wondering if I was normal and prayed to God that it would start so I wouldn't have to let my father do it.

"I prayed often during those years—mainly that God would make my father move out, something my father had threatened my mother with for as long as I could remember.

"Also in eighth grade, I had the opportunity to go abroad with some other students. My mother agreed to pay half if my father would.

"He said I could go if I screwed with him. 'You have to give a little to get a little,' he said.

"Needless to say, I didn't go.

"Freshman year was rough, and I have one example that will explain how my father treated me.

"First of all, he'd picked out a nickname for me—Ugliness. It was a name my younger sisters would call me for months—out of fear of getting on my father's bad side.

"It was the night of the homecoming parade and I asked if I could go and be back at eight P.M. He said yes. I then asked if I could stay until 8:30. He said, 'Screw me.' I said, 'No. Now can I?' He said, 'You just answered your own question.'

"I grabbed my shoes and ran out of the house in a fury with him shouting behind me.

"I returned home at 8:30 to find the door locked and the lights turned out. I knocked and rang the doorbell. No answer. I could see however that the TV was on and the car was in the garage—still no one answered.

"I went to my girl friend's house and explained to her how no one would answer. For an hour I was at her house calling my house but never getting an answer. Even my girl friend's mother called a few times, and she offered to let me spend the night seeing how afraid I was of going home.

"At 9:30 he finally answered and asked me where the hell I'd been. I told him that I'd been calling and calling. He said I was lying and told me, 'Get your ass home, Miss Smartass. And you're grounded for each minute you're late past the eight o'clock curfew I gave you.'

"I ran home in shock, confusion, and hatred. When I got home, he was standing there with pen and paper in front of the kitchen clock adding up the minutes.

"He grounded me for something like sixty-six days.

"All through my freshman year he wouldn't let me go out unless I let him 'give me a squeeze'—as he called it. To do this, I would reluctantly sit down on the bed and pull up my shirt, while my own father played with my breasts.

"It was a sick feeling and I became quickly reluctant to ever ask to go out.

"Then two events occurred that severed our relationship.

"One time when my mother was in the bathtub and my sisters were in bed, I was sitting there watching TV. My father was in a hideous mood.

"He came up from behind and put one arm around my neck as if to strangle me. He threw me to the ground and sat on top of me, pinning my arms down.

"His face was ugly, violent, and mean. He began messing up my hair. It was all over my face and I couldn't see or breathe but could do nothing about it since he had my arms pinned down.

"Then he began to make me slap myself in the face with my own hands. He was holding them and he kept making me hit myself.

"I was terrified and fighting him with all my strength. I was screaming and screaming but that just made him make me hit myself harder.

"This went on for twenty minutes. It seemed like an eternity. My mother finally came out of the bathroom and asked what the hell he was doing.

"He stood up and let go of me, kicked me aside, and said, 'Oh, she's nothin' but a goddamned baby.'

"I was crying and in hysterics. I ran into the bedroom screaming obscenities. I cried so hard I almost vomited. I wanted to die I was so mad and didn't know if I could take this life I was leading much longer.

"I contemplated overdosing but was so choked up I couldn't even swallow my own saliva.

"My parents went on screaming at each other.

"Then, when my mother came into our room, I told her everything that had been going on at night while she was at work.

"I did not get half the reaction I expected. She did not seem too shocked but was a little upset. She tried to discuss it with him but he told her to shut up or else he'd shut her up.

"Now that I'd told all, he did everything he could to make my life a living hell. He also mysteriously stopped molesting.

"I couldn't do anything. Not even read the newspaper or listen to the radio. I even had to ask to eat or drink anything. I had to stay in my bedroom, and if I entered the front room, I had to give a reason as to why I wasn't in my bedroom.

"He gave me hassles about washing my hair (I always had to do it on the sneak), buying clothes, my looks ("Ugliness"), and every little thing a person could imagine.

"I felt my spirit—my will to live—was rapidly dying. I felt I was a useless nothing. Most of all, I felt trapped.

"He began to be more physically cruel to me. One night he jumped me. He knocked me to the floor and sat on top of me. My mother was in the kitchen doing dishes. My little sisters crowded around to see what was going on.

"He began slapping me and calling me Ugliness. He pinned down my arms underneath me.

"My little sisters joined in. They began slapping me and calling me Ugliness too.

"My father had a lit cigarette in his hand. He began holding the lit end to my lips and I felt them starting to burn. He flicked his ashes in my face.

"My mother stood in the kitchen doing dishes as if *nothing* was happening!

"Finally he let me go and I screamed at them all and ran out of the house. But there was nowhere to go.

"I returned home, nothing was said. My father and I never really spoke again.

"A few months later I began to plan running away. My girl friend had a friend who lived in another state and we planned to go there by bus. We went, but after one day she decided she wanted to go home.

"I was too scared to go home. I knew my father would kill me. Perhaps literally kill me. He had a gun—a German Luger that he would always sit in the front room and clean. That thought haunted me along with several others, and I decided to stay where I was rather than to chance going back home. I had made my girl friend promise not to tell anyone where I was.

"However she did not keep that promise for long. Soon after, the police were calling the house where I was staying. Within a few days the police came around. They'd already contacted my mother and she was wiring me money.

"In the meantime I stayed at a detention home. It was nice except for the bars that covered every window and the locks on the doors.

"The counselors there were very nice. One of them asked me if I really wanted to go home.

"It was a difficult question. Of course I did not want to go home—but I told her that I did. I guess I was afraid of what might happen to me if I'd said no. However, the idea of never having to face my father was tempting. Yet I still told her that I wanted to go home.

"Looking back on it, I guess it was not actually my home I wanted to return to—but the town itself, my friends.

"Returning home after running away, the terrifying feeling I got on making that decision. I looked around that home and I saw the bars and screens and locks, and it all seemed no different than my own house except that in my house they didn't actually exist as material objects. At my house all my father's rules were those chains and locks and bars, and I was never told what would happen if I said no, so I said yes I wanted to go home instead.

"I couldn't bring myself to tell those people what they were returning me to. However, I did tell my roommate, and maybe deep down I was hoping that she would tell them for me, that she'd spare me the pain.

"I also lived with the dream that perhaps my running away would have an impact on my father—a big enough impact to make him stop it—and so I took the chance and got on the bus back home. Several times on the way back I was tempted to get off the bus and stay off but I only had fifteen dollars and I knew that wouldn't take me far, plus I was too afraid to go because I didn't know anyone at those stops.

"I figured if it was my time to die there wasn't much I could do.

"I called my mother when I arrived and asked how my father felt. My mother never really answered that question.

"Getting out of the cab and walking into my house was terrifying. My father was at the dining room table. My mother came to greet me. She asked me if I'd lost any weight. Then we went in her bedroom to talk. She said that she'd wired me the few dollars she'd managed to save and that she expected to be paid back. She also said my father had refused to send any money, saying, 'Let her rot in jail. Then she'll learn.'

"The next morning I found a note from my father stating how I was a rebellious brat and giving me a list of rules I would have to follow. The list took in every phase of a person's life—when I could wash my hair, which he said I'd have to cut, when I could eat, sleep, talk, also how many hours I could sleep at night, what I could wear, and last of all, that I was grounded until my sixteenth birthday. I was fourteen at the time.

"The police had suggested that we go in for family counseling, and I was hoping we would so I could bring that note along. But my father refused to go, and since I could not use the phone and was grounded, there was not much I could do. I thought of my counselor at school, but felt I just couldn't discuss my father.

"My father finally moved out about six months later—a year and a half ago. I did not speak to him for about six months before that and have not spoken to him since.

"Now I spend as much time as I can getting out of the house.

My mother, who when my father lived at home ignored those horrible things he did, now picks on me for every little thing. She is never happy with anything I do. If I'm home, she says I should go out because it's so peaceful when I'm gone. If I go out a lot, she complains that I'm never home.

"She also keeps saying that I only care about myself. I don't understand how she can say that—I lend her money whenever she runs out, which is often, and tell her she can take her time repaying me. I also try to do everything she tells me but when I do it she always finds something wrong with it.

"Also, the other day she told me that she thinks there's something wrong with me because she says I'm flat chested and have no bustline at all. It seems she loves to cut me down. Except for writing this, I try not to think about my father. I'm even considering changing my last name.

"I can't say that I actually hate him but I dread the day when he'll die and I won't be able to shed a tear at his funeral.

"If I do shed a tear, it won't be in grief, it will merely be tears—once prisms of hate."

Present Tense

Present tense. Now.

Today, *today*, my mother told me I was born illegitimate.

How very, very odd.

How can a baby be illegitimate? (Aren't the parents the ones who've done something illegitimate?) Does it mean I'm illegitimate now?

Then: "How come you *liked* your father?"

I'm floored. Fishing for *any* memory of him, vivid, I had no answer. I never said I liked him. Liked who? Who was he? Where does the mind go? She said I should like him. Told me he was a brilliant man. (If he was brilliant, I might be too—is that a clue?)

"I'd have killed him if I'd known," she said.

"Just as well then," I said. "They'd have locked you up. And he died anyway."

"I'd have killed him," she repeated.

"I don't know—how he saw me," I said.

"You know how he saw you?" Mad. Fierce. Pulled up to her full four feet, ten inches.

"I don't."

"He was drunk once. You were just born. He said, 'Look. Look what I've got here. A midget [meaning me]. And a bastard.' "

I looked at my wrist, the back where that nice bumpy bone is.

(You've got it too. I don't know what it's called.) How very extraordinary. How very odd.

Illegitimate.

I think of Piaf.

I hate it. I can't sing.

I push illegitimate around on my tongue. Roll it past the kitten who chases it. Pounces. Retreats.

How strange.

Born of two writers, my sense of myself was based on the stories they told. Now they change the beginning. How does that affect the middle, the rest?

A puff of smoke. He appears, looking dapper, young. Not to be outdone, I also drop years. My mother, too, retreats in time.

"What's all this rubbish?" he says.

"Get off the rug," I say. "You're getting soot on it."

He waves a manuscript in the air.

"Say your piece," he says. "But be quick. I'm working on a play. A light comedy about a romance in hell. The Devil's Own Theater has picked up an option."

"We were just talking about this and that," says my mother.

"Is it true that you always wanted a boy?" I ask.

"Who told you that?"

I gesture toward my mother.

"The way you put it," he says, "you make me sound queer."

"Well, dear," says my mother, "to be fair. The first three, no, let me see, six months, he was so proud. And so thoughtful. And so generous. And so—proud. He went right out and rented a penthouse, so I wouldn't have to drag a carriage up and down stairs."

"Yes, I've heard that story," I say.

"And he bought a camera and film and a piggy bank. 'We're going to put in five dollars a week for her,' he said. And I said—."

"You said, 'Oh, one dollar a week would be plenty.' "

"That's right. And he took a five-dollar bill right down to get change. And he dropped twenty quarters into the pig. Five years later, I opened the pig. And I spent the five dollars—."

"On food," we say together.

"You were big," I say to him. "I get the same sensation of

picked-up and put-down in a very fast, very sudden elevator, in jet airplanes traveling through a storm. Exhilarating, terrifying, grand. I remember your trouser cloth at the knee."

"Is that all you remember?" he asks.

"I remember a bed very high from the floor. Climbing off it as one would climb down from a wall. And a doorknob high over my head. I remember sleeping to the slapsound of cards. Drifting off to the sight of a black door rimmed in light. And waking to the same light, but no sound. Silence. I don't trust people who stay awake while I sleep."

"It's true," says my mother. "We went out. He went out. I had to go with him. He was—."

"Drinking. It's true," he says. "So I drank. I would have got over it in any case in time. Disgust for my own condition would have cured me. But you had to go and—."

"Betray you," says my mother.

"Don't interrupt," he says.

"Alienate your daughter," she says.

"Let me finish."

"Send you to—."

"You sent me to the psycho ward," he says.

"You were violent, drunk," she says.

"I remember you made me sit entirely still at dinner," I say.

"You played with your silver," he says.

"And you played in restaurants with the sugar and the salt and the pepper, pouring them all in a water glass."

"To make you laugh," he says.

"You laughed," I say.

"One should always be able to laugh at oneself," says my mother.

"And I remember if I dropped my spoon and you were talking, you picked me up from my chair and threw me in my room."

"You were restless," he says.

"She was a child," says my mother.

"I was frightened," I say.

But his attention is gone. He is settled in a chair, marking over his manuscript.

I pick up a pad.

"Who are you?" I write. "Yesterday, you were a man in a hotel room, smiling, and saying go on, undress; saying, with those words, I seduce you. As much as to say: I damn you with my body. Very well, then. Since incest, in this instance, is merely a figure of speech (your parenthood, existing solely in your sex, was over and done with before I was born)—very well, then. I damn you too."

A flash beam falls on my pad. He leans behind me, reading.

"It's a little late for that," he says.

"Tell me something," I say. "Tell me why you decided to rape me in a hotel room."

"Rape," he says. "Who said it was rape? Look. You've got a story here, but you've got the wrong handle on it. I see it as a romantic drama. A man and a young girl meet. He doesn't know she is his daughter. She doesn't know he is her father. They are attracted to one another immediately. A letter comes announcing the death of. . . ."

"The mother," I say. "Shit. I ask a simple question, I get a third-rate play."

". . . the confrontation scene takes place at the end of the second act. . . ."

His voice fades. His image fades. Only a great black smudge is left on my nice red chair.

"I was thirty-nine," said my mother. "It was my last chance to have a child. And he *begged* me to go through with it. On his *knees*."

"May I put this in the book?" I said.

"Oh, dear. I don't care. Next to incest, what does illegitimate matter? And we did get married a while later. By then, of course, I knew he was drinking. I didn't want to. But—I had you. And he wanted us—he always wanted us—to be a family."

"You tell me this now," I said. "Why?"

"Well—we were talking. It just came up. I never wanted to tell you before."

Never mind. I know why.

Families. Goddamn.

Is it possible to say forgive and forget?

Forgive and Forget

Maggie met me at the airport—a cheerful, handsome, *direct* woman. Though we'd exchanged size and hair length descriptions over the phone, it seemed as she strode toward me that quite probably we'd have recognized each other even without them.

In the car, it was she who was putting me at ease. Only once, when I asked if she had children, did she hesitate.

"I had children," she said. "Three children. I haven't seen them in years. I'll tell you about that later."

Although she'd just recently moved in, the atmosphere in her house didn't feel at all tentative. Details of a kind of carefree attention were everywhere. A vase of flowers that had reached their prime yesterday. Ashtrays, none full, none empty, placed for convenience, not centered for aesthetics.

"OK," she said, pulling her feet up under her on the large, cushy couch. "I'm presently thirty-six. I have been married four times, had three children. My husband died in March of this past year and that ended a kind of stormy marriage, but one which had been growing very consistently and which, for the year before he died, had begun to be a very mature and a very good working, solid relationship. The first one I ever really had. And it's given me a better sense of direction and put me much more in touch (although I hate that term) with myself. I'm in supportive therapy, primarily to deal with his death and the kinds of things that have resulted from that. And, on a wider level, to deal with stuff from the past, which includes an incestuous relationship with my father. That started at the age of three or four and continued off and on until I was sixteen and able to leave home.

"My mother came from a rather poor family and my father from a dirt-poor family. My mother was five months pregnant at the age of seventeen, by my father. When she asked him to marry her, he said no. Now he was in the army—and she said she was going to his commanding officer if he didn't because that was a terrible situation for a girl to be in at that time in that town. So he agreed. He was twenty-one.

"When they went down to get his birth certificate so they could get married, it turned out it had illegitimate stamped on it—which was, like, a riot.

"Well, she had twins. The girl died at birth, and the boy died at thirteen months from meningitis. Then I was the next child along. And I think—though in that environment divorce wasn't really a way out—they might have considered that possibility if I hadn't come along.

"It was during the war. I was born in 1941. He went overseas. And my mother had me, and we lived with my grandmother a while and then moved to a small apartment in the slums.

"I think I was happy with my mother at that point. I do remember at times she would be relatively affectionate. I remember standing on a chair and brushing her hair. Warm things.

"She was very pretty. She was very erratic. When she lost her temper, she really lost it. Would attack me, physically. Would really go. One of the reasons for that, I think, was she was very immature. She really got married as a child—and she had to deal with a very bleak, loveless marriage. Her relationship with my father was very masochistic, and I think she took her hostilities out on me.

"And you know it was the kind of background where people tended to be very obsessed with what will the neighbors think and cleanliness. So it was always sort of, "Be proper. You can't play outside on Sundays because that's not done. And if you go to someone's house, if they ask you if you want seconds, you must say no. It's not mannerly. If you go to someone's door, you mustn't look around their house. That's not mannerly.'

"They weren't religious. But I used to be sent to Sunday school as a child—mostly to get rid of me, to have the child out of the house. And—you should send your child to church, that sort of thing.

"I was an only child until seven. By then, my mother had lost two or three other babies that she carried to full term. Then, when I was seven, she adopted my sister. My sister was an illegitimate child and my mother had been in the hospital. I think she had been all psychologically prepared to have a child. And again, again, again they were dead, dead, dead. This was a child they asked her to help bottle feed because the mother had abandoned her. So she decided to adopt the child. Then later she had two successful pregnancies and had two boys, the youngest of whom was brain damaged at birth.

"So in my later years I was sort of a glorified baby-sitter. I didn't have the freedom a lot of kids had. I also had a couple of paper routes. But half the money from that went to my parents—as sort of compensation for loss of my services.

"I can remember having good, happy times. Playing with kids. Running around the block. Climbing trees. Playing in school. I was always painfully shy, though. And I always felt somehow unclean, unlike other people, like a freak. This was because of the incestuous relationship, I think. Starting at four.

"My father came back. He'd been all over the European front, Italy, North Africa. I think he'd actually been in a field hospital for about a year with a shrapnel wound. But back he came. And I remember him walking into the room looking—absolutely gigantic to a child my age. And my mother saying, sounding very proud, 'This is your daddy.'

"And he had a beard. And I had never seen a man with a beard. I remember just sort of looking at him. I remember him picking me up and putting me on his knee and saying, 'I'm your daddy.' And trying to hug me. And feeling his prickly beard and trying to pull away because I just couldn't quite put it all together. That was when it began.

"Now my mother—it was kind of a community thing—she would spend a lot of time in the street talking with people, the neighbors. And I remember she was outside talking to some women and I was in the apartment with my father. I remember him going to the window and looking out and saying, 'God, your mother really likes to natter. Look at her talking—blah blah blah.'

"Then I remember him taking his pants down and saying, 'Come over here.' And sitting on the bed. And I remember a feeling of total fear. Total revulsion. I knew it was wrong, even at that age. I knew that it was somehow perverse. At the time I remember being (a) frightened and (b) acutely uncomfortable with the situation. There was a hush, an intensity there that frightened me. And repulsed. Thinking, 'God, that looks really weird.'

"He wanted me to touch it. Touch it gently and then to do fellatio on him. To put it in my mouth. And I remember thinking, "Oh, it smells funny. It looks—ugly. It smells bad and the color of the skin is so weird.' And I remember him telling me then, 'If you ever tell your mother I will kill you.'

"And, he said, 'You know what happens to little girls if they do this sort of thing?' He said, 'They'll lock you up for the rest of your life.' Nice guy. And I didn't question it at all. He was totally omnipotent. I was totally afraid. So totally afraid.

"When he would walk into the room it was like a sinister force. That was a world where man is boss, man is king. At dinner, my father would maybe get a piece of steak. We would have lettuce and tomato sandwiches or macaroni and cheese. If there was any steak left, my mother would get some. And then if there was any left, maybe one of the kids would get some. If my mother would say, 'Maggie, come up. It's time to eat,' I'd fudge and say, 'Yes, be up in a minute.' But if my father would come to the window and say, 'Maggie!'—I'd go right upstairs. And he would be across the room. And all he would do is lower his paper and look at me and I would just freeze. A brutal man.

"And physically violent. He was the type of drinker that didn't take a drink every day. He'd go on toots. As though he would stay home and suffer his lot and carry my mother as a millstone around his neck—which he said openly. He would plod along full of loathing, being very sadistic toward her, saying very unkind, very cruel things to her and everyone around him. He would go along, go along—and then it would be as though he had had it.

"He would get dressed—get out of his old clothes into the one expensive outfit he always had. Perfectly cut, expensive clothes, beautiful shoes. Understated. Very elegant. And he would be getting dressed and my mother would say, 'Where are you going?'

"And he would say, 'I'm going out for a few drinks.'

"And it was as though—*ta-dum!* And everybody sat around and nobody said anything. And he would go out and come back at god knows what hour totally drunk. But I don't ever remember my parents going out together. Ever. Ever.

"He would go out and she would stay home and she would be frantic. He would usually have been with another woman, I think. Then a fight would come. He would come home and knock hell out of her. Really beat her up. She would get angry and call him names. And he would just go on beating hell out of her.

"One time, I was eight or nine, she was packing her clothes. Saying, 'I'm leaving. I'm not putting up with this and nobody has to live this way and blah blah blah.' And I remember feeling two things. Totally afraid in case she would leave me with my father. And she was saying, 'I'm not taking your goddamn children with me.' And I was petrified. I had knots in my stomach, but I sat there, not able to show anything. Completely stony-faced, silent. And she was packing, saying, 'Rags. That's all I have.' Throwing things together. And, 'I'm leaving.'

"And then he said, '*I'll* leave.'

"And I thought, 'Oh, thank God.' I remember saying that to myself. 'Oh, thank God.' Like a little old lady.

"Then I remember I went to a birthday party and I came back and he was lying in bed and she was sitting on the edge of the bed being very coy with him. And they had made up. And I said to myself, 'Oh, Jesus. So close—and it didn't happen.'

"It was a very destructive relationship. And they were very destructive. One of the difficulties I'm dealing with now that I've handled before in much more destructive ways is my sense of self. I always had these mixed messages, for which I'm very angry with them. It was, 'You can do better. You're bright and we're bright and you can do this, that, and the other thing.' I went to a school for gifted kids. I was always striving.

"But then on the other hand they would always say, 'You can't do anything right. You never do anything right. Look at the way you stand. Look at the way your clothes look on you. The way you talk. Everything you do is wrong. Constantly wrong.' The mixed message. One, I must perform for them and perform over and above everybody else. Two, it's never any good what you do. So not only was I abused sexually, I was also abused emotionally. Constantly being brought down. Whichever was worse, I sure didn't need both.

"I remember him masturbating in the bathroom. Saying, 'I'm going to show you something—how you make babies.' And he made me stand and watch him until he climaxed into the toilet. And I remember being frightened and repulsed and curious all at the same time. And kind of shocked. And thinking, 'God, how strange.' But being very afraid of him. My father was like a giant at that time.

"I remember him doing cunnilingus on me when I was little, a tiny child. And fondling me. And feeling nothing but anger, revulsion and having to deal with my rage and my fear and never showing anything on my face.

"He would tell me to tell him it was good. 'Tell me it's good.'

" 'It's good.'

"And, 'No, tell me like you mean it.'

" 'It's good.'

" 'No, tell me like you really mean it. I really want you to tell me.'

"I remember being so embarrassed and hating him so violently. I remember him coming into my room. I was about six. And pulling the covers back and putting his hands on my genitals and making me put my hands on his. And I was so petrified and so worried that my mother would know what he was doing. Because my mother was asleep in the same house.

"And I have come to feel later that from this point my mother had to know. I really believe that she was a silent partner in the whole thing because I don't think that you can live in a house with that going on for twelve years and not know that it's going on. I think she had to know. And, this may be purely speculation, but I really believe wholeheartedly that the only way she could cope with it and keep her marriage together was to ignore it. She had nowhere to go. Nothing she could do. Divorce was not a way out. Early in the marriage, I understand she once tried to leave him and go back to her parents. They said, 'You made your bed and you lie in it.'

"One night when I was nine or so, she said, 'Well, I'm going to the movies this evening and your daddy is going to stay home. Your daddy's going to take a nap. But, Maggie, you take care of the little kids, and if you have any problems, he'll be here.'

"And I remember being absolutely petrified, knowing what was going to happen. Another evening of the same bullshit. And I remember then saying—can you imagine how manipulative, so young?—'Can't I go with you?' Knowing the risk I was taking bucking him. Knowing I would have to deal with him later if that didn't work out—or even if it did, his venom from my trying to maneuver to stay out of his way. So much pressure created just by saying, 'Mother, can I please go with you?'

"And she went on just a tantrum, a tear. 'Goddamnit, I go to a movie about once every six months and you're so damned selfish and so worthless you can't even let me go to a movie for god sakes by myself without whining to come with me, and how can I go if you don't take care of the children and this is your responsibility,' and just blowing up at me. Me, sitting there just so frantic, saying to myself, 'Oh, god, she's going to leave me with him.' Knowing the minute the door closed, he would be in the bedroom.

"And he would say, 'Maggie? Come here.'

"And I remember him showing me pornographic pictures. And making me sit on a chair with my leg over the arm with no clothes on and masturbate. It was totally foreign. I just felt ludicrous and embarrassed and mortified. Humiliated. The anxiety was just incredible. And having him say, 'You say this. I want you to say that. Now I want you to say it this way and then do this and do that.' And feeling so ashamed.

"And then he would do cunnilingus. I remember just sitting on the chair watching his head between my legs, hating him. The hate, the hate was a living thing. I remember looking at his head and just wanting to take his hair and pull it out. At six years old.

"And he would sit across the room from me with his clothes off and masturbate or make me masturbate him, and he would read me dirty stories. And he would say, 'Look at your mother. She's had five children. What good is she to me? It's like sticking a sausage in a fireplace.' And tell me stories of how he had gone to bed with her sisters and her best friends and what they did and what so-and-so said, everything in detail.

"How did I cope? I compartmentalized it. I was able to sort of put it away. I remember lying there, crying, when I was very small and saying to myself, 'Some day I'm going to grow up and some day I'm going to get away from here.'

"And I did. Starting at sixteen, I had three very early, very bad marriages. Because I simply was not capable of adult relationships, of a healthy relationship with a man. In the beginning, I could relate fairly easily. But then a transference would come into it. I would become completely frigid. I would begin to act out all those angry things I had never been able to act out at the time.

"The first marriage—my parents just had a fit about it when they found out. They threw me out of the house. Finally, my mother came over and she cried. It was the first time I had ever seen her cry. And she said, 'I want you to come home. To visit. To get your things.'

"So I went home and I went to my bureau. And my father came in and closed the door. I opened a drawer and there was money in it. I said, 'What's this?' And he said, 'You're a married woman now. If you cooperate, that money is yours,' meaning if I went to bed with him. And I said, 'I don't want to cooperate.'

"That first time, I stayed married for two and a half years. I had a boy, a child. It seemed to me that my need was to be somehow normal, to be a mother and a wife. Somehow be normal. That was the only form of acceptance I had been raised for. Someday I would be married and live happily ever after.

"It didn't work. It wasn't normal. It was awful. Because after a little while all of the old experiences would come flooding in on me. All of the unexpressed anger would come out right in the middle of intercourse or something. I would just suddenly be ready to kill somebody. It was all of the rage that had been backlogged, never expressed.

"And then when I was pregnant, I would just schiz out. Because when my mother was pregnant, I had seen her beaten up so many times. See, my father would say, 'Well, look at her. She looks like a goddamn cow. I don't want anyone to see me walking down the street with her. God, look at her. She's out to *here*.' So when I was pregnant, I would feel so ugly and so unsure of myself—even more than usual. I was shattered. My ego was so damaged that when I was pregnant any sort of criticism at all, real or imagined, sent me off into total rage. Three rapid marriages. A child in each one. All doomed to begin with.

"All young, passive men. I didn't want to trust anybody. I wanted to be in control. During the second marriage, I began having an affair with a man who was ten years older and quite wealthy, who sent me to business school and was very kind to me. He really began giving me the idea that you can't just go through life living from day to day. You have to take charge of your life. You're not always going to be able to count on being cutesy. You're going to have to develop a little substance, something that is you. So from the business school I at least began to get a sense of something I could do. And now, finally, for the first time in my life I'm trying to put down roots—and to deal with all this.

"It's taken me years to be able to verbalize all this. And the first time I went to a psychologist I was twenty-three. My second marriage was breaking up. And so I went to a psychologist. And he tried to make me do fellatio on him in the office. Isn't that too much? Don't you love it? My protein count. Christ.

"And *now* I could deal with that very effectively. But then I was just a scared little girl. It was like panic and 'I don't want to embarrass him.' Back to that primitive response I'd been trained to so well.

"And when I wouldn't go back, he said on the phone, 'You're running away from yourself.' And I thought, 'My god. What is wrong with me? What is it that I do to people? What is wrong with me?' And feeling dirty, feeling guilty.

"As a kid I felt that. It was my fault. I was unclean. I was dirty. I was guilty. I didn't fit in. A sense of being tainted somehow. You're keeping so many secrets to yourself. So many skeletons in your closet. You hear other children saying my father this and my father that. But you're so guilt stricken and so guarded you can't say anything about your father. So while I do remember having fun sometimes with kids, I also remember feeling like a little old lady, being much older than my years.

"And I was really an acting-out adolescent. My anger was beginning to spill and I was really angry. I was always leading people to act out in class. Laughing. Raising hell. Interested in boys. About the only way I could really relate to them was seductively.

"And that brought down just crushing abuse. I remember once when I was eleven I had a crush on a boy at school and he kissed me. I got home a little late because I'd been waiting for him to work up the nerve to kiss me. And I got home and my mother said, 'Where have you been?' I said, 'I was with so-and-so.' 'What happened? What did he do?'

"I said, 'He didn't do anything.'

" 'What did he do?'

"And, 'Let me see your clothes,' and holding up my panties to see if there was anything in them. And calling me a whore and a slut.

"And my father would call me all sorts of names and would storm around saying, 'You're no goddam good. You're a whore. You're a nothing. You're this and you're that. You're bad through and through.' Just the whole verbal abuse that he heaped on me. They would turn even the most innocent relationship into a really dirty thing.

"It's hard to know which was worse abuse. I think that the 'you're no good, you're a whore, you're nothing'—that constant theme was almost or as bad as the sexual abuse because it was constant. But the *big* thing was sex. It was the sexual thing that made me so crazy for so many years. And I felt that the only way that I could have relationships with men was on a sexual basis. That that was the only way I could be accepted—if I put out. That was the only tool I had. Nothing else.

"But their constantly calling me a whore—so therefore I am. So therefore I can go to bed with anybody. It's a vicious cycle.

"And certain facets of myself that are there now developed then. I sense immediately when any conversation takes a deviant curve. I tend to avoid sexual confrontations or certain sexual conversational interplays. I can tell the moment there's any special interest a man takes in me, when he's been sexually affected by our relationship. It's like a sixth sense. And I remember as a child being able to do that. To try to change the subject. Somehow put brakes on it. Get it going some other way. The sense of panic, of desperately wanting to be in control, has never really left. And that's a hell of a burden.

"But my last husband, when I'd flip, he'd just say, 'Cut that shit out. I haven't done anything to you so don't take it out on me.' And I think that's right. I think that because your mother had roaches all over the house doesn't give you the right to be an obsessively compulsive housekeeper for the rest of your life and say, 'Well the reason I'm like this is because my mother had roaches in her house.' And you're sixty-eight years old. There comes a point where you have to say, 'That was what happened. But now I have to start doing something else.' And basically that is what has happened.

"Now my father—I keep skirting the issue because some of these things are quite painful for me to be talking about. So if I get upset, don't worry about it. I can deal with it. Anyhow. I had intercourse with my father when I was eleven.

"I remember starting my period then. I was with a girl friend who'd had her period and her older sister who'd had hers as well. I was at their summer cottage for the weekend. We were there and my period started. I was absolutely paralyzed. How do you go to the bathroom? You know, rushing to the bathroom every two minutes to peer at my crotch and say, 'Do you just sit down and go to the bathroom?' Couldn't believe this was actually happening to me. Now what's going to happen? And the thing I was totally afraid of was 'how am I going to tell my mother?'

"Sex was a no-no. You just didn't talk about it at all. And I remember hanging around and hanging around and goddamn she was cooking something in the kitchen, and I just kept going in and out, in and out. And she kept saying, 'What do you want?' And I would say, 'Nothing.' And then I would go back out and hang around and think, 'Oh God, I've got to tell her.' And I would go back in again, and she would say, 'Would you stop hanging around here?' And so I'd go back out again. Finally, the kitchen was right next to the bathroom, and I just said, 'My period started this weekend.' And I went in and shut the door to the bathroom and thought, 'Oh, god, now what am I going to do?' And I stayed in there for thirty minutes. I didn't know how to come out. How to look at her. What to say to her. Anything.

"And I finally came out and moped around the kitchen kind of looking down, and she said, 'Well, um, that will come every month and here's some money to buy some sanitary napkins. You have to get these and wear them, and you have to take lots of baths and keep away from boys.' That was my sex education.

"My *formal* sex education.

"And when my father came home shortly afterward—he'd been away for a while—I was thinking, 'Oh no. He's coming back. It's going to start all over again.' And I just hated it, hated it, hated it. And their bed was an open-out in the living room. And he was in bed the next day. My mother went out of the room and he said, 'Hi. Come on in.'

"And I kind of sidled into the room, hung about the doorway. And he said, 'Well, you're getting to be a big girl.' And I remember this body odor. I don't think he was a smelly man, but I'm very aware of the smell of a body from that particular time— that comes to me every once in a while, an awareness of that. And he says, 'Your mother tells me your period started.' And I thought, 'That fucker.' I thought, 'Why did she tell him? Why did she tell him?'

"And he says, 'Well, you're ready for it now, aren't you?'

"And just absolutely panicking. Panicking.

"And a week or so later I was alone with him and he brought out a condom—the kind that you washed and dried and put powder on or something, and then stuck it on. And he said that, you know, this was going to be it.

"And I remember him penetrating me slowly. I remember lying on the bed just shaking and thinking, 'Oh, god, what is he doing? Oh, god, what is he doing?' Absolutely no enjoyment at all at that point. Totally petrified. And he said, 'You know, I have to use this all of the time. Because if you ever had a baby, they would lock you up for that. And besides it would probably be crazy. That's why people are born deaf.' That sort of thing. That, I'm sure, didn't help with my pregnancies later.

"Fury, you know. Just fury. On top of everything, you know, above everything, he was invading the only relationship I had— which was my relationship with my mother. He was alienating me by saying, 'Don't you ever tell your mother about this or I will kill you.' Not only did he abuse me, but he took away the only relationship I really had. Annihilated that completely.

"I do remember once, my mother had to go to the hospital for a kidney infection. I do remember him getting into bed with me and caressing me and actually enjoying it that one time. I remember thinking, 'God, this feels good,' and the guilt and the surprise of enjoying it. Not the intercourse. I was never able to. I always wanted him to get it over with and leave me alone. I figured I'd paid my dues for a while and that he would get out of my life. But that one time—I felt just terribly guilty about that. And terribly surprised at the sensation.

"I knew it was wrong. I was being used. I was being abused.

"And you know I went back there later. After my second marriage. I had my two sons with me. I had to go back and take a look at my parents. Because that was when it was really flooding in on me. At twenty-three, twenty-four. I said, 'I've got to go back and do a little reality testing. Go back and look at these people, see how I feel.'

"I was just beginning to think about my past, to talk about it a little more.

"I went back. I walked into the house. And there was this kind of aging man, much smaller than I remembered him, who didn't frighten me at all. I felt kind of sorry for him. And I walked up to him. And I put my arm around him. And I said, 'Hi, dad. It's good to see you.' And he had tears in his eyes.

"I was there several weeks. Later, one night, he said, 'Let's go out for a drink together.' And that produced anxiety. I thought, 'Uh-oh. When he goes out to drink, he usually drinks too much and my mother is angry at him. Therefore, if I go out with him and he drinks too much, she will also be angry with me.' An uptight kind of feeling. Yet wanting still to relate to him a little differently.

"Wanting to have a warm, good, person-to-person relationship with him. Yes. I wanted him to be a father to me. I wanted a normal relationship with him.

"And we went out and had a few drinks. And sitting there in the bar, his eyes filled with tears, and he said, 'You know, this is your second divorce. Your second divorce. I know that it is because of the things I did to you as a child—that that has to have some bearing on what is happening to you now. And I want you to know that I don't know why I did it. And I'm sorry.'

"And I reached out and patted him on the arm, tears in my eyes. And I said, 'It's OK.' And I was feeling, you know, what a mature, giving human being I am—feeling benign, good about myself.

"And we were going up the road, arm in arm, and kind of laughing. Because with all the other stuff, he really, as an adult to an adult, he was a very clever man, with a good sense of humor, very dry sense of humor. We were laughing going up the street and then we started talking about it again. And he said, 'Yeah, I know. It was really too bad.'

"Then he says to me, 'But you know? You are a very good-looking woman. I would still like to take you to bed.'

"And I thought, 'Oh, shit. Have I been had.' I really remember thinking that. 'Oh, shit.' Thinking, 'Forgive and forget. The little Girl Scout leader. Oh, shit.'

"And I went back another time seven years ago—and it was just awful to watch them abusing my brothers, making fun of a brain-damaged boy. But I don't correspond with them any more. Don't ever write. I always had that need to keep in touch, like the good little daughter, and go back and, 'Am I good enough yet?'—you know, hoping something would change it. And it's like so many abused kids keep going back and trying to make it OK. Trying again and again and again.

"I kept going back saying, 'Here I am. Is it OK yet? Am I all right? Am I good enough? Am I good enough? Am I good enough? Finally, I thought, 'Fuck this.' I had good relationships with friends. And here were these unlovable people and why in the hell was I expending all of my energy trying to love them? Why was I looking for their approval? They were just abusive parents. My brothers were physically and emotionally abused. I was sexually and emotionally abused. And my sister, the adopted child, was for some reason their little pride and joy.

"Now. How did this leave me equipped to deal with my own children, one with each marriage, each of the first three marriages? Well I was with the first husband for two and a half years. Then I took the child with me, Danny, then a year old, and went to stay with a relative. She was really a very cold, strange person. And it just didn't work out. I was trying to work and take care of the baby and I really wasn't able to. And things sort of went from bad to worse, until my coping ability was zero. I was, at that time, nineteen.

"And Danny's father came down, trying to get us back. And I allowed him to take Danny back. I said I was just not taking care of him well enough. He was being shunted from pillar to post. 'You're at least living with your mother. Take him back with you.'

"Well, by the time he was three and a half, I had remarried. I'd had another child, Mark, who was a year old. And that marriage was going sour. And I decided to go back to work in order to earn some money and make a stab at independence. And I had been fretting and fretting and fretting. I couldn't even watch a television program about kids that were abandoned or had run away or about unwed mothers who had to give up their children or anything without just dissolving in tears.

"And I thought, 'I'm getting my kid back.' Danny.

"So I went to a lawyer. I wrote to Danny's father. I said, 'This is it. I'm going to get my child back, and if you do it this way, easily, then you can have visitation rights. You can cooperate or I'm really going to give you a rough time.'

"It was such a dumb thing. I went up to get him one weekend. They were waiting for me. I got on the next train with him, which was like ten minutes later. But. To me he was still the year-old son that I'd given up. Now he was this three-and-a-half-year-old kid that I didn't know, and he didn't know me.

"I didn't even know how to relate to a three-and-a-half-year-old child. I just didn't know what to do with him at all. And it wasn't good, you know. There was no real warmth. I was very uncomfortable and it was just bad.

"Then I went through that divorce. And went back with the two kids and visited my parents. That summer, we came back and went to the beach and had a pretty good time. Later in the summer, Danny was to go up to his father's and—they didn't bring him back. They had decided they were going to keep him there. They were Catholic and it was all about my not sending him to Catholic school.

"At the time, I was working for this social worker. So—I was going to go up. I was going to do this. I was going to do that. I had no money at the time. And I was newly married—the third time. But I was going to go up and get Danny.

"Really irrational. 'I'm renting a car. I am going up. I am getting my son from the play yard at school, and I am driving out of that state and nobody better touch me.'

"And my boss said, 'Wait a minute, Maggie. Let's talk about this a little. Don't be crazy. He has been with you. Now he's with him. He's like a damn package back and forth, back and forth.' He said, 'In the name of love, you're going to tear this kid in twenty pieces. Leave him alone.'

"Well, I finally had the state go and do a home visit, which I knew would be fine. They said the child seemed very happy. They had his little paintings and stuff all over the kitchen and he seemed very much at ease.

"So I agreed to leave him there. And never see him again. I just somehow was not able to go back and forth to see him and leave him, see him and leave him.

"So then I had Mark and my daughter, Mandy, had been born by then. And that marriage had gone damn sour. And I sat and I thought and I thought and I thought. And I went to see a psychologist for one visit. And I said, 'You know, I need your help. I just don't know what to do. It's just this damn pattern and I'm so unhappy and this is my third marriage and I've had three kids and my life is a goddamn mess and what am I going to do? What am I going to do? I have to stop this pattern.'

"So he said, 'Well, what you're really asking me to do right now is make you love your husband. And I can't do that for you.'

"And I thought, 'Well, that's pretty logical.' But I thought, 'No. I've got to do something different. I've got to stop this goddamn cycle. I've got to stop it. I don't understand it, but I've got to end it.' So I sat and I thought. And when I threatened to leave, my husband said, 'If you think you're getting Mandy, I've got news for you. If you think you can get her, you're going to have to work. You turn your back for one minute and that kid's gone. You'll never rest.'

"So I sat and thought it over and I thought it over and I thought, 'Well, the worst thing that could happen is that I lose my kids.' So I decided I was going to give them up.

"And Mark at that time was seven and a half. And his father, a good old boy, a nice guy, had just remarried—a nice girl. And I called him up. I said, 'Hey, you know my life is just a mess and my marriage is at the point now where it's going down and I really think some people can't be married. Right now, I seem to be one of them. I've got to somehow get away and figure out what in the hell it is with me because I just create such a destructive environment. I have to somehow deal with that.

"I said, 'I adore Mark. He adores me.' He would say things like, 'Oh, mommy, you're so neat.' He just beamed at me. But I said, 'He really needs a father. He needs a man around. And what's going to happen is what's always happened. I'm going to go out and find a father for him. And I can't do that to him anymore. I want you to consider having custody of him.'

"And he said, 'Oh, I would love to have custody of him. In fact, I would like you to sign adoption papers.' And I said, 'No, I won't sign adoption papers. But in order to protect him from what I did to Danny, I will sign permanent custody papers. So that if a year from now my life changes dramatically and I get the self-indulgent ᵃwish to have my child back, I don't come waltzing in and snatch him back. Because I really think I would do that again. That's something I have to protect him from.'

"So I told my then husband that Mark was going over there for a vacation. I took him over. The thing I didn't do that I really regret to this day is—I didn't talk it over with Mark. At that time. I just didn't. I just took him over there.

"I took him over there and took most of his stuff over and I wrote my husband a note. I left my daughter Mandy with a baby-sitter. She was then a year and a half old. In the note I said, 'I am leaving. I just can't take it any more. I can't be married to you. I don't love you. I have to make the break. I have to leave. It's the only way.'

"And I left. I got an apartment. But there was still all kinds of hell going on around me.

"I was at a friend's house a few Sundays later. She was a woman who had five or six kids and she was kind of a mother figure. Big open house. Lots of meals. Lots of mess. Lots of kids. Lots of noise. And a very sensitive, warm, funny human being. I was over there having dinner and somebody said, 'Your husband's at the door with your daughter. At the front door.'

"And I said, 'Oh my god.' He'd seen my car there. I thought, 'Oh, Jesus. He knows I'm here.' So I said, 'Well, I don't want to involve you. I'll talk with him on the porch.'

"And I went out.

"And the baby, Mandy, her eyes just filled up with tears and she said, 'Mama, mama.' And she was trying to laugh but she was crying. A year and a half old. And she was saying, 'I love you, mama.' And he put her down. And she had her hands around my legs. And I picked her up. And I just unknit her hands. And I said, 'Take her.

" 'I don't want to see you again.

" 'And I don't want to see her again.

" 'Ever.'

"And I went in and I closed the door, and that's the last time I've seen either of them. I haven't seen them.

"People say, 'How *could* you?'

"I tried it the other, messy way. The self-indulgent way. Muddling along and not being able to cope and somehow trying to do it and doing a damned inadequate job.

"The reality of it is that I really didn't know how to be a mother.

"And since my fourth husband died, I realize—it's time now to get off my ass and do something else. It's time. If I'm ever going to change—. It's like having the mother with the roaches so you're obsessive-compulsive. There comes a point when you just have to say, 'Hey, this isn't what I'm striving for now.' I don't know what degree of success I'll have, but I plan to keep trying.

"I just wish I had been able to cope with less human wreckage along the way. Goddamn. I mean, I'm pulling myself out of it. But what about the people whose lives I—the children? They have to be saying to themselves, as I said to myself, 'Why me? Why did this happen? Why did she abandon me?' I said, 'Why did they do this to me? Why couldn't they love me enough? Why couldn't they have left me alone? Was I so unlovable that they couldn't respect me as a human being and care about my needs instead of using me as a public accommodation?'

"When I think of the fact that never, with all the anguish that I have gone through, all of the rage, and all of the hurting, the emotional hurting, that I went through—which had to be apparent. So that anybody who had an IQ of more than one point above a ripe cucumber could have really looked at me and seen an obvious emotional trauma—

"I mean, what about my needs as a child? What about my needs? Goddamn. How can someone do that to another being?"

The Psychic Center Violated

When I first received and read a letter from June, I was afraid of it. I filed the letter—written on the back of a resort flyer—tried to ignore it, to forget it. I really didn't want to know.

Was there such a thing as emotionally terminal incest?

"I had an incestuous experience with my stepfather. My very first memory, at my earliest age, was when I was one (but I might have been three). The neighbor, who later became my stepfather, was baby-sitting for me and my cousin while my mother and father were out. I was lying on my parents' bed naked, my cousin was standing up in my crib looking at me, while this man was orally copulating me. I was deeply shamed and wanted to cover myself with my hair. In all the years that followed till now I'm possessed with long hair as a form of covering. Also I feel this man's actions contributed to me not having a mind of my own and not being able to say no to men. . . .

"I feel I owe him something because he raised me like a daughter, and yet I hate him for subjecting me to his adult wills at such an early age that I can't think for myself. I want to destroy every female child's vagina so it can't be used in an adult way."

Try as I might, it was a letter I couldn't manage to lose.

June came into my apartment serenely, carrying a half un-painted board she had picked up on the street. It would make a bookshelf in her apartment. We began talking about where she was now, what her interests were.

"Well, raising your Christ consciousness, trying somehow to survive on the planet Earth. Getting land, growing food. Learning how to be your neighbor's brother. To survive. Since the whole structure of Earth, according to some sources, is going to change and alter. The farthest remote place you can be is suggested by some sources to be best because the first wave will be the cities.

"I've visited a foundation in Virginia Beach that was built around the readings given by Edgar Cayce who died about fifty years ago. The people were beautiful. I felt balanced for the first time. Because for myself I don't agree with the heterosexual balance. So when I went there I saw beautiful people. I expected to see women all log-cabinish. I didn't. I saw very beautiful, feminine women. The men were also very beautiful. Everybody had beautiful hair. Definitely masculine, the men, but they were pretty.

"Every job that was done—building the house, putting on the roof, cooking in the kitchen, side by side, man and woman—no duties separated because of sex, none.

"I only stayed there two days. But they've been there four years. And it's been a year-to-year struggle and they've gone through many, many changes."

"Did you grow up in the city?"

"Uh—the last twenty years. The first twenty I spent on the West Coast.

"Then I hooked up with a man and we sort of hitchhiked here, and I just never left. I'm afraid to go back anymore because I have a deep feeling of, you know, things are going to happen to the West Coast first. Even before I read things that Edgar Cayce said and other people—I had a deep feeling inside that I don't want to be anywhere on the West Coast.

"Of course the entire earth is cracked, not just the main fault lines. But it's OK. I mean we're not supposed to be afraid. That's not the purpose. Because by having fear, this attracts these things to happen to us. But by losing this fear and learning how to change our situations and adjust and be flexible and to accept things with all the lovingness that we can—this in fact can change the entire force. I mean, these things don't have to happen. But what is said is that if you allow yourself to change in these ways, that whatever must happen will happen to you gracefully. If you resist, you will weep bitter tears of sorrow.

"See, even when I was seven years old I was digging caves for my family for protection—before I knew what I was digging them for.

"It's also said that the people from Atlantis are being reincarnated at this particular time because we have the same situation confronting us. Like they had high technology and made holocaust out of it—like we're beginning to do now. And so the same people are given the privilege to face it again. So like my inner feelings could be from a knowledge of a time like that, or it could be an oversensitivity of the time to come."

"What was your childhood like?"

"To me, it was normal because it was my childhood. And looking back I liked it because that's what I want to get back to now. But then I didn't like it.

"My mother married a friend, my father. Then I was born. When I was in third grade they were divorced and my mother married my father's best friend. And he's the type of person that has to be punished. And my mother was a strong, austere woman who didn't like to have sex and liked him to work. And he doesn't like to work and he likes to have sex.

"I guess I was ten or eleven when they got married.

"My father is still alive and my stepfather is still alive, but very, very sick. My original father is my ideal in a way. Very carefree, nonprejudiced. In those days when prejudice was running rampant we had one black boy in the school. And of course if you so much as looked at him, your name was mud. My father—'dance with him, dance with him. He's such a great dancer.' My father was helping me destroy my reputation—which I loved him for!"

"Were you sad when they got divorced?"

"Well, I don't recall anything. They told me that's when I shut up and never spoke again. I guess it upset me in some kind of way.

"But I don't feel—they just said I withdrew from then on. But I don't feel it and I think too much is placed on that. Because I think I'm an ingrown personality anyway. People sometimes don't look at that. And I visited him every weekend—going back and forth constantly. I loved it. Then when I got in my teens it gave me a great opportunity to be the biggest delinquent I could get away with being—because my father lived in the city. And I took full advantage."

"What was it that happened with your stepfather?"

"The first image that I remember—that first thing I remember in life—and I used to think I was one, but I guess I was three—I used to think it was a dream for years and years until I got grown and realized that I don't think a baby would have dreamt that.

"My stepfather was not married to my mother at that time. He was just baby-sitting with me. And my cousin, who was two years older than me, was standing up in my crib. And I was lying on my mother and father's bed. And all my clothes were off. And he came in and he went down and orally copulated me. And I remember my hair. I wanted to cover myself with my hair. I thought it was a deep, deep shame for a child like that—you feel deep, deep shame and my cousin was looking down and I just didn't want her to look. And I attribute my neuroticism for my hair to that. Because I always have to have long hair. I feel that the hair hides me, gives me a personality. Without my hair, I'd be nothing.

"See, I thought I was one. But I asked my parents when my cousin was living in the house with us. And they said I was three. So that's why I say between one and three. Because I feel I was one. I've had that thought all my life. But I must have been three.

"Then—between then and the age of thirteen, he was—in front of my mother and family—constantly grabbing hold of me and picking me up. How can I explain? He'd—all right, say this was my back. He'd pick me up under my legs and under my arms and then his hands would be right inside my thighs. He'd definitely be getting a sexual thing out of how he was holding me. But nobody could see. Nobody knew how he was holding me. And he was getting away with this in front of the family. And kissing me. Running and grabbing. Chasing me all over the house constantly. And grabbing me and kissing me and all like that. It was always mouth-to-mouth kissing."

"And you never mentioned this to your mother?"

"Never to this day. But I always wanted to mention it. Not to her. But to everybody else. I wanted everybody to know. But not her.

"I don't think she'd have dealt with it. I don't know why. I really don't know why. You know you have a protection for your parents. I didn't care so much if my father knew. See, I was always testing my father's love too. I always treated him mean and shocked him with details of my sex life. I used to always do this. I don't understand why either.

"When my mother died, I told him what happened to me, but I didn't tell him who. I wanted him to guess so bad. But either he didn't guess or wouldn't say. So, at the same time, I'm protective toward my stepfather who did all this, too. I mean I don't really want to crush and destroy him, but on the other hand, I do and I have.

"One time later I wrote a letter and left it for him to read—very cruel things about how he destroyed me, and how I was going to destroy him. It was what I felt. And the next day I saw him walk away from the house with his shoulders bent over. He looked like he aged twenty years. I was so sorry. I was really sorry. I was glad and sorry at the same time. That I did that to him. Glad and sorry.

"But to this day I have to go out and take care of him because he's a really sick man. And I don't feel—I mean he was a good provider.

"He got me a horse. You know, he fed us and clothed us all those years. He took care of me. And to me, that counts for something, you know. He told me once that when he was seventeen he did something he could never forgive himself for, and he would never tell me what that was. So the only thing I could figure out is that he had sexual intercourse with a child with his penis. He never did that to me until I was older.

"Then he stopped grabbing and kissing me at thirteen until I was fifteen. And then he wanted to have sexual intercourse with me and I wouldn't let him. Now he had apparently drawn the conclusion that I was having sex with everybody. And I was strictly a virgin. But he didn't understand, you know. He didn't think it was fair that I was going with everybody else.

"So then nothing else until nineteen. Now this is odd. I willingly went to his house after I'd moved away from home, and I had to get really, really very drunk. And we had a sexual affair. And then one more time. The second time I didn't get drunk.

"And what these things did was they filled me with a deep, deep depression and a disgust. Yet there was something about my fantasies. It's always him. His bald head. Going down. You know?

"That association that I have—that I enjoy on a level—that I can't accept. Because then I experienced nothing but wanting to die.

"Then again when I was twenty-eight, when my mother died. I had nowhere to go. My husband beat me up. So I went back with the kids. And he was going to take care of me the rest of my life, because I had always lived in poverty as an adult. He was going to take care of me and it was, gee, all I wanted was to be taken care of at that point. I was just tired.

"And I thought, 'Well, OK,'—all my kids and everything. So the first three nights we had a sexual affair and that's when the depression started setting in. And it got worse and it got worse and it got worse.

"I had run from my husband, who almost killed me, to him. And then when my depression got so bad I just had to die or something, I packed up again after two weeks and came back East. In other words, it was from my murderous husband to earthquake and my stepfather. And then I ran from there back to the other fear, the husband. Only I didn't stay with him when I came back.

"See, before I understood my beliefs, I used to put all the blame on my stepfather for my being a wishy-washy person who could never say no to a male. Could never say no. That time I was back there with my kids I told him what he did to me when I was a baby. He said, 'No, no. It wasn't me.' I told him, 'No. It was you.' He said, 'It was that cop. That cop. When we went to a movie and the cop was baby-sitting.' It wasn't that cop. It was him. Because I remember seeing him on the street the next day and I was so afraid. And I was holding so tight to my mother's hand.

"And I definitely have a fear of authority. There must be some reason why I'm a yes person instead of a no person. When somebody wants to abuse me in some kind of way—I know that I feel I'm supposed to. How can I say no to this male? I must say yes. It's their right or something like that. Definitely, I feel those feelings.

"My kids were all males. I'm afraid of males. My kids pushed me around. Just a mess, you know. So I used to blame him before I understood that we come into this life by choice. I believe in reincarnation. I believe that our spirits choose situations that we have to work out. I believe I came into this life with certain weaknesses anyway. But I understand that these are areas that I now feel determined to find some balance in before I die. Or at least die trying.

"See I could never say no sexually. From sixteen on. And I certainly felt a sense of shame. I mean it was something I had to do. I was so driven that I would go to a park and pick up five and then leave that park and go pick up five more on the street. And all this could be in a day's time now. Just crazy, crazy, crazy—and just a nothing, nothing, nothing feeling. And the depression of die, die, die.

"It was like that.

"And throughout my adult life when I found myself in a situation where I couldn't say no, then that same overpowering destruction would come on me as a result of the act. And my oldest son has the same qualities. He's seventeen now. He started running away when he was eleven, was out on the street—you can understand if I don't put a term on it. He feels like nothing—but he is just driven, driven, driven.

"He and his brother got the worst of it as kids. His brother got more than he did. But when two kids are treated the same, they can react oppositely. Like the older is bisexual and very self-destructive. Whereas the other one will have nothing to do with a dirty kind of life.

"See, there were two husbands. The two men in my life were both brutal. The first was the most brutal. The second one, the father of my fourth child, was not brutal to the kids. He was brutal to me. He beat me up twice, not too bad, and the third time it was very, very bad. That's the last time I had anything to do with him.

"Then I went with one other man because I still couldn't cope with my kids. I was like a three-year-old child with kids. You wouldn't believe. There was no way of explaining my inability to cope. All they can do is blame me and hate me today. So this man came in the house who was very terrific as far as setting down systems in the house to try to get ahead with the food, to understand what was going on with school, and just to live like a human being. Because I just mentally blocked everything out. And it was so—anyway, a year of being with him turned into a very, very brutal thing.

"But the first husband was very, very bad on the kids. He only hit me twice. When he did, he went like this—and broke my eardrum. Second time, he went like this—and broke my nose. So I was deathly in fear of him. Because he didn't play. The oldest boy was first beaten up really bad by him when he was three months old.

"And I was passive. Because, again, in my mother's home, the mother, whether she agrees or disagrees, must not disagree in front of the kids to her mate. So the only position I felt I had a right to was to show no disagreement. And I resented it so, but there was nothing I could do according to my belief and my training. And having these three babies and no money. I couldn't get away. I simply couldn't think for myself. So I couldn't get away. I had to stay with him until a situation provided itself. Which—a situation did provide itself. He helped the situation come about.

"See, he knew that I always figured I'm homosexual, although I've been involved with all these men. I always figured I'm homosexual. I don't know why I had such a fear of that. I didn't when I was ten or twelve, but then my girl friends suddenly decided they liked boys and put me down. I couldn't face the rejection and I didn't continue.

"Well, he brought a girl home. Because we'd been talking about how we had to separate. We were destroying the kids. We were destroying ourselves and our love for each other and love for the family. We were going to separate.

"He was on drugs. I don't know if I mentioned that to you. That was why he was out of sorts. He tried to be good by cold turkeying all the time. But he's an impulsive pill taker, drug taker, everything all at once.

"And it holds his brain like that and the slightest noise, he'd just have to crush it. And, of course, it's coming from the kids, so he crushes his kids. I had all this understanding which made it hard too. Seeing how hard he tried and all of that. See, when you know too much it makes it very hard.

"So he brought this girl home. And she was gay. So then he left us that night. And we hit it off just like that.

"So he came home the next morning and he knew we'd been together and he went on this killer rampage that beat all. I had just gotten paid because I was working at the time. Where she lived, somebody had just left an apartment right next door. See how that worked out? It was—the timing was perfect. So I went with her. But, what happened was—I also had a nervous breakdown. And I went in the hospital. But when I came out, I stayed with her for about two years.

"The kids were in a children's home while I was in the hospital. It took me ten months to get them back out. There were three of them I had at that time. And she helped me.

"I wasn't able to rule them. I couldn't take care of the responsibilities in any area for raising a family. I just didn't want the responsibility. As a kid, I would go into the woods and pretend I was a wild horse. Because a wild horse had a long mane, and I would throw my hair.

"But that relationship wasn't satisfactory. So after two years I met my second husband, the baby's father. Much better improvement. Each person was an improvement. I mean, he was almost really sane.

"We tried a bisexual thing, but he couldn't deal with it. This is when he tried to kill me. This is what he couldn't deal with. Today he's a very good father. He's got six kids by his new wife.

"But see, it's a funny thing, too, about what happened to me, because I react the way I wish I wouldn't. Like my oldest son who at eleven would get arrested, and he'd been with a thirty-eight-year-old man. He looked like six, he was such a little kid. With this very big man. He'd get himself in positions where he'd be molested. He'd seek it out. But what I saw was this child molester. And I hate them, and at the same time I'm unable to do anything and unable to feel anything.

"See? I'm unable to feel anything. I have to pretend anger. I guess what I'm saying is I'm showing you a pattern. That I feel nothing. So that's the only way I can show it meant nothing.

"Or maybe it didn't mean nothing. Maybe that's why I feel nothing. But I still to this day feel nothing. I can't feel.

"When I think about grown men raping young children, I get very upset. I want to kill. I have feelings of rage inside. But as soon as it pertains to my own child, I go dead with feeling.

"And I know that I ought to express feelings for my child's sake, so I start pretending anger and rage. And one time I beat him up mercilessly. I beat him up to show him I was angry. I didn't want to beat him up. I didn't feel that anger. I didn't feel anything."

"You mentioned in your letter something about not being able to be around little girls?"

"Um—I used—I'm getting over a lot of my negative urges. I'm getting over them. But I used to—like I told you, my stepfather would hold me in these crazy ways and pull me apart with his fingers and things like that. I get urges to do this to children, to babies. I get a feeling to destroy.

"I have never done it—no, that's a lie. I'll go back in time to when my youngest sister was one year old and I was twelve. I was changing her diapers. She was one—like the age I thought I was when my stepfather went down on me. And when I was changing her diaper I had that flash of what my stepfather did. And I had a very strong feeling to go down on her. Now I didn't. I don't know—I wasn't in touch with what the feelings were. If it was vengeance or desire—I have no idea. I just connect it with the flashback. I didn't do it—I fought it.

"Then my first really close girl friend, about seven years ago. She had a daughter. We lived together. We stayed together two years. I was cruel to that child, like those men had been to my kids.

"All my capability of authority and control came out in a very aggressive way on this little girl. She wouldn't get potty trained, and I would treat her like I would treat a puppy who wouldn't get trained. I'd make her stay on the potty maybe all day while her mother was in school. Maybe eight hours. And she's a very neurotic little girl. I love her. That's the funny thing. Today I love her. I've had to fight with myself to get rid of these ugly feelings toward her, though. Coming from what, I'm not exactly sure.

"She would have these hysterics and she'd fight. Screaming. Tantrums. And any kind of tantrum sets me off. I can't be around it. It makes me violent. And I definitely got violent with her. And I had urges—I mean, not urges—but thoughts crossed my mind that I wanted to rip out her vagina, to destroy her.

"And I thought to myself, maybe the reasons for wanting to destroy a female body, a child female body, is because what my stepfather did to me shouldn't have happened. You shouldn't try to make an adult out of a little baby. So if you destroy the physical, the genital—if you destroy the sexual part, then that takes away the womanhood. And she's therefore a child."

"And yet you talk about having compassion for your stepfather."

"Uh-huh."

"How do you explain that?"

"He didn't hurt me. He didn't put his penis in me when I was a child. And men do these things. And I feel grateful to him that he withheld that part of his sickness, because he certainly wanted to do it. And I feel he was definitely sick in that area.

"But I've just gained a lot of understanding through the past couple of years. Any time I condemn somebody, put somebody down, right away quick that feeling comes on me. I experience the same thing.

"I should give you an example so you'll understand what I'm saying. Since we're talking about my stepfather right now—in the past few years, I've been plagued—and to me it's a plague—I've been bothered with sexual fantasies that I don't like. Of very grotesque things happening. Incestuous things. Torture things. Rape things. Slave situations. Now some people say how healthy they are, how stimulating they are. They torture me. I think they're wrong.

"I think I'm building myself up for maybe another life of these things happening to me or me doing these things. So, but these sexual fantasies have made me understand that if a person has a sexual illness, it takes over. And maybe they have no control."

"Did you ever hate him?"

"Uh-unh. Nothing mattered too much. Like I can't deal with feelings at all. I'm insensitive to smells, to flowers. I'm insensitive to anything of any beauty or pleasure. And I think I could maybe pinpoint that it's a cover-up. When I see a beautiful, beautiful rainbow it's so pretty, but I can't put it into my functioning. It makes me want to cry or scream or tear it apart. So I just block it out and don't deal with it.

"There's a deadness there. Where I should feel.

"My third son. When he was about seven, I had to go to work.

My girl friend was in the house. And some guy who always got stoned on acid came in just as I was getting ready to leave. Now I should've taken care of the situation. I just took it for granted my girl friend would stay until I got back. But she wasn't thinking either. She was young. So she walked out of the apartment.

"When I came back from work four hours later, he had my little boy with no clothes on lying across his lap and he was kissing him. And I saw all this. He had this very strange look on his face. So the only thing I could think of real quick was not to put trauma on my baby. So I just very calmly changed the situation by having him do something.

"That was a child molester. I ought to know. But, see, I wasn't angry with him. I was sad and sorrowful for my son. I would wish anything it didn't happen. But I couldn't even get angry.

"Instead, I felt subjugated.

"The same way with my stepfather. Like he had a right. But I don't feel logically that they have a right. But emotionally, I'm completely in their control.

"And, see, I neglected my kids bad. I didn't know how to be a mother. See, now that they're growing up I get along good. I can relate to them as people. I couldn't relate to them as children. I can't relate to a child or a baby as being somebody that I'm responsible for. I think there's a great, great lack in this area.

"My mother and me never touched. And my father—when my real father touched me, I always thought of incest. It was a feeling I had of sex when my father would hug me and touch me, and I was very uncomfortable. We just weren't a touching family and I'm not a touching person. I can't reach out and touch unless I'm in bed screwing. I can't touch. You know how people can touch? I can't do any of that. I'd like to learn to do it. And yet I always felt I was well off.

"Because he didn't hurt me. He didn't internally hurt me. Psychological rape he definitely did. When you take somebody at such an early age and do a sexual number, you definitely have got that person in psychological control, plus warped in some kind of way.

"See, I wasn't allowed to grow up. I wasn't allowed to—when children play around together, you're ready for different things. You're ready for different stages at different ages. When you're ready for different things, you experiment with different things.

"But if an adult comes along and takes you and does this before you're ready—it's like a spiritual experience or a psychic experience.

"They say drugs can only take you five levels. You can't go any higher. If you go through meditation, you can go very high. But if you're not ready and one of your psychic centers opens, and you haven't purified your thinking and your thinking processes, you'll be caught up in destructive elements that are all wrong. And you'll have terrible, terrible experiences.

"Like some people who take LSD. They're opening up their psychic centers, but they're not ready; so they see horrible things. And they experience horrible feelings and they jump off roofs and things like that. But if they are ready, then they're in heaven. They experience angels and glory."

"You think that a sexual experience before five—."

"Destroys you."

"Do you see yourself as a survivor? Or do you see yourself as maimed?"

"Oh, I'm a survivor. I don't look at myself as being maimed because each day is gonna be a new day. I know my kids have been touched and scratched up. They may carry that through their lives. But they, just like me, they have to take the day and mold it. And it can be done. And it's OK, whatever has happened. Because you can try to erase it."

As June picked up her bag, her board, we chatted a bit about the good stuff one can find in the refuse of others. Then, at the front door, for some reason I said, "Is there anything else about it all that overwhelms you?"

She looked surprised. Then she grinned. "My whole personality," she said, "overwhelms me."

And we both really laughed.

Insist: The Pornographic Principle

But can't (as any number of fellows have insisted to me)—can't there *ever* be such a thing as happy sexual involvement with one's own children? Why can't you love them as your children and also love them sexually? Sex, after all, is a form of love, an expression of affection.

Because, I have answered back, when you speak of someone's being just like a father, are you describing a sexual relationship? Why is it necessary for men to eroticize all positive, affectionate, even sensual responses? And why are men such victims of their sexuality? And I go on and on answering their questions with questions, and we don't really get anywhere.

Which closet are you going to stuff your wife in while you and your kid play?

Well, suppose we let her play too.

Happiness. OK, now suppose you and your wife want your kid to come play in bed—but she insists she's got a Campfire Girl meeting she wants to go to. Are you going to leap back into parent-power role and make her stay home?

Oh, that's silly.

Is it? Once you've eroticized the relationship, broken down the dividing lines between parent and child, where are you going to renegotiate the boundaries?

116

Well, you've got to admit children are sexual.

And you've got to admit parents are powerful. And I think you probably ought to admit that children are anarchic. They learn to control their own impulses largely from parental example. Mainly, I think you've got to admit that when you sexualize a child to fulfill your adult, male needs, you are socializing her to subjection. Florence Rush, social worker and author, said in a paper presented at the New York Radical Feminist Rape Conference in April 1971,*

> Sexual abuse of children is permitted because it is an un-spoken but prominent factor in socializing and preparing the female to accept a subordinate role; to feel guilty, ashamed, and to tolerate, through fear, the power exercised over her by men. . . . The female's early sexual experiences prepare her to submit in later life to the adult forms of sexual abuse heaped on her by her boyfriend, her lover, and her husband. In short, the sexual abuse of female children is a process of education that prepares them to become the wives and mothers of America.

That's only because society imposes the guilt? Only because of our culture?

I've got this vision. You've eroticized all affection: Every hug is a grope. Susie skins her knee falling off her trike. You finger-fuck her in consolation.

You're getting absurd.

Maybe. But little kids are needful, dependent creatures. When you sexualize them, and sexualize affection for them, it is something you are *doing to* them. You cannot say they wanted it—no matter how you elevate the importance of childhood sexuality. If they depend on you for their ring binders and their Band-Aids, they're going to do anything you say.

You mean you've never heard from a happy, sexually abused woman?

Yes. Annabelle. To begin with.

Annabelle?

*Reprinted by New York Radical Feminists, *Rape: The First Sourcebook for Women* (New York: New American Library) p. 73-74.

"I am not quite sure what to say or what you want to know, but it is important that you write your book to educate people and I really want to help.

"First, I hate the word *incest*. It seems like a dirty thing to everyone when they hear that word, and loving someone in your own family is beautiful and is not dirty at all. It is just plain love and it just happens to be in your family. A long time ago someone said it was wrong because they were ignorant and didn't know, so now everyone says it's bad and dirty and against the law.

"I really don't know what's so bad about it anyway. I think it is more natural than trying to fall in love with some stranger and let them make love to you and then just leave you because they never really loved you anyway. It is natural for children to love their folks and for them to love their children from the time they are born. So if you already are in love, what is so wrong about expressing it just like you would with someone else?

"I think everyone is worried about having children that will be retarded and that is not true. I read a whole series in the newspaper about incest (God, I hate to even write the word). They said that studies prove there is no more chance of having a retarded child from your own Dad than from someone you aren't related to at all.

"Third—I think that the love feeling with your own Dad makes making love with him even more beautiful. I made love with only one other man and I liked it physically (because he was bigger—ha, ha), but the love feeling just wasn't there and I would never do it again. I am glad I did it that once so now I know the difference.

"Since insist [sic] has to do with sex, I have to tell you something about that. I won't tell you the sex details because you might not need that, but I will if you need them later to help you.

"I am nineteen and I have a job at the variety store. Dad is forty-three and he works nights. I am kind of pretty (if I do say so myself—ha, ha) but not beautiful, and I have a pretty good figure but I am a little chubby. When I was real, real young, I used to come home from school and Dad was usually home because he works nights. Mom was always at work. I don't remember everything from the beginning because I was about six, but Dad and I used to play and kiss and wrestle on the bed a lot and get naked together. I really liked it a lot.

"I knew right from the start it wasn't right to do because we had to keep it a secret from Mom, but I liked Dad a lot more anyway. . . . I never knew why it was wrong because we loved each other and it was beautiful.

"I'm not really saying this right. First—I have to say that I would never tell this to a man but telling you you will understand. Second, it is not fair or right to say it was beautiful when I was real, real young. I didn't really know about sex much and didn't get sex thrills like I did later. What I did mostly was do it because Dad liked it and I was real close to him. This is real personal but what we did was oral sex to each other. It kind of tickled me is all because I couldn't climax yet but Dad could, and I knew it made him feel real, real good because he said so every time and I liked to make him feel so good. He never tried to go all the way up me with intercourse until after I could climax, when I was almost through fifth grade, but (besides sucking) he used to just rub it against me and push up just a little and do it all over me when he climaxed.

"I know you will think he was taking advantage of me but I don't think so because now we are in love like two adults and it grew out of being so close when I was young. He got pleasure out of it and I got pleasure from giving him pleasure and that is what sex and love are about no matter what your age or even if you are related. I also have to say we didn't do it every day. I went to a friend's house two or three days a week and stayed until five or half-past five when Mom got home. Even if we did do it sometimes, we only did it for a half hour or so and then went fishing in the boat.

"That was when I was real young. When I was almost through fifth grade (or it might have been sixth, I'm not sure), I found out why he liked it so much and I climaxed first. Boy, you know I really wanted to do it after that, and Dad was so good (and still is) to think of me first and try to make it feel good for me because he loves me a lot.

"So when I was in eighth grade I had my period and we had to use protection (rubbers) until I was sixteen and got the pill from Social Services. I didn't tell them it was Dad, of course.

"So about two years ago Mom and Dad got divorced and Dad moved to the next city, and twice a month I would go stay with him on the weekends and just be his wife all weekend long, and we would go out on the boat and out to dinner and all and we still do. Dad and Mom are still good friends but don't see each other a lot, and he is careful never to say anything bad about her except they just couldn't get along too good, and the only thing he ever says is that he likes to make love to me better. Mom is kind of straight and doesn't like to do some of the things we like a lot. We are real open and free together and like to look at sex magazines and take pictures of each other naked, and he likes garter belts and heels and hose and special bras and pants and all, and Mom didn't like to wear them for him but I do because I feel real sexy and it pleases him. (It's kind of funny at first but then it's fun.) And we love to talk dirty sometimes, which Mom would never do.

"It has been so wonderful and beautiful except for one time, and Dad was really sorry about that. Last year one Saturday we went out fishing on the boat (naturally—ha, ha) with this fellow George all day. We drink pretty much beer but we don't really get drunk at all. Anyway George brought all this hard liquor, which we never drink. Dad got kind of drunk and was getting real silly and sexy with me right in front of George and saying how pretty I am and feeling me above the waist and pulling up my sweatshirt to show George my bra and saying how do you like that, George. I was kind of drunk and I wouldn't let him do that otherwise but I didn't care. I was getting kind of hot, too, I guess maybe. So George was kissing me and feeling me under my sweatshirt, and we were kind of fooling around and went back to the dock and the apartment for dinner and had some more drinks. I got sick in the bathroom but went and had another drink, which didn't help any. So we were just sitting on the sofa all together and kidding and fooling around, and they were kind of both kissing me and feeling me. I think I was getting sexed up, too, which didn't help; so Dad said, 'Show George how pretty you are in your garter belt and panties' (the special sex pants I leave there all the time). God, I just went right in and changed and came out.

"So to make a long story short, Dad said will I let George make love with me and him all in bed. We didn't do it immediately but got fooling around, and Dad really wanted me to so I said OK. So we all three did everything half the night and didn't eat dinner at all. So the next day was really my fault because I was sober but it was raining like mad and too much to fish so we stayed home and pretty soon George said let's go to bed. So I asked Dad and he said will I do it for him so I said OK only we didn't go to bed and we all did it right in the living room. George called this real, real fat girl he knew who came over. She was real pretty if she would lose about fifty pounds, and we just all kept doing things until late at night, even with the girl and me together, and Dad had to drive me to work and was I late. I only did it with George one other time when Dad was working overtime but it was only oral love and not intercourse. That was my fault, too, because I was not even drinking, and I think I just got sexed up because George is real handsome and real, real big you know where and can do it three or four times, which I like a lot instead of only once or twice. I have to admit that I might do it with him again as long as Dad does it with me, too, so I would not be sneaking around cheating.

"Dad doesn't have enough money saved this summer and I don't have a dime saved, but next summer we are going on vacation to Mexico and get married and I will have fake ID and all so they won't know who I really am, and we are going to be husband and wife and have children (three I want), and all because we are so much in love and have been for so long and always will be.

"One thing that I have to say is that I am not a Lesbian and neither is Mom but I wish we could make love a lot. She really needs love since Dad left and doesn't like the boyfriends she has had. It wouldn't hurt anyone and we are getting along really super this last year and love each other a lot. I have done several things to try to get her to think about it, and I know she is from what has happened, but it's hard for her because she is older and set in her ways. I really liked it with this other girl a lot and Dad liked to watch and I know Mom would love it too. I would like it with her I know because she is real pretty and young looking and all.

"One thing I didn't mention is something special only Fathers and Daughters can have together. It's a special feeling when Dad is up me. I keep thinking this is my own beautiful father and not some guy I don't even love, and when I do oral love for him, which he likes a lot, I look at it and feel it and think this is the thing (prick) that made me and in my mouth I think this is the stuff (cum) that made Mom pregnant with me. I try real hard to taste and to get the most out of it when he is up me inside. I think it is such a beautiful feeling, my Father up inside, and he is giving me pleasure and I am like Mom when they were married. I think that this is a special love feeling a girl can't have with anyone else but her Father.

"I'm not saying this right at all. I'm not a very good writer, and if I don't tell you what I mean, it's just stupid to write at all. What I am saying if we are talking about me doing oral love to Dad is the really special feeling you get from holding it (prick) in your hand and knowing this is your own flesh and blood and that the taste is the same as what went to Mom to make me and pretty soon one day we will make more babies from his love juice up me. It's just so special I can't tell you.

"What I would love the most is Dad and me and Mom all making love together in bed at once, but I don't think that will ever happen. When I have kids, I will make love with them. I know this Lady who did it a lot with her boy when she was divorced and was depressed and needed love, except I don't know if she was depressed really because one of the boys at work pointed out her and her son, who is about twelve, and told me, so all I really know is they do it. I will, too, and I think we would have a super close family if Dad did the girl. . . . We can all make love and sleep together naked. I am not a Lesbian and my daughter won't be either, but that doesn't mean we can't make Lesbian love once in a while as long as she has intercourse a lot with Dad and stays straight.

"I want to tell you that I dropped out of high school but I have never been in trouble of any kind. A couple of times I let a boy feel under my bra and pants but never did anymore then and that's nothing when you compare what everyone else does. I have never smoked dope and went home when people did. I practically never miss church (except that Sunday with George) but I don't confess that Dad and I make love because the priest wouldn't understand. I talk to God about it though and I think he understands OK. When you look at all the animals that do it in their families, like baboons, then you realize that it is natural and he [God] meant it to be. I think he planned for people to have sex these days just for fun or he wouldn't have let the pill be invented. I think God likes things that make the family closer and more loving, and I wish all families just did it right from the start and stayed together and forgot about boyfriends and getting married and then divorced and finding yourself alone to raise children. It would make us all a lot closer and there would be less crime and dope.

"What I did was read my letter over and I am not saying some things right, and I know you will find one thing you don't like. I think you will say Dad should have waited till I was eighteen and then asked me to make love and he took advantage of me when I was about in first grade or second. I don't think he really did though. I know you will say I was too young to know when I was six or seven and he got me to do oral love to him. What I have to say is I really liked it right from when I started. It wasn't sex to me then, I don't think, but Dad loved it and it felt good and it's nice to make him feel good when you can because he works hard to support us and loves us. I don't know how to tell you how I felt when I could make him climax because I probably don't really remember, but I know I liked it every time he squirted. And I think you will say it's not love if I get dressed all the time in sex underwear, but I think it is really sexy and like it too. What happened was that is how some of the girls in the sex magazines are dressed so we just got a catalog to order. He didn't say I had to and only that I would be real sexy and pretty, and it was my idea to get some.

"I bet you will be mad about George, but I am just telling you that because it is how I discovered the difference in making love and sucking with your Dad and another man. If I wasn't related to Dad, I would rather make love with George just for hot, dirty sex because he is so big (prick), but just having Dad be my Dad is what makes our lovemaking so special. It was just hot sex with George and no real feeling.

"I am not saying I will never do it with another man before we are married (but *never* after). I get real sex hot thinking about George sometimes but I don't call him up. It just isn't the same.

"I think you know a lot about insist [sic] (God, I hate that word). I would tell you everything you need to know for the book if you will tell me a few things I don't know. I am real, real close to Dad but I can't just ask him everything. I think I know the answers but I am not sure.

"We like to play a lot of games with sex because it makes it a lot more fun. Usually I dress real sexy in sex underwear but sometimes we like to play this game and we do it a lot more lately. What I do is wear my old school uniform with knee socks and all but with the skirt hemmed up real, real short so my pants almost show and wear my hair in braids with bows and have a sucker and talk like a real little girl like he says and call him Daddy instead of Dad. Sometimes we take all afternoon if it's raining out and we play like it is the first time again. Sometimes we play like I am a bad girl and he spanks me with my pants down and then makes me do oral love to him like for more punishment and sometimes we play this game like I am a strange little girl and he gets me in the bedroom and rapes me but really we are just playing. I don't like the rape one so much unless I am real hot. Or sometimes we play like I am a strange school girl and he gives me some beer and I play half passed out and he undresses me and does everything to me.

"What I think is Dad liked me for sex more when I was real young and we play like I am again. That is OK with me. What I really worry about is when I get older. Will he think I am too old and not marry me or want a divorce? That would be so terrible. I only worry because we do those games like that more and more. Would you tell me what usually happens when I get older?

"The other thing is he had a lot of dirty magazines of little girls who are about eight or nine to eleven or twelve. Some are American ones that just show the girls undressing and posing naked but some he sent away for are German and Swedish and show little girls with men actually doing *everything*. He is always saying I had a body like this one or that one when I was her age, and like, 'Boy did you like to do that when you were her age' (like sucking), and do I remember? That kind of bothers me too.

"You know—it is really stupid. I am nineteen and have had sex experiences for thirteen years on and off now but I really don't know how men think about sex. What is really weird is that Dad always likes to sit and watch me get dressed and undressed and always has me masturbate a lot when he watches naked and masturbates too. When we were with George that time, he told me to lie on the floor and show him how I did it so I just did and that was OK and I still don't mind doing it except that it still seems strange to me to show off like that. He tells me what to do, like, 'OK, up your bottom now a little,' and now do this or that. He got me these two vibrators and I can climax like crazy with them and tell him when I am about to (cum) and he watches me go crazy. I like to cook for him a lot and kind of wait on him at the table and make him comfortable and he likes to be dressed while I am naked or in my sex underwear so he can watch me. That is OK with me, except it is kind of hard to just sit down and eat like usual."

"This is being continued after the July Fourth weekend. God it takes so long to write. I am glad I did not send this Friday. I think I was misleading kind of but I did not try to be. What it is that I don't want to admit to myself is how Dad is changing but I really should. What it is is that we really had a beautiful relationship up to the time Mom divorced Dad. It was just perfect. We didn't do it too much but a couple of days a week after school and sometimes if Mom would go to the store or over to her friend's for an hour where we could do it real quick sometimes and love a lot.

"I don't think I changed but I think Dad did when he moved and started getting kind of weird with me, like letting George make love to me and all like I said and the garter belts and turning on his recorder when we made love and having me make sex sounds and talk dirty and all to record it and having me dress in my old school uniform. I am really getting my head together because of this long weekend—mostly when I got upset and went home on Monday. I think I was right to do that and maybe Dad will see what is wrong and change now.

"What happened was I went down for the long weekend and we had plans for a really super time. We had a minus 3.1 tide and we were going to dig clams and get oysters and have a wonderful time on the beach way out alone where hardly anyone goes. So when I got down there Saturday, his boss, whose name is Pete, and his wife were there. Dad picked me up and said pretend I am his girl friend and not his daughter because they won't know, so I said OK. So we went to this beach when the tide was going out in Pete's big camper and were going to stay overnight. Pete is real thin but real nice and real, real, funny, and Jane is his wife, who is about forty-five, and is kind of pretty for that age but wears too much makeup and jewelry and fancy clothes for clam digging, where you get so wet and dirty, and smokes all the time and drinks like a fish even in the morning. She has perfect hair and huge earrings and all. So we left her at the camper and we got tons of clams and oysters but we couldn't build a fire to steam and fry them so we took them home. We really had fun until then and I really laughed and laughed at Pete, who is always joking.

"It was kind of like with George, and Dad was kissing me and feeling me in front of them and saying they were just jealous because I was young and pretty and said you should see me without clothes on if you like me now. So pretty soon after supper, about five, we were all having a little too much to drink, and Dad said will they stay in the apartment instead of the camper, so I said we only have one bed, so Pete said that's great and why not. So I got that funny feeling, like with George, and I was kind of mad at Dad but he told me in the kitchen to please do it because Pete is his boss and thinks I am only his girl and I guess I was kind of sex hot anyway so I said OK. So pretty soon Dad said why don't Jane and me get dressed for bed and wear my good nightie, which is the one you can see right through even with pants on and give this other one to Jane. What I kind of didn't like was he was telling Pete wait until he sees me in that. Jane was real nice when we went in to change and said did I always swing and that they do a lot, so I said we always do, too, so she said she could wear my other nightie OK and it was real sexy, too, and let's really put on a show for them and it will be a lot of fun but to really tease Pete along, and then we will kid them and tell them we are too tired tonight and we don't feel like it.

"God it was real sex hot going out and they were clapping their hands and whistling at us, and Pete just pulled me down on the sofa and kissed me. What was real weird was Dad never touched the girl with George and for some reason I wanted to see him do it up Jane and watch him. I wasn't jealous for some reason but wanted to see him that's all. Anyway we just kind of switched partners, and Dad was kissing and feeling Jane, and I was getting real hot watching him. What it was was I could never watch before because it was with me. It's kind of a shock to watch your own Dad with a Lady, like you can't believe he ever did those things before. It's real weird.

"Anyway, we didn't really just start doing it right away. We had a drink and were dancing in our nighties with them in their shorts. It was kind of dirty the things we were doing but OK, and I was getting kind of sex hot mostly from watching Dad. Jane was really being super dirty. She wears so much perfume that the room really smelled.

"Anyway Pete was kind of kissing me and all and I couldn't see Dad, and he said, 'Look at what Jim and Jane are doing. Do you want to too?' God, it was really a shock. Jane was having oral love from Dad naked. It really seemed hard to believe. So I won't go into detail but I just wanted to tell how weird that was seeing your own Dad do that.

"So anyway Pete and I did everything right in front of them, and we brought the double-bed mattress with sheets in on the living room floor, and all got on it doing everything. Pete was so small that I was kind of embarrassed for him but he was real nice and loving.

"So Dad said pretty soon, 'Let's all get Annabelle,' so he practically jumped on me and told Pete and Jane what to do to me all at the same time. I really had a funny feeling about Dad for some reason, and Pete was kind of hurting me in the bottom, and for some reason Jane was talking to me and being real sweet and doing oral love on me but I couldn't see her because of my position but I kind of got to like her and was thinking about her and not Dad and Pete, and I got to thinking even more how I would like to make love with Mom.

"So the rest of the evening we drank and fooled around naked until Dad said show them your garter belt and things on. I didn't really want to because I was real tired but I did, and they all clapped and whistled at me and fooled with my body all over, and Dad said, 'Show them how you masturbate.' I didn't want to so Jane said she would help me, and Dad said, 'Good, I like to see a woman with Annabelle the most,' so I just did it for him, except Jane made me so sex hot so I said let's all get Jane and they came down on the mattress and we did, and I really made her climax like mad even after all evening, so she said, 'Come over and visit me sometime alone.' I said OK but I won't really go.

"So I said, 'I am so tired and let's go to bed.' God, I almost said Dad right in front of them. So he said, 'No, you sleep with Pete tonight and Jane and I will stay here on the mattress,' so Pete said, 'I want one more drink,' so we were sitting on the sofa and Jane was practically asleep with her eyes closed. So Dad came in with some blankets for us on the sofa and them on the floor and said, 'Look at her. Just one more time.' And he just got down with her and she wouldn't open her mouth so he did intercourse up her front and up her bottom right in front of us, and Pete was kidding him like it wasn't even his wife and saying she likes it best in the morning and you won't get any more tonight. God, it was so weird so I asked Pete didn't he care if it was his wife and he said not when he could get me. So Dad just pulled the covers up on them and went to sleep. That was what bothered me the most all night was him sleeping with Jane and not me.

"So Pete said, 'Let's go sleep on the box springs—they are padded enough with the sofa pillows.' And we took our covers in the bedroom, and the bathroom is off from the bedroom and he said do I like to play in the bathroom. God, I won't say what he wanted but it was with peeing, and I said no but let him watch me alone and I was real embarrassed so we didn't do anything else but kiss once and he was real sweet and said I was real good to make love to. So when he went to sleep, I went in and got between Dad and Jane and he said, 'Go back to Pete,' but then he went to sleep. I was real, real mad so I turned over and cuddled with Jane naked and she felt real good, and she woke up real early and was surprised to see me and kissed me and we hugged and hugged and she felt me a little but I didn't feel her and I had my eyes closed pretending it was Mom and felt real good. Then we went back to sleep until ten o'clock.

"So I said, 'I am going to 11:00 A.M. mass,' and they laughed and laughed so I didn't go, but Jane said she was sorry and she should have driven me over. So we took showers and dressed and had breakfast, and it was going to be about a minus 2.6 or .7 tide so Dad and Pete said let's go clamming, but Jane didn't want to go and was spending hours putting on makeup and perfume and fixing her hair and I was still mad at Dad so I said I will stay with Jane.

"So pretty soon she said, 'They will be gone all afternoon and probably stop at the bar and do you want to come in the bedroom with me? So I said, 'I never did it all alone with only a Lady,' and she said, 'You did OK last night,' so I felt real funny being a Lesbian without the men there but said OK, and we went in and undressed each other like she said. It was real strange being with a Lady all alone like a Lesbian, and I was kind of scared and decided I would try to play like she was Mom because she is only a couple of years older and has a good figure like Mom. I said I was kind of scared right to her and she hugged me and kissed my cheek and was so sweet, and I said right to her, 'Will you play like you are Mom?' so she was kind of funny and said OK and I was calling her Mom and she was saying I was her sweet Daughter and it was really like she was.

"So I forgot about Pete and Dad and they came in and came in the bedroom, and Dad was saying I couldn't wait could I and Jane said it was her not me. So Dad said, 'Pull the covers off and let us watch you two make love,' so I said I didn't want to be watched. He wasn't very happy and said, 'OK, Pete, I guess it's our turn and I will take Jane in the other room and you can have Annabelle on the bed,' and he said, 'She is all yours all weekend like I told you.' God, I got so mad.

"You know what's so stupid is I know Dad is fooling around when I'm not there but he says he is not and I am the only one but I can see how he liked Jane and only did it up me once all the time when they all three did, and I just don't like to think about it, but writing this to you, I have to, and I thought about it all night and have really been honest with myself and think Dad still probably loves me best but told Pete he could have me like I was his property and not his daughter and said to them that he would bring me to one of their swinging parties and could trade me for any woman he wanted because I am young and pretty so I wonder how much he really loves me.

"What's so dumb is I am just sitting here writing away and I don't even know what you want to know or what you need for your book. I think it is real, real important to educate people about Fathers and Daughters but I don't know why they really do it up them myself. I think it is love but maybe after a while it's just sex. I guess it could be like married people falling out of love after a while. I don't think swingers are in love anymore but just want new sex. The more I write the less I know anything.

"I am going to phone Dad pretty soon and see if we can talk and make things right and move in with him right now for all the time. I could get a job down there and clean house and cook for him and all. But I guess even if he won't, I will just keep seeing him as long as I can if we are alone and it's only us and no one else. That is better than nothing and no love from anyone at all."

By the time of her next letter, Annabelle had reset her grip on the situation:

"I want to help you with your book because that is real important but what writing does is make me think and I came to a conclusion even in this letter that I was so worried and it is all natural. Like lots of married people swing and are still in love. If I want to marry Dad, then I have to start thinking like a wife to make his sex life happy. As long as he doesn't make me do it too much, it should be OK to do it with his friends once in a while.

"What I am going to do is surprise him and play little girl with a new skirt and blouse and braids and ribbons and knee socks and all and say to go ahead and have Pete and Jane back down for a weekend. He will really like that. I will just play real, *real* young and they and Dad will like me more. I think having the right attitude is real important and I haven't had it for a while. I just wasn't thinking about it all before but now I am prepared. It's not all that different. In fact I was just kind of bratty that time and I don't blame him for getting mad. . . .

"So what I am saying is I am kind of changing. I like sex with Dad a lot and even with his boss OK but I am beginning to like it most with Jane and want it all the time with Mom. Mom used to wear her robe and a long nightie and doesn't wear her robe and wears a shortie lots with me now because she read the Lesbian books I had. I could tell when she borrowed and returned them, and I think she really wants to get together with me but she is like me and doesn't know how to.

"You know what is really funny. Maybe this will help you understand. I got to love Dad doing it up me a long time ago and I don't like to even think about anyone else. His friends are OK for once in a while but not for long. I think a real young girl gets used to this and doesn't want to change. Dad seems real secure and all and I don't know what some boy would be like. What it is is we kind of get trapped right from the beginning. I figured that out. I am just plain scared to try someone new for making love and to live with. I know Dad real good and don't know anyone else. It's kind of a trap but a pretty nice one.

"Boy, I just get thinking more and more things about myself. Do you masturbate a lot? I always did and I do now more than ever before—about two or three times some days. It isn't always for sex but just because I get depressed and really down and have nothing to do. I have a girl friend (but not for sex) and I don't have a boyfriend really. She is engaged and I don't see her much and I used to get asked out a lot in school but I never wanted to go out much. Lots of times I like to go to bed real early about 7:30 or 8:00 P.M. and just get naked under the covers and fool with myself for an hour before I climax. Do you ever like to kind of hurt yourself for sex? Sometimes it is kind of fun. I like to tie a string real tight around my nipples sometimes. But mostly I like to be real slow and just fool around. Sometimes I wish I had lots of friends but most people are not really your friends and are just using you and you can tell when they are.

"I have to go to bed now so I will say good night. I like writing to you a lot."

The next letter brought a lift of spirit:

"Boy, I just have to write right away and tell you what a wonderful weekend I had and how really super Dad was. It was all because I figured out that before I was kind of letting him do what he wanted with me to please him instead of me really trying hard to make him happy. . . .

"I did like we played a couple of years ago and went out the back door and around to the front and rang the bell and said, 'Mister, I am lost and will you help me.' God, he just went right on from there like we always did it everyday and got me to come in and sit next to him on the sofa with my skirt way up and says, 'How old are you little girl?' So I say, 'Ten,' and he says how pretty I am and I have pretty pants (panties) and can he touch them and do I want to touch him and do I want to touch him naked and can he pull my pants down, too, and I talk like a real, real little girl all along and pretty soon we are naked. I always call him Mister, like I don't know him, and he calls me Little Girl, like he doesn't know me and says do I want to suck his lollipop and get vanilla milk shake, he will show me what little girls like (oral love) and so finally he pretends like he wants to take me in his bedroom for intercourse and I pretend like I am scared. So I try to get away and get dressed and he grabs me and pulls me in his bedroom and ties me to the bed and I play like I am crying and begging him to stop but he does it up me anyway, and by that time it is dinner time so we stop and barbecue really nice steaks and baked potatoes and peas and a glass of wine. I still play little girl, dressed again, like I decided to stay with him and I keep calling him Mister and all.

"I didn't go into any detail because you will get the point but what was different was always before I was kind of following what he wanted and I really thought it out before and now *he* was playing *my* game and I really liked it and so did Dad."

Pete and Jane came and this time everything went swingingly. . . .

"Anyway, I just wanted to tell you that everything has changed so much since I started writing to you. I have so much to thank you for by making me start thinking. Jane helped, too, because I told her I thought we were going bad so she told me a lot that helped. Boy, I'm going from a dumb girl to a happy, swinging housewife (pretend) in just a few weeks. Tell me if you need more information."

Next word from Annabelle was that she had moved in with Dad. Mom was mad. But all was really wonderful. They had joined a swinging club.

"I am going off the pill and stay away from the other men and I will get pregnant with Dad and have my own wonderful little baby with him and then go back on it so I can have fun with the others. We go to a different house each weekend and there are about fifteen people there who all get naked and have fun. Boy, we get about five or six of us on the bed at once, and they have a lot of Polaroids and all and everyone loves me and Gail, who is the other daughter. I gave her your address because she did it with both her folks since she was seven or eight so maybe she can help.

"Dad and I are really in love. We are going to get married in Mexico next year. We learned lots of new things to do from other people on the weekends that we never thought of so it is much more fun. All the men and some of the Ladies just love me and are so nice to me.

"Mom phoned up and said am I working yet so I said not yet but I will soon. She said where am I sleeping so I said on the sofa so she said, 'No you aren't, you are sleeping with Dad,' so I got mad and said, 'So what?' and said, 'You wouldn't hardly ever do much sex with Dad so he deserves it and I am and we're in love so that's just tough,' so she said, 'What are you doing? Are you doing intercourse and oral love and all?' I just said, 'Every day and so what?' so she hung up. Boy, wait until I have my baby. She will be so mad."

But that was not to last. By the time Annabelle sent off her next letter to me, she was back with Mom. And mad at Dad:

"You said what is sexual abuse of children. I don't think that it is any kind of sex itself. I mean, maybe some Dads really hurt girls between their legs on purpose, but I am thinking of any kind of sex with children that doesn't really hurt but is real, real dirty. I think that is OK even if the girl is real young, like about seven or eight or something.

"What I think is sexual abuse is only when your Dad doesn't really love you and just pretends to and you find out later that he doesn't. That's when sex with your daughter is wrong.

"I kind of have that kind of thing. I think Dad loved me a lot when I was real, real young because he didn't have intercourse with me until I was old enough and not when I was too young to climax. He used to do it on me and all over me, squirting his stuff, but not up me. He did it up me with his tongue but that was so it didn't hurt me. And he always would let me suck him to get his vanilla milk shake in my tummy whenever I wanted to because I really loved to even if he was busy doing something else. I just had to ask and we would right away and he never said he was busy.

"I think that I thought he didn't love me the first time he let that man do it up me and when he let Pete do it and said I was all his like he told him.

"So I think children really love sex. Boy, I loved it with Dad a lot more when I was eight to twelve but not as much later.

"You said what makes *hurt*. What that is is when your Dad is just using you. I have been so dumb about that so it is all my own fault. When I moved in with Dad, right away we went to this sex group that Pete and Jane belong to with about fifteen different people. Boy, there is no love there. Everyone just wants more and more sex even if you hurt. I thought it was fun at first because they do a lot of sex things we never heard of that are real, real hot and we used to go home and do them. Some of the things are real dirty and everyone watches and takes Polaroid pictures of you. But they don't even really love you but just want sex mostly with me and that one other daughter because we are a lot younger than everyone else.

"Anyway, it was kind of exciting at first . . . but I figured out that Dad just wanted me to go with him to play hero with a young girl and not for love, since he hardly ever paid any attention to me but mostly with this other young girl when he had a chance.

"What I am saying is that it isn't what you do but if it is for love. *Used* is what you call being hurt.

"I think the other thing is the men are always wanting me to do Lesbian love with one or two or three of the Ladies, and Dad is the worst about getting me to do this because they all like to watch that for some reason and get hot. I think that is taking advantage of me and is not love. So anyway I am saying that people who are together just for sex and not to be watched and not to use me is OK and not sex abuse.

"The very worst was the second weekend when Dad never touched me but we were there for two nights. What Dad said was get to know every man there and do everything with him and he said to suck and fuck every man there this weekend and there were nine men with him but he never did me so it was eight. What was real bad was he said, 'Make sure you do it in front of me and not in one of the bedrooms.' Boy, he just watched me like mad and he said, 'Hey, there is only one man up Annabelle and she needs more so some of you other guys get up her too.' So they would and he said, 'Give it to her real hard,' and what was worse, he said, 'Now suck him,' no matter where he pulled it out, like up my bottom without washing first, and kept telling me to suck real hard and said, 'Look at her suck everyone and all.' Now that is using me to get him hot or something and I hate that.

"What I am trying to say is I like all kinds of sex and even a lot of tying up and spanking and all but I hate to have to do it always with someone else than Dad and it is Dad who makes me do it for him and not for me at all.

"So what happened the last week is Dad went off fishing during the day with his friend and I went up to see Jane twice but Dad never made love up me even once so I found that he was going fishing with this Lady and I bet he was doing it up her all day and not up me. So I just waited for him to go to work and moved back with Mom.

"She was nice and said she wasn't surprised so we stayed up real, real late and talked a lot, and she kept saying am I doing it with Dad so I finally said yes and I really cried and cried and Mom was real, real nice to me. So we just sat there practically all night and we just drank this whole half gallon of red wine of hers and we got kind of smashed and so I just told her about everything from when I was in first and second grade and thought we would be real friends because I did. But you know what? She knew all the time. She didn't really know everything but really knew a lot so I just told her the rest and about swinging and all and why I left Dad, so she said it was good and really hugged me tight and was real loving and tender and understanding and has never been this understanding before. So I said, 'Mom can I sleep in your bed with you tonight?' So she said OK if I remember she is my Mom and not another woman, so I said OK and I always sleep naked so she said not with her I won't so I said OK. So we brushed our teeth and went to bed and talked a lot more and I promised to go to church again every Sunday but not to confess what I did ever to the Father but not to ever do it again unless I was married. And if I would promise, I could stay with her and not to worry about anything. So later she said I had more sex all my life than she ever did and do I need to keep having it, so I said maybe I might a couple of times with this girl I met that I told you about, so she said she wished I wouldn't but at least I won't get pregnant and we laughed and laughed at that.

"So I said, 'Mom did you ever do it with a woman or a girl?' She said no. So I said, 'Did you ever want to?' She said every woman wants to some time in their life but they just don't. So I said, 'I like to be in bed with you.' She said she knew I had ideas about her for a long time but to forget it, so I said, 'Can we just once?' and she might like it. She said that is what she is afraid of, so I know for sure she thinks about it, too, and wants to but she is afraid for some reason. So I think pretty soon maybe we can try it and she will really like it but not for a while.

"I am not ever going to see Dad anymore. I have been so dumb time and time again but now I know for sure that he is just using me because that's what all men finally do.

"So what I really think is that Dads sexually abuse their children and Moms don't. They just really love them. I just hate the thought of getting married and getting divorced and all and like the idea of staying with Mom, who will take care of me because she loves me. It seems real, real secure with her and I know it is not with Dad. I like to feel secure and I think that is why a lot of girls do it with their Fathers and some do with their Moms, too, except it is love with your Mother.

"So if a girl wants my advice now I would say it is OK to do it with Dad until you are about thirteen or fourteen but after that he will lose interest in you and abuse you sexually by letting other people do it up you so it is best to stop at that age, and if I did, then I would still like Dad and not be mad at him like I am.

"I still think Daughters like to do it best with their folks so I would suggest that they do it with their Moms after about thirteen or fourteen so they will still have plenty of sex and still never be sexually abused.

"The only other thing might be if the parents never got divorced like they always do, then it would be best to do it with both of them and save their marriage and keep the family together. What you could do is take care of the problem of dads wanting only real, real young girls by having only girl babies for your Father (except maybe Moms would like you to have boy babies for them—I don't know but they probably would.)

"It is really terrible to grow up though. Dad and I were really close until I was fifteen or sixteen, and I used to sit in school and hardly wait to get home to have sex naked with him even when I was in second grade and third and fourth and especially when I was in fifth and sixth when we did intercourse and I could climax. God, I wish I was young all over again right now but I never will be. What I worry about a lot is Mom thinks I am too old and that is why we aren't doing it yet. I think if I was twelve or so we would.

"I have to go now and I hope this answers your question. I am at the same address again so it is OK to ask me questions. Mom says she promises I can sleep with her Saturday night if I wear my nightie, so I said, 'What if I just take it off anyway?' She said maybe it might be OK and we will see Saturday, so that is what I am going to do."

And so, it would appear, the socializing-by-sexualizing sometimes backfires. But if it hadn't—can this be what *anyone* wants the wives and mothers of America to be?

Gone Fishing

We were fishing in the unpredictable waters of my mother's memory.

"When *did* you get married?" I asked.

"Just before you were born."

"But you said I was illegitimate."

"No. I never said you were illegitimate."

"Yes you did."

"No. What I meant," she said simply, "was we were married—somewhere in Massachusetts I believe—by a justice of the peace whose wife was the witness. But you see your father was still married to his first wife, who'd run off to Africa, so he couldn't find her to get a divorce."

"I remember you showed me an early letter from him telling you that you were finally divorced."

"Yes, well, he went to Mexico when you were about five or six."

"And got two divorces?"

"Well, he didn't really get any. You see, Mexican divorces weren't recognized here at that time."

"Then when I was in boarding school and you remarried him you were really still married?"

"Well—but in between he'd married your brother's mother."

"And then you were divorced again?"

"Again—in Mexico. And Mexican divorces still weren't recognized here at that time. So then he married again and when he died they wanted to give me the Social Security because they felt we were still married, but, of course, I didn't take it."

"Do me a favor," I said.

"What?"

"Make me a flow chart."

You can sit over there—next to Jenny.

The Grisly Details

"Dear Louise:

"I hope all is going well. I've got a job. Classes start next week. And so it goes.

"In the meantime, I've been trying to get this together for you. And I'm settling down to it (cup of tea, kitten asleep in the sun, Cris Williamson on the stereo). (Actually, I'm hoping the typewriter will make it go faster, and thus be done with it. I admit my cowardice quite freely.)

"I wasn't quite sure how to organize (organize?) all of this, and I keep finding things I had completely forgotten about. I finally decided to just go ahead and give some of the longer fragments that I remember, as I think of them, and fill in anything else I can think of; then let you deal with figuring it out, or making sense of it.

"I would like to hear from you after you've gotten all this for several reasons—to answer any questions, fill in gaps, know that you have it; but mostly because it feels sort of shaky to be doing this at all, and I guess I want to be sure that it's acceptable.

Take care and good luck,
Jenny"

"So—going on the assumption that what you want is basically a factual rundown, fleshed out with feelings and impressions then and now:

"It was to a large extent a progression. Always a fair amount of general touching, horseplay, 'exposure,' etc. The first solid impression that something was different. Sitting beside daddy on my bed, his putting my hand on his penis, and then pushing my head into his lap, nothing said. I had some idea of what was being asked for, and tried to figure a way out of it. After brushing my cheek by, he did tell me to use my mouth. Whereupon, I repeated the same. This time he didn't say anything, and I hoped that I had fooled him, but was scared that he might figure it out. Next, being pushed backward onto my bed, being kissed good-night. Strongest sense from that time—that it was thoroughly gross, scared of getting caught, and of its happening again. And so it did, occasionally. I believed that I had him fooled.

"Waking up and realizing that daddy was sitting on the edge of my bed, hands under my nightgown, leaning to kiss me. Mostly startled, then some panic that he would realize that I was awake. Mostly, I couldn't figure out what was going on. Then daddy lying on the inside of the bed, touching/kissing all over. Trying to be relaxed so that he wouldn't know that I was awake. Afraid that I would be caught awake—and a lot of why/what confusion. Besides that, confused as to why it all felt so 'strange.'

"Daddy lying on top of me—pushing and pushing. Very heavy. And not getting very far. Really scared. And, again, terrified that he would know I was awake. Daddy on top of me again. This time rubbing up and down. Seems like this was after the preceding time—another time—because of relief that he wasn't pushing anymore. But it returned.

"Many, many fragments of being touched, moved, etc. Chronically afraid that I would get pregnant, and therefore get in trouble. At the time I thought that I would get in trouble because I thought I knew too much of what was going on—and obviously I wasn't supposed to know. And though I thought at the time I was very worldly-wise and knew lots about what was going on and to some extent some of my information was accurate, mostly my information was either missing or misinformation or woefully inadequate.

"After my dog started sleeping on my bed, she would growl if anybody came near my bed and lunge at my father if he came within a foot of my bed. A source of some satisfaction. Perhaps that is part of what ended it.

"At the time, there were recurrent nightmares. Two of which I have had again recently (opening old closets revives many a skeleton). First is/was a very black place. I am lying on my back, very near the edge of the end of the space, which is indistinguishable from the rest of the blackness, but I know it is there and that it is light on the other side. It is curved. The only other thing present is a pair of hands that never stops moving and an unrecognizable face. The other, much briefer, primarily involves a naked man, standing in the doorway with an erection. He doesn't move, but I know that he will sooner or later. OK. I didn't say you had to be interested. I was just telling you.

"Now is a good deal harder, mostly because it is something to be reckoned with yet. I keep feeling that I haven't given enough in the above, but perhaps with what you have, you can get some sense of it. It's hard as, to a large extent, I'm not sure where I am with it. Sometimes I get angry briefly or frustrated in trying to figure it out or whatever, but mostly I ignore it, which I have had a fair amount of practice at.

"It seems that every time I get this far in getting anything written, I get really uncomfortable with whatever I've written and want to tear it up, start again, and get it right. Maybe that's the best indication of where I am with it.

"One thing more. One of the side pieces was that I was also convinced that mom would walk in any minute and that I would be the one in trouble. No, it never occurred to me to tell her because they always took the same side, and I guess I figured this was no different. Also, I seem to have been thinking I was just as implicated as he was. *Assumed guilt* is the term, I believe.

"Somehow, mailing it feels very final—but so it goes."

Touch Me Again and I'll Kill You

"You just have no idea," my mother said, "no idea how traumatic this has been. I feel like such a fool. I mean I built him up to you. I *wanted* you to see him as brilliant, see his good features. I am furious. I have never been so angry in my life.

"Now that it's sunk in. Finally. God, am I stupid. How could I have been so stupid. You see, at first—I really didn't get it. When you first told me, it didn't sink in."

Disbelief. A normal reaction. It's not the same as denial.

"Of course, he did have some good qualities—."

"Like what?"

"Well—you know he really did have a hard time of it, a very unhappy childhood—."

"Phooey," I said, before she could begin the litany of his early childhood miseries.

Here we were, two adult women, both kicked in the head by the same guy. Why were we trying so hard to *understand* him?

I knew what she was going to say next.

"Well, dear—I guess it was partly my fault—."

Why is it so important that your father or your child's father have "some good qualities?"

Some women have a resonant toughness. They go "phooey"

much sooner. And they seem to spring back somewhat more quickly.

"Okay," Jill said. "I was assaulted by my father when I was eight. It ended when I was twelve.

"My father didn't contribute to the support of us children. My father drank a lot although he wasn't necessarily drunk when the assaults happened. I remember chewing gum on his breath and maybe alcohol, but he was never drunk.

"My mother was a responsible, strong woman. One of the first traveling saleswomen—worked her way up from an eighth grade education. Had a strong background. I never told my mother. I didn't know she was that strong. I was eight years old.

"It's a classic example of children following the authority of their parents: afraid to go against him and afraid to hurt the woman. Afraid to hurt mother. There was no reason to hurt her or bring it up. He hurt her enough.

"I thought my father was weak, a name dropper. I had no respect for my father whatsoever. He was just terrible to me. I didn't like him at all, but I pretended to until he died, and when he died, I didn't go to the funeral.

"I had an awful guilt feeling. We were taught that sex was wrong. And I knew it was wrong with my father. Actually what he was doing was oral. I didn't perform it on him. He performed it on me. One time he did attempt it when he thought I was asleep and he came up with his penis to my mouth. But I just turned my head and pretended like I was asleep, although I was awake. Wouldn't accept it.

"The worst thing that could happen to a kid, I think, because she doesn't know these things exist until they begin to happen to her.

"When it first began, my sister and I were lying in bed and he came in and rubbed—put his hands up both our legs. And then afterward, we both said to each other, 'Did daddy do that?' And we both agreed that he had. But he never did anything more to my younger sister, and my older sister was never involved in it. It was just me. And so later he said, 'Come upstairs. I have some pennies I want to give you.' And I went upstairs and then he had me get on the bed, and he began doing all of these things, caressing me, and doing all of those things. And it became a chronic thing.

"I wasn't so much frightened—more upset that it was happening. I used to cry a lot. I was a very sensitive child at that age and used to cry all the time. And my mother never knew why I cried so much. At the least little thing. And then it would seem like my sister and I would have arguments and my mother would either spank us both to get the right one or not believe me. And so that hurt me all the more because I was getting everything.

"I felt very, very rejected and I planned to kill him. I was going to kill him with an ice pick. I had it all planned because I had read somewhere that when you pulled out the ice pick—you know—no hole. And when you're twelve you begin that—I don't know how long I thought about killing him.

"But I first tried blackmail. Not, 'Don't do it anymore,' but, 'If you don't give mother some money this week, I'm going to tell her what you do to me.' Oh, I was real clever.

"I was a fighter for causes and I am a fighter for causes right now. I'm into a lot of things right now. But at that time it was bad. And one time my girl friend was staying all night with me and my father came in and ran his hand up my leg and said, 'Come in the other room. I want to talk to you.'

"And I knew my girl friend was awake. She didn't say anything, but I thought she was awake—hoped she wasn't. And when I got in there, he had me lay on the davenport and this time he just laid on me and just rubbed between my legs, and when I recall it now, I don't even recall a real erection. Whether he had a problem or not, I don't know.

"But anyway, he said to me, 'Do you want to read a book on this?'

"And I said, 'No, I don't. I'm no baby.'

"And he said, 'You're not going to have a baby.'

"And I said, 'I didn't say that. I said I'm no baby.'

"And then I was embarrassed at what he had done to me in front of my friend—and all the other times when he would stop me and say 'wait a minute'—and play with my breasts when I was on the way out and all of my friends were out there waiting. This was the final straw.

"With a lot of force, I pushed him on the floor. And he looked up at me with startled eyes and I said, 'If you ever touch me again, I'll kill you.'

"I think with me the fact was I actually disliked him so much and as years went by, the more I matured, the more I disliked him and the weaker he seemed to me. There was something the matter with him. If he wanted sex, why didn't he go out with another woman? And he just got to seem so bad. Much worse than I thought of him when I was a child. In my mind I lost so much respect for him and everything he did.

"It wasn't hatred so much as the fact that he seemed like such a jerk. Just such a jerk to me. I thought, 'Oh God, how could anybody have liked him? I don't understand how my mother could have married him.'

"But my mother was a strong woman and she was a good influence on all of us. We're positive. We're success-oriented. And it has to do with my mother, I'm sure.

"But you see it's all these attitudes toward women. How does it go that a man can take advantage of women? Why does he feel he can take advantage of a two-year-old or a five-year-old or a seventeen-year-old or an eighty-nine-year-old? Why? It's because the society says that men are better than women, and that if a man wants something he is entitled to it, and the women have to nurture men and take care of men. And men to me are very weak, very weak.

"But I work in lots of things and go forward and have strong, aggressive tendencies. And I think this experience gave me aggression.

"Once I pushed my father off and threatened to kill him, and I meant it—I learned that aggression was something that protects you.

"Protects one."

Orphaned, Emotionally

Carla's therapist had suggested she get in touch with me. She's a slight, very pretty Puerto Rican–American, twenty years old.

"Sometimes I feel about eighty, though," she said.

"I just moved into a new place with a girl friend of mine. Been living there about a month now. We have been planning for years to move in together but it didn't work until recently. It was fun moving in in a way, but after a while it got frustrating. Because everything went wrong—like we found out that the shower leaks and my landlady likes flooding us with her hose, and the place has cracks in the walls.

"It's a two-family house. Brick. Beautiful neighborhood, though. Every time I move it's to a nicer looking neighborhood.

"When I was a kid, we lived in a project. People weren't too nice and we kept to ourselves mostly. I didn't like it. Until I moved out two years ago and I started doing what I wanted to do. About two months after I turned eighteen. I moved in with my sister first, and then I found a room.

"And my mother had a fit. And my father got so mad he tried to choke me as I was packing. And since then we've hardly spoken two words to each other. Not that we ever talked much anyway. I get along a little better now with my mother.

"She's very—as far as we're concerned—she's a very domineering lady. But she is the real homebody type. Her husband comes first—and then her children.

"I guess that is the way she was brought up. I mean she was married at fifteen, had her first child at sixteen, and all she knows is what her mother taught her—to be with her family. And her husband—she really thinks a lot of my father—so he always came first.

"Both my parents were born in Puerto Rico. They came here when they were in their teens. They knew each other in Puerto Rico and I think they came here a year apart from each other. They lived in the same neighborhood when they came here, so I guess that's how they got married. My mother doesn't talk about the things that happened before. She likes to keep it to herself.

"I wish she would talk. But she's not the type. Anything that happened before any of us were born is a blank to all of us.

"And there is one thing I wanted to ask her for years. My oldest brother happens to have a different name from my father and he looks like my mother, which none of the rest of us do. I have always wanted to know about that. But I couldn't ask her. She would hit the roof.

"And see he never struck my oldest brother. And my oldest brother always called my father by his first name. My father never really considered him his son, I think. Because I'm sure he isn't.

"And it was like—he's not my son, so I can't do anything to him. Like—he's not my possession. I think that's what we all were. That's why he got so mad when I left. To his mind, I'm sure it was an insult that I would leave his home before I got married.

"I would say the way he thinks of the family and the way he thinks of women is fairly typically Puerto Rican. His attitudes about—you should respect the parents no matter what. And the woman is to serve the men in her family and that's it. So I would say part of it is from that and part of it is just that's the way he is. He wasn't too happy as a child.

"I heard very little about his father but I know one thing. When he was living with his father and his father's mistress, he told us about one time when his father was punishing him for something and he told him to sit on his knees and he left him there for six hours and he said if he moved he would beat the hell out of him. He was about ten. And the mistress told him to get up when his father left—and he had to get back down before he came back.

"But up until about the age of six—when you're very small and you don't think too much for yourself, my father likes you. You know, he used to play with us when I was about four. Then the only other happy memory I have after that is where he used to sit and comb my hair because I had very long hair. And he used to put it in pigtails for me. He loved doing that. And this is the last thing I remember about him that way."

"Was he abusive?"

"To my mother, no. There were times that they would get into really heavy fights. There was one fight when he hit her with a broomstick on her head. And it was something to do with us. Some argument over the kids and he hit her on the head. But he never hit her again. But they had some pretty heavy fights sometimes.

"To everyone outside the family, my father is a very pleasant man. He's very friendly. He's funny. He always makes guests feel welcome. But sometimes when I see him with people, I can't help but laugh. Because he's so different—from the way I think of him."

"How do you think of him?"

"I think he's a rotten son-of-a-bitch. See, there are seven of us— four girls and three boys. I'm fifth. Most of the time he ignored me. He singled out my brother, my second oldest brother, and my second oldest sister. He used to like bothering them. He once tried to strangle my brother with a rope.

"My brother—I think he had cursed at my father. I believe that's what it was. And the one thing you didn't do to my father was to curse him. And he got so mad at him that he took the clothesline out of the closet and started wrapping it around his throat. And it took my mother, my sister, my other sister, and my brother to get him off.

"See, my father didn't get violent that often. But when he got violent, he really got violent."

"So he singled those two out for abuse?"

"Yeah."

"Not for fun."

"Well, my sister for fun. For some reason he seemed to dislike them the most."

"You think sexual abuse is a form of dislike?"

"I think in his case, yes. Because the one sister he liked—the only one in the family who could really have a conversation with him—he would never touch her. But the other sister—he used to hit her if he hit anybody. He used to call her names all the time. And she was the one he sexually assaulted the night before he hurt me. She ran away the next day.

"At that time, my mother was in Puerto Rico, and my sister ran away. And it was just my brother and myself. And I used to kiss my father as a habit every night before I went to bed. And that night I went to kiss him and he hugged me and said, 'You're never going to do that to me, like she did.' You know, leaving like that. And it was the first time in years that it occurred to me that maybe he loved me. So, you know, I felt good, and I said, 'No. I'm not going to do that to you.'

"And then the next thing I know a few hours later he's in my room.

"And—it's hard to explain. He didn't have intercourse with me. But his hands went everywhere they shouldn't have. And as much as I tried—like I tried to pull the covers over me and I tried to pretend that I was sleeping—but I think he knew I was awake because I did that two or three times. As if I was cold or something. And as if to pacify me, he started rubbing the back of my ears. To this day, I can't stand anybody doing that to me.

"At first, I couldn't understand exactly what he was doing. Then—I was mostly afraid.

"My father weighed about three hundred pounds in those days. And I always had a fear of him. My mother would use him as a weapon against us. 'I'm going to get your father after you if you don't cut it out.' And I was very afraid of him. And I thought if I did something against him that he would do something. He would maybe kill me or something. It surprises me that I really believed this. Then, after the fear, it was mostly humiliation.

"Humiliation and embarrassment.

"At twelve—that was the time when I was first becoming aware of sex in any form. That's why I felt—he was using me. And I tried to talk myself out of it. I tried to pretend I was dreaming. That he hadn't showed up after all and done what he had done. After he went back to his room, I just stayed awake all night.

"I helped him fix his breakfast as usual and I had just about convinced myself it wasn't true. And that night I found him in my room again. Only this time I got up the courage—before he came near me—to get up, go to the bathroom, and pretend I hadn't seen him. And I did the same thing the next night. After that, he stopped coming.

"I think I stayed in the bathroom about a half hour each night. But then—after that, I don't know whether it was because he didn't have the opportunity or he didn't feel like it or what.

"But—my father. If there's one thing I knew then it was that your father doesn't touch you the way that he did. It was just instinct. I never had any real sex education. It wasn't discussed.

"And now my father—I don't know if he remembers what he did or not. I don't know. Maybe it's because he acts so normal. He doesn't drink or anything. So maybe it's not that he doesn't remember it. It's just that he doesn't feel anything about it.

"He wasn't the affectionate type. As a matter of fact, he never touched me until then. I don't know if that's why I knew. I just knew it was something he shouldn't have been doing and that I shouldn't have allowed him to.

"*Now* the worst part is that he shouldn't have done it. For a few years, it was that I allowed him to. I felt guilty about that for a while. And the fact that I had to admit to myself that my body responded—that made me feel worse.

"Because I went over the whole thing, and like, at the time my mother used to buy me gowns that were—well, that night I happened to be wearing something that you could see through. And my body was just developing, and that plus the fact that I hadn't really done anything physical to stop him. And that I felt some response in myself, which I now know is something that everyone feels no matter who's doing it to you. But those things all together made me feel like it was my fault. I had somehow enticed him or something.

"And for a long time it made me distrustful of any man. I still am, though not as much. I felt like someday whoever I happen to marry might turn out the same way. Or that, you know, I can't trust a man because all he wants from me is sex and nothing else. It lowered my self-esteem to the point where I got into one really lousy relationship with a man a lot older than I was. And when that relationship broke up—I was always a very emotional person—but I got really nutty. I yelled at people for the slightest thing they did or said, and I would go into rages at anything and depressions constantly.

"It was like after I moved out I was very insecure and I felt lost. And I was—like I spent most of my time in my apartment, and everything, everything in my mind seemed to revolve around what had happened with him.

"I think because I ignored it for so many years that it was catching up with me. And my attitude toward men—I started to realize what it was. And when I look at it now—I see I was looking for a nice father.

"All these years I had dreams that he was doing the same thing again. I would wake up in the middle of the night and I could swear he was in the room with me. And this is even after I moved out of the house. I was afraid to open my eyes and find him there. And during the dreams he would start to beat me up. These went on—I had them constantly. Now if I have a dream, it's usually every two or three months, which is terrific compared to what it was. And I don't have the one where I think he's in the room with me. I don't have that any more. I think I finally killed that ghost off."

"Did you have flashbacks?"

"During that one relationship, a couple of times. The one time I remember most is a time where he wanted to have sex and I didn't. I wasn't feeling well. And he started trying to get me excited. And I wanted to kill him. Because for that moment I felt like he was violating me. Trying to get me to do something I didn't want to and right then and there I never screamed so loud at him for it. I really wanted to kill him.

"And I have one very good friend. And sometime around then I told her about what had happened with my father. At first she didn't believe me. She thought I had made it up. But then a year or so later she told me that she believed it but she couldn't understand how he could do it. Because her father would never in a million years go near her.

"But that's one reason I came to see you. I remember what it felt like for a long time and there was nobody else who had gone through it—except for my sister and she never discussed it after she told me the one time. And it was like I know what it feels like to be alone with it and to have it affect you, to have it on your mind for a long time, and digging into your life. So I figured if I came here—between me and whoever else you talked to—maybe somebody who had had it happen to her would at least—if it couldn't help her resolve it—it would let her know she wasn't alone.

"I think for most people it's traumatic. It's something that stays with you as long as you're alive. You remember and that's it. Like after you get over it, you just remember it.

"Like I've gotten over it—especially in the past year. But sometimes someone will say something to me or I'll be talking about something else that somehow connects with what happened. Like the other night with my boyfriend. We were talking about families and how kids should be brought up and how we were brought up, and all of a sudden it hit. I remembered. And for a while I just sat there very quiet. I couldn't say anything. I don't kncw. It's—I can't say everyone is going to carry it around the way I carried it around. Because I'm the sort of person that sort of simmers. And I just simmered with it. Whereas if you stand up and face it right away—.

"But your father's supposed to love you and protect you, and if he does something like that, it's the biggest betrayal there is. What you really need from a father is just love. You don't need a physical thing. That's for the husband and wife. But a kid is not a father's wife. She is something they created together that should be—you know, you teach them. You love them. And that's it. That's where it goes. As far as I'm concerned any sexual relationship is just using her.

"I think it's just like sometimes parents look at their kid as being theirs. She's mine. I can do what I want. And she can't complain.

"And I think my father was kind of smug about it. I think he knew that I knew what happened and that I would never say anything about it. Because he knows I was afraid of him that much.

"He always knew I was afraid of him. I mean when a kid sees her father try to strangle her brother, that's frightening.

"But I think the main thing that helped was my therapist accepted it as the truth, and that he held me guiltless, especially being a man. Even being a man he can see that my father was the one who was responsible for what happened and not me. He got me to the point where—it's a strange combination—but I still hate my father, but I pity him as well. Before, I had no such feeling as that. And the fact that he is a man did help a lot. If it had been a woman, I could say—'She's a woman. She understands.' But for a man to understand—it shows me that there are men in this world who can see it for what it is. They're not all the untrustworthy bastards I thought they were. It helps.

"But knowing what I do about my father, I would say the only way he could have rationalized it is that the man has the power. That he's a man. That he was my father and as far as he was concerned he could do whatever he wanted. As if I were a couch. To him, I was a piece of property.

"And to me, being betrayed like that, I felt like my father was gone. Since that day, I have not considered him my father. As a matter of fact, when I speak to my brothers or sisters, I say, 'Is your father home?' I say the same thing about her. I always say *your* father and *your* mother. It was like what I thought were my parents—what I thought they were—disappeared overnight.

"It's like making you an orphan emotionally."

"You never told your mother?"

"Not directly. Indirectly. I got into a mood one night when my little sister was six. Maybe it runs in the family—but my brother was experimenting with my little sister sexually. It had happened the year before when she was five. Then when she was six I got into this mood about it. And I realized she didn't seem to remember what had happened. But I said to her, 'Remember. When mom goes away, make sure she takes you with her.' I said, 'Don't ever be alone with him.'

"My brother was about fourteen at the time. And I said, 'Don't ever stay alone with him—or with your father.' And she didn't understand why. And I said, 'Don't say anything to mom. Just do what I tell you.'

"She went and told my mother. It's the way she was in those days.

"And my mother came to me and said I was just like my older

sister making up those terrible lies about my father. That he was a perfect father and a good man and I had nothing to say against him. So I quit right there.

"Except one time. What was it she said to me? About why I disliked him so much or something? And I said, 'If you knew what he was really like, you would hate him as much too.' But she never came straight out and faced it.

"And see, when my sister left, she'd left a note for my mother telling her what happened. Telling her what he had done. And I think my mother, in the back of her mind, believed it, because she never went away without him again, and she never left my little sister alone with him.

"But I had decided it wasn't worth it. She wouldn't accept it. And now with her health the way it is, I wouldn't want to do anything about it now anyway.

"I wish she had left him. I wish she had had the courage to face up to it and had left him because of what he did.

"I think there were times when she really wanted to kick him out, when they had a really big fight, and she knew she couldn't because she had seven children and a six-room apartment that she'd have to pay for if she did. So I think that had something to do with it. Plus the fact that I think my mother is basically an inse cure person and if she thinks my father is the most handsome, friendly man in the world—I think she was afraid of losing that. Him above all.

"For me now, the thing that I want most is to be loved by somebody, by a man. To be able to return it and for him to be the kind of man that I'm hoping for, something totally opposite of my father. Someone I can trust.

"Because if something like that happened to my children I think I'd kill him. I think I would snap if I found that out. I would murder him. Or at the very least put him away.

"That's the one thing that always aggravated me: I never knew when it happened to me that there is such a thing as going to somebody outside your family and saying, 'This happened to me. Get me away from him or put him away or something.' They now have where they'll put the child in a foster home and try to rehabilitate the father—or just take him away permanently, whichever is best."

"Which do you wish had happened?"

"You've got me there. See, the question there is that this is me and there were other people involved. As far as the rest of my family is concerned, I would say it was better that it was left alone.

"Without money, you know, my mother would have wanted to kill me for taking her husband away and for having her family wrecked financially and probably emotionally. So as far as they're concerned, it was better that nothing was done. As far as I'm concerned, for my own feelings, it would have been better if they had taken me off.

"Because for the six years that I lived with him since, there was a constant fear of having it happen again. And any time he touched me or came near me I wanted to throw up. So I think it would have been better if I had been removed at the time. It would have saved me a lot of fear. But for everyone else's sake, it was best left alone.

"See, I don't know which is more important."

Brothers and Sisters

Brother and sister incest, so the recitation goes, is perhaps the most prevalent but also the least and least often traumatic.

Certainly I received any number of letters from brothers claiming they had screwed their sisters and would love to talk about it. I spoke with a couple of them and their stories, though eagerly specific, sounded reasonably tame (was I getting jaded?).

Some I was grateful to for providing moments of lightness in an otherwise dark morning's mail. The fellow, for instance, who stood ready to tell all if I would: (1) Promise anonymity, (2) Tell him my story, and (3) Send a nude photograph.

If the relationship is equal, kids experimenting sexually would seem to present no real problem. And I'm sure that happens often, and I'm sure it's OK. I did not, I must say, hear from sisters with happy memories. Perhaps that can be chalked up to a lingering female reticence. Perhaps.

"It started when I was three," Tess said, "and it lasted until I was twelve. And what my brother would do is he would say to me, 'Do you want to play doctor?' And he was like a great big guy. He was nine years older than I was. He was twelve. And it was just terrible. He had this great big prick. I don't clearly remember the three-year-old part. I remember when I was six.

"See, I know it was three though. Because when I was in therapy I went back to the doctor and got all the lab reports. And I wanted to get all the facts from the doctor. And she said, '1943—gonorrhea.' And I was born in 1940."

"Good god. How did he have gonorrhea at twelve?"

"Well, in the summer we had a house in the country and he was like doing it to all the kids there. And that was during the war. And there was a lot of gonorrhea at that time. And I can't remember how they discovered it on me. But I can tell you what the doctors did—how they treated it then. I can remember the doctor would come to the house. And she would do these things called smears, which are very, very painful. Like she had these little glass slides. And she would cut. And it was very painful. And, of course, as a child I thought, 'Oh they'll see that it happened. They'll see the marks, the signs. They'll see that it happened.'

"And they would take me to the hospital. I can remember one time my mother telling me we were going to the zoo and the next thing I knew all these doctors are tying me down on a table. And the ether mask over my face. I found out recently that what they did in those days was they'd give the child a pelvic exam, they'd put them to sleep. And one time I can remember the nurse coming in with these awful needles. That's when penicillin started coming in.

"But what I don't understand and what my big gripe about the whole thing is *why* didn't anybody protect me? Why did all of this keep happening?

"See, my mother is still alive. And when I started realizing all this had happened, I got very angry. And my mother said, 'Oh well, I got it from these girls that lived next door.' Totally denying it. Absolutely denying it. I don't remember my mother ever coming to the hospital to visit me. I had a nurse who stayed with me in the hospital.

"My mother was very ambivalent. She could be very nice for a short period of time. But then she would just cut off and push me away. She's a very charming woman, she just wasn't a good mother. She should've just been my father's lover—she should never have been a mother.

"She took these dancing lessons and she traveled a lot with my father. Just the two of them together. And we had a bunch of servants. But it happened a lot. I can remember friends of mine—you know, also from super-rich families—where the mothers would be off. And they'd be raised by help and be sexually abused by their brothers.

"But like my brother was so rough on me. He was so much bigger than I was. Like as a little six-year-old you don't even have any moisture or anything. It was kind of weird. It was like in a little bit and then out, in a little bit and then out. It was very painful. It really hurt.

"I didn't yell. I kept all that inside, you know. I didn't tell because I was too terrified. It was, why me? Because I felt guilty, you see.

"I mean I had agreed to it. He said, 'Do you want to do it?' And I had agreed to it. Because he was so big. And like I would have done anything to get contact with my brother. I was much younger. And no one ever wanted to bother with me. We lived a very isolated life. This big house with a lot of ground around it. I was dependent on my brother—there was no one else to play with. I would have done anything.

"My father was a very withdrawn guy. But the thing is when I grew up I had lots of dates and everything, and my parents were always very concerned about my virginity. Who I went out with. And that I married the right man. Which is so ridiculous. Here they didn't care at *all* that I lost it when I was three. And that's what's so crazy about the attitude toward women and toward girls, you know. It's OK to rape them. But then when it comes to who you're going to mate them with—then you've got to be careful, pick a person with a pedigree.

"I still have a little bit of the guilt. Because even though I've been *told* that I wasn't accountable for it, that I was a child—the fact is that I agreed to it, you see.

"He'd say, 'Do you want to play doctor?' And I'd say yes. And I really didn't at all.

"I just wasn't assertive enough. I mean there weren't any assertiveness-training classes for three-year-olds, for six-year-olds.

"And I never wanted to talk about it in therapy. And then when I got older, there was one psychiatrist who said, 'Well, it was just playing doctor,' you know.

"But *playing* doctor implies you were playing it equally. And that's the guilt. That I did agree to it. But when you stop and think that I was only a little kid. How could I stand up to this great big brother and say no? I think that would have been a lot for a little kid that age. I wish that I had stood up to my brother. But I agreed. But I didn't like it. I really hated it.

"I found a wonderful gynecologist recently. And I said, 'Why did the doctors allow that to happen?' And she said, 'You don't think you're the only one who went through that with gonorrhea do you?' But I guess I always thought that I was the only one, you know.

"But you know—I never ate with my parents. But you would think that my father, if I wasn't around, would say, 'Where's Tess?' 'Oh, she's in the hospital again—.' Don't you think? And what's really weird is he was a doctor.

"Two really horrible memories I have are of the doctors having to pin me down. Getting more and more people to pin me down. So they could examine me. I'd be kicking and screaming. And just the humiliation of all these people over me pinning me down. And then putting the gas mask on me. And the feeling of 'Oh, my god. What are they going to do to me?' And losing control. And, 'They're going to find out.'

"And whenever I go to a gynecologist my legs ache for days after. And I can hardly hear what they say sometimes I get so anxious.

"And see, I feel that the fact that I was brought up in this super-rich environment—I was exploited. The blue-collar worker's daughter is taught how to fend for herself. She's taught how to be practical. I was taught how to be helpless. How to be dependent. I was taught how to be exploited. I was sent to dancing class. I was taught how to curtsey. And I was taught all that kind of nonsense that has nothing to do with the real world. I was taught to be sub-missive to men, how to please men. And taught never to say no to a man.

"But I went back to see this doctor—after my therapy. And I asked her why in the world she'd allowed this to happen. And she said, 'I just don't understand your generation. You talk about sex just all the time as if it's nothing. And I just don't think that's right at all.' See, she thought I shouldn't even mention it. But then I looked at the names of these doctors, like who had been in charge of me when I was five or six and all, and these were leading doctors at one of the best hospitals in the country. I guess it was that nobody was going to expose my father's daughter. They all wanted to be on his good side. I mean he was the leading doctor at the hospital.

"Nobody ever sat down with me. I can remember just crying and crying and crying and crying and crying. And nobody ever sat down with me and said, 'Little girl, what's the matter?' Nobody. Never. Never. Never.

"And I know that my mother said to me once, 'Your nurse says that you're into something with your brother.' And I was just terrified. But that was the end of that. He was sent to a psychiatrist, but that was all. But it was still going on.

"But see my therapist now—he works in a clinic. And he said if I had been a clinic patient even in those days, they would have blown the whistle with the first lab report and pulled in a social worker or pulled me out or done something. But the fact that I was a private patient—. He said the private doctors wouldn't try to stop something like that because—you know, they got a lot of business out of it.

"But why did my mother allow it to go on? I don't understand. I don't understand.

"But then again. I was married to a man who was having an affair, and I look back and I say, 'How could I not have known about it. It was going on under my nose. Why didn't I see it?'

"I think rich people have kids as a social thing. So they can send out Christmas cards with their pictures on them. It's a very upper-class thing to have a lot of children. You have four or five or six children. That's a man's property. You know they say, 'Oh, we have all these children,' and people say, 'Oh, well, you must be a good person.' But really they have nothing to do with the children. They have servants to raise them. And then whenever we'd get too attached to the servants, they'd fire them. And get other servants. Jealous.

"Understanding that strata—the rich WASP—it's very hard. Nothing's been written about them. They don't talk about themselves in any analytical way. But they're very isolated people. They're probably the most isolated people in the country.

"They have their own areas in which they live. They go to their own schools. Really, nobody knows about them.

"But I can't sort this out for you. If they didn't care about this happening to me at three, why did they get so worried about my virginity—and send me to an all-girls fancy school and examine every boy I went out with for pedigree? I had to marry the guy I married because he was from a fine old background. It didn't matter how I felt. I remember when I was engaged and was thinking of breaking the engagement, my mother said to me, 'Oh you can't do that. There are so many parties planned before the wedding. People have all these travel plans. You can't do that. It would be too embarrassing.'

"The girls are just something to raise like a race horse. You keep them tied up until the right stud comes along and then you mate them."

Rape. Really

There doesn't seem to be any way around it. When your twelve-year-old Johnny invades six-year-old Susie, it's a no-frills flight. (And it's no flight.)

No caresses. No bribery.

Barbara wrote:

"I'll start by telling you that I am the third oldest of ten children, and I was raised on a seventeen-acre farm not far from where I now live, and where my mother still lives. This past month I observed my fortieth birthday.

"The first incident with my brother Bobbie, who was seven years older, occurred shortly after I turned six years old. I really can't remember much of what my life was like before. However, I do recall that even at that early age I knew and loved every inch of that farm. Most of my memories are of work, caring for the animals, working in the house and fields, and wandering through the woods. I have to think I was a happy child to that point. The only exception would be memories of Bobbie even then displaying tendencies toward mean, sadistic-type behavior, especially when forced to baby-sit. This was manifested in tying my pigtails to the banister, sticking my head in a bucket of water, or tickling me until I was exhausted. Fortunately, this did not happen often as my father worked away from the home, which meant my mother seldom left the house. I mention it only because it played a significant part in my feeling that I had to submit to him when the first incident occurred and all the others that followed.

"I can still see the details and hear the conversations. It was a painful, frightening experience and, not really understanding what was happening, I tried to put it out of my mind. Then, within a few days, it happened again and again, and I soon realized this was to be a regular part of my life.

"For the next five years, there were countless repetitions and I spent the whole time in constant terror and fear, feeling revulsion and shame; and as I grew older and understood more, feelings of guilt were added to the above. Then, during the summer of my eleventh year, Bobbie joined the army and I could finally go to bed at night without worrying what might take place the next day. From then until I was fifteen, the incidents lessened because he was not often home. He married when I was fifteen and I thought that would be the end. However, he returned home a few times after marital arguments and so I was not yet free. He did make the army his career and shortly after his marriage took his wife with him and never again came home to stay.

"It was months before I finally realized I would not be faced with this anymore and decided to try and forget the past and make some kind of life for myself. However, it wasn't until after I finished high school that I was able to accept a date with a man. I dated a young man for several months, but that broke up after I either would not or could not submit to his demands. A few months later, I tried again, but that also ended when I walked home after escaping from a wrestling match in the car. That night I realized any sexual relationship was more than I could handle and I would not date again.

"My next eighteen years were spent in what you could call self-imposed isolation. I had an extremely poor self-image and as a result had no friends and made no attempts to make friends. My time was used strictly for working and making sure my younger sisters were not subjected to what I had experienced. This was a real obsession with me and did not leave me until they all left home and went on their own. During this period, I successfully built a wall around myself and obliterated the past from my mind.

"Then in 1972 my father died, and for reasons unknown to me at the time, I began to feel restless. In 1973, when my youngest brother left home, I started to feel tense, nervous, and constantly upset. Again, I did not know why. I changed jobs, thinking that would help. I started to go to school and that caused problems with my mother who couldn't understand why I was no longer satisfied to just work and stay at home. Then, for the first time in my life, I developed a close friendship with a young woman. We had long, deep conversations and during one of those I told her of my experiences with my brother. To that time, I had never told anyone and still don't think anyone in the family knows. About six months after the disclosure, this friendship began to have problems—although she insisted the thing with my brother had nothing to do with the difficulty.

"From the time I told her, my life has been in a constant turmoil. Nightmares that had plagued me as a child suddenly returned. I had difficulty sleeping and difficulty functioning in everyday activities. It became impossible for me to deal with my friend's rejection of me. My self-image and self-confidence hit an all-time low, and in addition, my brother's thirty years with the army were coming to a close and I could not see how I could possibly handle that. In 1976 I started psychiatric therapy (I'm still not finished). I have made some progress. I can at least look at myself in a mirror without diverting my eyes. Earlier this year I finally removed myself from my mother's home and now live in my own apartment. I'm going to the state university nights (and will go full time next year) to try for that degree I wanted as a young girl, although there are many times when I feel it is too late. Those are the pluses. On the minus side, I have no hopes of ever being able to have a meaningful relationship with a male; the nightmares are still with me; I still have difficulty thinking I'm worthy of anyone's friendship, especially since my one attempt failed so miserably; I have negative feelings about my mother; and I still don't know what I will do the next time I face my brother.

"I have no difficulty intellectualizing the situation. However, my guts won't let it go; and no matter how much I tell myself it is all in the past, there are always reminders, especially in the area of what I term a ruined life—mine. I just hope I still have the strength to reverse some of the damage and salvage some happiness in the years ahead.

"If you would like to get together, I think it is only fair to warn you that I do have difficulty remaining composed at times; so if you can put up with a few tears, I'm willing to give it my best effort."

There was an immediate and striking contradiction between Barbara's sturdy build and the initial pallor of her presence. She reminded me of Bashful. Her fingers played with one another. It was easy to read what it had cost her to come to this meeting.

The beginning of my transcript of the tape of our conversation reads: (Opening Talk about Living in City V. Country, Mostly Inaudible). But soon:

"What's my mother like. Let's see. My mother is a very quiet homebody. She never worked out of the home. She was married when she was very young. Seventeen, I think. Just did nothing but raise a family—ten kids.

"She's alone now. Since my father died. He was a quiet, unconcerned man. He worked out of town five days. He'd be home on weekends—sometimes. I mean he provided for us, but he felt his responsibilities began and ended with that. As long as we ate and were clothed, that was it. He was not involved at all in raising us, except as a disciplinarian when my mother would—blow her stack. After being cooped up with these kids, you know, every now and then she would really blow up. And then he would take over as disciplinarian for that one particular incident. I never had any close feelings about my father.

"But now she won't leave the house. Just won't leave it. She doesn't drive. There's no bus service. She's sort of isolated.

"A couple of my sisters live around the area. Up until the time I left home, I did all the running around—whatever she wanted. But now they have to assume some of the responsibility.

"I go there Sundays usually, because I have to keep the grass cut, stuff like that, for her. She's not helpless. My mother is in very good physical condition. But my mother only knows housework. Other than that, she never did anything physical—even living on a farm, she never did anything as far as the farm was concerned. It was just taking care of us kids. Washing, ironing, cooking—.

"Now—she's a TV addict. That's about it. She keeps the house nice. Since I left, she got a cat.

"But it was a very difficult thing for me to leave, really. And I'll tell you. The first couple of weeks, maybe even the first few months, I had a tough time because I had other—you know, other problems I had to try to straighten out. But now I just feel great having left there.

"For a while there I thought I just couldn't make it. Although I've never admitted that to too many people. It was not necessarily being alone, because I'll tell you I've been a loner all my life. Even being in such a large family—my grandmother lived with us too. But I still felt alone most of the time, because I did keep to myself quite a bit.

"And I started having the two recurring nightmares that I had years ago. One was—I always sleep on my stomach with my arms under me. And this nightmare I had was always of lying in bed, sleeping, and someone trying to turn me over. Even lately when I have it I never know who this is. I never see who this is. But I'm trying to call for help. And there's a strange twist to it. Up until the point when I left home, I was calling my mother—but I couldn't get it out. It was one of those where you're trying and trying and nothing comes out. And there were certain variations to it. Like the last time I had it, at home, my sister was there. And in this dream or nightmare, whatever you want to call it, she came upstairs and she said, 'What do you want?' And I said, 'Tell mother someone's trying to get me.' And she—she says to me, 'Well, mother says it's in your imagination, you know. There's no one here.' And then she left.

"And then, after she left, it continued. And then all of a sudden—I do eventually yell because I've waked my mother sometimes—I finally yelled, 'Help!' Out loud.

"But since I've left home, I don't—when I'm calling for help—I don't call my mother. I just say, 'Help!' And I wake myself up. And I'm usually in a sweat. And my heart starts in pounding. And I'm trembling. And it takes me forever then to get back to sleep.

"Of course I have to assume that that's related to my brother in some way. The other dream is definitely related. The last part of the time he was home, when he was on leave, I slept in a bedroom downstairs with my older sister. And there's the living room next to that—like a sitting room with a studio couch. And that's where he would sleep because he used to come in late from camp, just come in. So he didn't have a bedroom at that point.

"And he used to come into the room where I was and put his hand over my mouth, so I wouldn't yell when I woke up. And then he just led me out of the bedroom. And so this nightmare is somebody's got his hand over my mouth and it's definitely him. Definitely him. There's no question about it. But I wake up as I'm coming out of the room, I wake up.

"Now I can't really pinpoint when those stopped, but I would have to say I can't remember having them after I was twenty years old. And as clear as I can remember, they started when I was about fifteen. After the incidents had stopped, the nightmares started. But then I didn't have them anymore until approximately a year and a half ago.

"And at first, early, those—the sexual incidents did not occur in the house. It was in the woods, in the barn, in the truck, in the wagon. Just out. All over. Any place on the farm.

"As I recall, the first incident was merely—uh—primarily it was just intercourse.

"I was six. He would have been twelve, thirteen. I remember it being terrible, painful, burning. I know I had problems after for a while going to the bathroom or whatever, you know—.

"Even then, though, I knew it wasn't right. I didn't know what it was. I knew it was not right because of the fact that he said I couldn't say anything. Tell on him.

"I remember where it happened. I know we had a lot of woods and we had this one section off between the barn and the house, and when we wanted to play, we'd go there. We used to make our own play areas. And we'd sweep out, take all the leaves out of an area where there were trees around, clean it out, and then we'd mark off rooms. We'd draw rooms.

"And I was playing in there one day, and that's where the first incident happened. And he came in.

"And the incident itself, he said to me, 'I'm going to do something. It's OK. But if you ever tell anybody, you know what I can.

do.' And he said, 'But you're going to like it.' And then—that was it. And I remember crying. And I had no idea what was happening. Of course a few years later, going to school, I picked up a lot about what was happening. But I have to really say I didn't understand all of it then either. I know we got into conversations at school, like girls will, and I know from a very early age that I became terrified of becoming pregnant. Not knowing I wasn't old enough to do that.

"Then before he left home, I would say it happened regularly. I would say it would occur at least once a week—in the beginning—when I wasn't too clever. Later on, it was much less often. I spent most of my life finding hiding places.

"I did know that farm very well.

"And I'll tell you. It went from ordinary sex, regular sex, to oral. Just totally oral sex. Which, no matter how I tried—I mean I threw up and everything—but I do have to admit that later as I got older, and this I didn't really understand then either, there were times I was actually looking for him.

"After he'd left. When he'd joined the army.

"I couldn't understand till later on, but I realized that being stimulated is, you know, a pleasant feeling. That would have been after I was eleven years old, twelve. Up to that point, no.

"And I didn't know why I was feeling this pleasure, you know. I was really feeling pretty damned guilty about it. I couldn't stand myself. Because I didn't know what was happening to me. Why? It terrified me. Everything terrified me. Why *now* all of a sudden, do I sort of look around for him—when he's not around? Why do I wish he were around?

"But when it came to the point where he was around, on leave, home—I still did not really want it. There was something in me that felt differently when this was actually happening, but I couldn't understand what it was. But still—my head kept telling me, 'Hey, this is absolutely wrong. You don't want this.' Intellectually, I knew this was still wrong. I did not want this to happen. I knew how I was going to feel after it happened.

"I hated myself, especially at those times, later, when I was responding. I often felt, well, gee, maybe this is why it's continuing. You know?

"Well then—eventually—how can I say this? Eventually, does

that mean that because of the fact that I no longer resisted—I mean there was no point in resisting—does that make it OK? No longer force? Or not.

"I'll tell you. I just lived in constant fear most of my life. I just didn't know which way to turn, where to hide, what to do. At that time, I didn't see how I could stop it. I don't know. All I know is from the time I was six until I was sixteen I—every day of my life I just wanted to die.

"I'll tell you what my fantasies were. I wanted to get an incurable disease. I didn't—really didn't—know how I was going to make it through this life. But there was this. The only escape I had at that time was school. I really worked at school. Working, even then, as, you know, a small kid, was the only way. I kept myself absolutely frantically busy. I did most of the work around the house as a kid. My mother didn't have to ask me twice. Never had to tell me to do anything twice.

"I was there to keep myself busy, to keep myself close to her. Maybe that would help. Keep him away. I don't know what. But that's the only thing that got me through.

"The other thing was I always had goals. When I was younger I had dreams of going to school, of becoming a librarian. I was going to be a librarian at a huge library. And then when I realized I couldn't do that—there were no finances when I was in high school—I knew I was going to have to work when I got out of school. But I spent a lot of time making sure my younger sisters had it easier than I had it.

"I watched over them like a hawk. I wasn't going to let anything like this happen to them. Like I would say, 'Nancy's six, she's ten years younger than I am. She's six years old, so now that makes my brother Arnold twelve, thirteen years old. Do I see any signs of anything happening there?' And then I'd say, 'Well, gee, Patty's now six. That means Arnold's fourteen—.' So when I got out of school and I went to work, I spent a lot of money on them to help put the two of them through college. Three of them actually went to college.

"See, for a period of about eighteen years I pushed this whole thing to the back of my mind. To the point where I rarely if ever thought about it. And the way I did this was I just kept myself tremendously busy. I've worked two jobs most of my life: a full-time job and a part-time job. And I kept that farm—well, my mother's seven acres—beautifully manicured. I came home from one job and either went to another job, or I'd come home and work at the house.

"Right now I work for a real estate firm, a full-time job. I never was trained for anything except clerical work, office work. And I work for a small business part time.

"Now I do it more or less because I want to. I'm going to go to school full time and I just want the money. Right now, it's for myself that I'm doing it. Although I'll tell you, I have to keep myself busy. I really do. There's no other way I can—I can make it. No way.

"See, I never told because—I just knew my parents. I knew them. I knew there was no way, even as a small child, there just was no way I was going to ever have been believed if I went to them. Plus the fact that I couldn't go because he said he would get me one way or the other, eventually. I mean I was just afraid of him, real frightened.

"As clearly as I can remember, I was always introverted. I was not aggressive in any way. I think now this was partly because of the fact that my mother was very busy. I was not my mother's favorite child. I was not a cuddly kind of kid. I wasn't one that anybody really showed any affection to. Although I never showed any myself. And my parents weren't affectionate with each other. But they were with some of my sisters and brothers. My brother Bobbie was the favorite. He was six years old before the second child was born. And then of course it was bang, bang, bang after that.

"And they would protect some of their children—but not me. I'll give you an incident. We were discussing this the other night. This related to that business about how my brother would react when he was forced to baby-sit. My mother and father would always say, 'Look, we're going out now. Bobbie, take care of the kids. We'll be back at such and such a time.' And, 'Do this'—we always had a list of things to do. Well, once they were out of the house, it was, 'You do it. You do this work.'

"And if you didn't, he had all kinds of ways of making you do it. And one of his favorite ones was he'd fill a bucket of water. And he'd say, 'Now either you do it or your head goes in there.'

"So one time I tried telling my mother this. 'You know, I wish you wouldn't go out. Bobbie doesn't treat us right when you go out.'

"And she said, 'What do you mean?'

"And then I said, 'Well, you know, he's too rough on us.'

"And she said, 'That can't be. He's not like that.' Because he wasn't to her. I mean he could really be a very charming young man. But this was directed more toward me.

"So when we were discussing this with my mother—my sister and I—I finally said to her, 'Well, gee, how come I took most of this and you never intervened or tried to help me out?'

"She said, 'Well, when he was at you, at least he was leaving me alone.'

"So everybody was more or less taking care of himself. But my mother said to me, 'Well, why didn't you say something to me?'

"I said, 'Well, mom, I did try. And you said that it couldn't be. He wouldn't do something like that.'

"I mean these things happened when I was about four. I remember one time I didn't want to do something. And he tied my pigtails to the banister so I couldn't get up. Move. I was stuck there. And another time we were having trouble with the commode: The commode stuck and the well would go dry if the thing just kept running and running and running. And my father wasn't home, hadn't come home, to fix it, and my mother had to go somewhere. And she told Bobbie to just stick around there and deal with this water problem. And that guy took off. He took off with his friends down the hill. And all of a sudden I realized—now I was smart and I don't know how old I was—but I realized this water was running, and if I didn't go in and do something, we were going to get killed. He was supposed to be there.

"Well, I had to sit up in that bathroom for two hours and hold this thing, because I didn't know what to do with it to fix it. But I knew if I held up that ball, the water would stop running. So two hours I spent in that bathroom.

"Now he comes back. I mean he knew when my mother was coming back. So now he comes back. And of course he knew how to stop it. But there was no way I could tell my mother that he'd left. You know. Because he could be really mean.

"And see, I spent most of the time when I was real small just crying through the whole thing. I don't cry loudly. Never. I tell you, most of the time I was completely stiff when I was small—when he'd be bothering me. I mean I just clenched my fists and cried and tried to get through it. Then later, as I realized this was going to be a thing, a regular occurrence, I just became very blah about it. Just nothing. I'll tell you what I think about it now. I don't know how I made it. I really don't.

"And even now I just do not feel comfortable around men. I just have such a lousy opinion of sex right now that I just don't want it. I just want no part of it.

"And in the last two years I think I saw Bobbie maybe once for about ten minutes. That was at Thanksgiving. I'd seen him before at family functions. I had no problem then. But this time it startled me, started things coming back to me, coming out again. It came as a shock to me. I was coming from work, and all I was going to do was change and pick up a friend and go into town. And I walked in the house. I didn't recognize the car because he had a different car. And I walked in the house and he was sitting at the kitchen table and I was just floored. Just taken aback. And all I said was, 'Hello.' And I went around the corner, went up the steps, and changed my clothes. And sat up there a while trying to compose myself. And when I did come down I said, 'I'm sorry, but I have to go right away. I have to pick this friend up.'

"And I left. And I was just so shaken by it because I just suddenly realized—we never actually settled anything. I never said to him, 'Hey, look. This is it. It's never going to happen again.' All I did was, after fifteen, I just never was there. I never let myself get into that position where I was ever, ever alone with him again.

"And my anger right now is primarily directed at him. I'd like to tell him what I think, you know. But as for telling my mother—I just figure, what would be the point? After all these years, why make her life miserable?

"I do have some bad feelings about her now. I guess I feel she should have protected me more. I feel she herself got me in a lot of positions where I was with him when I shouldn't have been. Because I was such an easy child to tell to do something. I would do anything for her. When he needed help with anything, she always made me do it. No matter how I'd plead, 'It's not my turn, it's not this—.'

" 'Well, you do it.'

"That bothers me. I would have to say from day one I never talked back to my parents or argued with them or refused to do something.

"I think probably a lot of my obedience or my makeup was that I was trying to please. Get some kind of recognition or attention from my parents—because it just was not there. It just wasn't. Nothing was there.

"And my friendship with—this woman—this recent friendship—was just the catalyst. That started this whole thing again. Because up until that point, as I said, I did nothing but work. And then I got involved with this young woman and we got along really well. We just went around together. There was nothing sexual at all.

"She's the daughter of one of the women I work for. And Beth, the daughter, came home from college one day and I happened to be delivering some papers to her mother, and we got to talking. We found we had a lot of things in common. And then the next weekend when she came home, she called me and asked if I could come over and visit. And so this evolved into a real talking kind of a friendship, you know. I think she knows more of my inner feelings than anybody else. So that opened up a lot of things. And plus my brother's thirty years being up now.

"You know, when I was fifteen years old, I thought twenty-five years is forever. And then—here it was. I'd have to face this thing again. But Beth was the first person I ever told. The first person I ever talked to about it.

"And she was quite shocked by it. More upset that it had ever happened. And she felt she liked me and anything that had happened to me that wasn't good—. But she's in a lot of emotional trouble herself now. Just so completely depressed she can't see people.

"But I'll tell you what I look forward to now. The only thing I hope to gain by therapy is the ability to relate to people and to make good friendships. Not an emotionally dependent kind of friendship like I had with Beth, just some good friendships. Plus I want to get rid of the guilty feelings, which I'm beginning to make some progress with. They tell me that I will be able to relate to men sexually, but I can't see that. As long as I can function and make some friendships that are normal.

"I sometimes wonder—if this hadn't happened. I—probably never would have been a forceful person. I don't think. Although I think I probably would have started looking after myself much earlier in life. I would have left home much quicker. I would have gone out on my own. Because—most of my life I've felt that I might as well stick here you know, the way things have been. Where will I go? What will I do? Who—who will be interested in me? You know, you have this, you might as well stick with it. I really believe that kept me down more than anything. The fact that my self-image was just terrible. Without that—I would really have taken care of myself much better.

"The fact that it continued so long—. If it had been an isolated incident, especially if it had happened when I was so young, I would have understood I had no control. But it lasted so long, and it made me feel there was something in me that made him continue. It was my fault in the sense that this continued. Plus—nothing was ever resolved about it.

"I never went up to him and said, 'Hey, if you ever touch me again, I'll kill you.' It was—a lot of defects in me. First of all, I wondered what there was about me that he picked me instead of my older sister. She was really a better-looking girl. I wasn't too attractive when I was young. I was real heavy. And I had the worst acne problem you've ever seen as an adolescent. So I'd say, 'Well, gee, why me?' What was there about me—that it would be me and not her?

"And I often thought: Can people see this? Is this something that shows? You know, maybe, if I get too close to someone, will they pick this up right away?

"And—that it would be my fault. I was supposed to be in control. It's me. It's my body. That—it's only natural for a man to try and it's up to you to draw the line.

"And, of course, I never did consider marriage—because of the sex thing. I felt that there was no way I could ever become involved with a man who didn't know that something had taken place in my life. I mean, definitely I was not a virgin. And I just felt someday I'd have to explain if I ever got to that point. And not knowing how I would ever handle it, that just decided it. It wasn't for me.

"I just decided I was going to be terribly self-sufficient. In those days there weren't too many self-sufficient women, either. But then when I got out of school, I just felt that there was no way I was ever going to be able to depend on anyone but myself. And I'm stubborn in a lot of ways. No way will I ask anybody for anything, even my mother—I wouldn't ask her for a dollar. All the time I stayed with her, I paid my board the first thing off the top of my salary. I just determined I was going to be a self-sufficient woman.

"It's like my father said no women in his house were going to drive. So I had to sneak to do it.

"And he had a truck that he used. That was always there. So when he was gone, he had the car, right? So I drove this damn truck in and out the lane, in and out the lane, till I learned how to drive. Then I'd have to walk all the way down to the corner gas station to get enough gas to put back in the truck so that there'd be the same amount of gas left.

"I'll tell you. I do have a tremendous amount of energy even now. Like I'm forty years old and yet I go seven days a week. And I really go. Sometimes I wonder if I'll run out. But I've done it for so long.

"Talking about trauma, though. I'll tell you. For—this is what?—almost thirty-five years ago that a lot of this started happening? Well, aside from how I felt at the time, in this past couple of years, the trauma I've felt is a pressure. Something that's gotten to me as if I'd come completely aware. Suddenly.

"Hey. I'm forty years old.

"I didn't even live.

"I let it do that to me.

"And then all of a sudden, I say, 'Well, gee whiz, you know. Time's running out. You've got to make a start in this world somewhere.'

"And hope you don't run out of gas in the meantime."

The Pillar of the Community and the Pillar of Strength

Removing the girl from the home to foster care (or a detention house) is an antique solution—but by no means obsolete across the country. There are no statistics available on how often that happens, nor on how often the father is removed or arrested. Most professionals I talked with agreed that it is probably the girl who is most often removed if only because it is far simpler to get the girl out than to drag the case through the machinery of the criminal court system to get *him* out.

The thrust of most developing programs that deal with incest families is therapy for the whole family—court-remanded therapy in those states that mandate incest be reported to the justice system.

It's troubling that a major part of these treatment programs—while helping the father understand he has done something wrong and take responsibility for what he did—ask mother to swallow her share of the blame, too. "The father rapes and brutalizes," said Florence Rush, "and it turns out to be the mother's fault and responsibility. Has anyone thought of the fantastic notion of getting rid of the father?"*

That's exactly the notion that's a crucial part of the crisis intervention program at the Sexual Assault Center of Harborview Medical Center in Seattle. "We ask the fathers to leave voluntarily

*Reprinted by New York Radical Feminists, *Rape: The First Sourcebook for Women* (New York: New American Library) p. 71.

for an interim period," says Lucy Berliner. "And it's amazing. They do. It's like nobody ever thought to ask them before."

Harborview social workers then direct their efforts toward supporting the mothers and helping them learn they can cope on their own. The girl is protected. The mother is free to choose her course of action—freer, probably, than ever before. And most of them choose not to go back to their husbands.

This is not the most popular approach in the country. But it's one I'm partial to. Again, by no means are all mothers in incest families *or nonincest families* ideal parents. Many of them are more than capable of making their children neurotic. But it is daddies who hold the reins on father-daughter incest. If they don't commit it, it doesn't happen. And with a close to fifty-percent divorce rate—with people divorcing over a difference in preferred style of eggs—why, when a man gets caught sexually abusing his daughter, is it suddenly vital that the family be kept intact?

We all know that if a woman gets caught doing anything her husband doesn't like, including get older, we nod sympathetically as he packs his bags. There's no elaborate social machinery to forestall that.

But—foster care.

An interesting sidelight on the idea of placing sexually abused children in foster care comes up in the story told by David and his sister, Sara. David is thirty, a social worker. Sara, twenty-six, is a housewife and mother.

"My father grew up in a rural area," David said. "They were like tenant farmer types. And his family finally moved to the city where his mother was a seamstress and his father got a sort of a minor office job. He had been injured in the war. As a matter of fact, one of my recollections of my grandfather is that he was constantly ill. He was always either bedridden or very frail, a very weak sort of person. And then the depression came and my father had to quit school. And he went to a trade school and lived at home to help augment the family income. Then he went into the service and married. He was a very smart man. He should have been college educated had it not been for the depression, where money had stopped.

"And he was very communicative, outgoing. Very effervescent.

The pillar of the community type. Lots of friends—more so than my mom.

"And my father's opinion, for my sister, was very important. My mom's opinion for me was very important. We sort of take after the opposite parent. I take after my mom. I'm very introverted, very studious, college educated, advanced graduate work. My sister attempted college, but that wasn't quite her bag. But she's very mechanical. And my dad was very mechanical. Very effervescent. Life of the party type person. Always doing for other people.

"That was one of the biggest surprises we had. Was when he died. And we were driving to the cemetery. We had like a half-mile to a mile funeral procession. The government agency he worked for had sent out like limousines filled with people from where he worked. He knew incredible numbers of people. Very strange.

"And it's funny because he was like the favorite uncle with all the nieces and nephews. It was like—'Uncle Herb's here. Uncle Herb will fix my wagon or fix my tricycle.'

"My dad—it was like an adventure with him. 'Oh, good. Uncle called. He's stuck in a snowdrift and he's eight miles away and it's a blizzard outside. Fine. I'll put on my coat, grab my chains, and here I go.' Or, you know, 'His plumbing is stopped up? OK, good. I'll be right there.' 'Oh, the next-door neighbor needs a ladder? Well, I'll just go over and I'll help'—and he's out on the roof the next thing you knew.

"That was one of his better sides. He was very outgoing. He was always doing for people in the neighborhood. And my mom was always at home in the backyard. It was a nice blend.

"The thing I was jealous in a way of was the kids in the neighborhood. Like my cousins were extremely fond of my dad. He was like the idolized dad of the neighborhood. The guy that was out there and could throw a football. And could run. And would repair bicycles. If the neighbors would coast in with their chains off their bikes, there was dad with his tool set putting the chain back on.

"I didn't get it because I didn't ride a bike. I was a handicapped kid. I had a congenital leg problem. So I didn't learn to ride a bike until I was like twelve or thirteen. I had to have training wheels, which was a big gaffe in the neighborhood. He was very stern and gruff in voice. In mannerism. But the kids just loved that. They would hang all over him and would come out and watch him fiddle under the hood of the car or dig out of the snowbanks. He would slide down the hill with them. And wax their runners. That kind of thing. Incredible—in doing things for other people.

"If the fathers needed help or the kids needed help, they would call Uncle Herb—and he would be there. But with me he was very cold and distant. At least my recollections are that way—my sister's are different. He was not patient. I don't think he really tolerated me well until later. Until I was like in high school and I went out for the football team. That made him very proud, because he was a track star in high school."

"See, my father was—he didn't really have time for us kids," Sara said. "But he was an idol. I don't know if it's just an idea kids grow up with, but you idolize your father. We put him on a pedestal. So I could never really hold my father—hold it against my father for the things he did.

"My mother was a paragon of strength. She was just the epitome of strength. Whenever she said, 'Don't,' you didn't. Because she's a very stern disciplinarian. But always—the pillar of strength.

"My father was a good man as far as doing things with the family—picnics, going to parks, going camping. My husband doesn't do any of that, but his spare time he spends with both kids. And he plays with them like I think a father should. Two boys need their father more than they need their mother. And I don't believe my father gave much of himself to us until we were older. The time he spent with us when we were younger was for his jollies—the incest part. But he didn't really spend time with us, play silly little games like mom used to, until we were older and he took us camping and stuff.

"Everybody loved and feared my father. Feared because he was a big man. Well, big by a little kid's standards. And when my father whistled for us—when he whistled, you hustled. You got down home to dinner when he whistled. He was also a disciplinarian. Controlled anger, though. I think he and mom helped each other. Because mom made sure he didn't lose control. And yet dad helped mom open up. She's an introvert. She's a stay-at-home person.

"She sort of guided him as to discipline and how hard. And finally she said no more spankings. And we didn't get spanked. Reprimanded seriously, but not spanked."

"Both my parents were strict disciplinarians," David said. "We were made to toe the line and had very definite expectations placed on us as far as helping around the house, doing household chores. At a very early age, like six, we were required to do the supper dishes, make sure that one of the two bathrooms in our house was clean. And our bedrooms were kept clean and that meant making the bed every day and all.

"Usually, my father would phone in every morning when he got to the office. He called in to whisper sweet nothings to my mother every morning at, say, a quarter to seven. And she would give him a progress report on how we had done, if the beds were made and so on and so forth. And if not, we would be disciplined, usually spanked, by him. She would swat us, too, but he was really the heavy in the drama.

"He would go out of control. One of my most vivid memories—I forget what triggered the incident—but I remember the punishment for it. He went from his hand to a paint paddle to a leather belt until that snapped. So I would say he got out of control.

"What triggered the incest was—I'm the oldest of three children. The middle child died at the age of three, so there is a four year difference between myself and Sara. Well, when the middle child died, two things happened. One was, my mother started back to work as a nurse. And she had to take some extra courses so she'd be out a lot. And the other thing was, we started taking in foster children.

"The first young boy we took in was four years older than me, so in effect he became my older brother. He was going through puberty and started to ask my dad questions about nocturnal emissions, erections, and things like that. That's where the incest started. It was sort of like my father got him to expose himself and they went into manipulation.

"And I sort of walked past it a few times and didn't exactly know what was happening. I would ask questions like, 'Why did John have his pants down?' And my dad would say, 'Well, I'm just explaining something to him that I will explain to you when you are grown-up.'

"So I sort of started to ask the same questions John did. John and I shared a bedroom, so it would come up in talking, or he would wake up with an erection. And I went to my dad to ask him. And he started the same sort of thing. You know, 'Take down your pants and I will show you how that can happen.'

"I don't know why he did that. But at first it was fairly normal and natural and I guess we were fairly sheltered. We didn't think anything abnormal about it. When it became abnormal was when he would make John undress and have us manipulate each other. And then he would join in. He would undress and enter into it. Then it got a little worrisome.

"Well then, through a series of circumstances, John left our home after about four years, which made him about fifteen years old. Within a few months, we had a younger foster child, a boy, who was five or six—my sister's age.

"And then my father got into not only me as far as sexually, but he started involving my sister and this other fellow, making them do similar things.

"And I was forced into sexual acts with him. In other words, to give him a blow job. Forced in the sense that he would hold my head in position. He was holding me in position and saying, 'Do this. Now do that' and forcibly moving my head.

"This was mainly in the evenings. Mother was in night school. She had to update her qualifications, so she'd be at classes. And then my dad changed his working hours so he was on day work and would be there when we got home from school but left before she got home.

"And as far as the early sexual stuff—in a way it was one way I got close to my father because he did not engage in the nor- mal—'Let's go out in the backyard and play catch,' or, 'Let me show you how to ride a bike or fix a car or do carpentry.' He was very impatient with me. I was a klutz. I was uncoordinated in a lot of those areas. So in a way it was a very special—it started out as a very special relationship just between him and me."

"The first time I can remember exactly," Sara said, "I was about four years old. And we had a foster child at the time. I don't know how old my brother was but my brother was there and the foster boy, who was older than my brother and myself. And my father called me in and he said, 'OK, Sara, lie down on the floor.' It was the bedroom floor. Um—'Lie down on the floor.' Anyway, I did. And that was my introduction to sex. Right there. With the two boys and my father looking down at me.

"Four years old. I had no concept of right or wrong. I didn't know it was wrong. It's funny. You know, he had us kids parading around naked and he had us do a few other little goodies. But he was never really a participant. He was on the outside. And he was getting—some hand jobs, masturbating. I had to use two hands. And when he was ready to, you know, well anyway—come, I was usually called over to finish it off. And I know that at the end of that I got a mouthful of sperm.

"He made it like a treat. You know, 'Here's some cream.'

"Terrific. Well *now,* needless to say, I mean I cannot go down on my husband. That just completely nauseates me."

"But when it got into the physical force aspect of it," David said, "I got very resentful and felt very abused. Sort of mutilated, if you know what I mean.

"That sort of feeling began when I was nine, tenish. I began to feel different. Like I knew my friends' parents weren't doing the same things to them. I mean I didn't ever mention it. It wasn't something to just drop casually into the conversation in the play yard. But I would just feel kind of bad about it.

"And when the business started with my sister—well first of all, pretty soon after that second boy left, the one my sister's age, we got a third foster child, whose name was Mary—who was my age.

"I was then about twelve or thirteen. And about that time, my father was very anxious that I should experience intercourse. I had started to sexually mature. So he was putting Mary and me in very compromising situations and using her as a live demonstration.

"He was manipulating her and saying, 'Now if you really want to turn a girl on, you do this and you do this.' It was like sex ed with live demonstrations. And then finally it reached a point that he kept wanting us to have intercourse. And I was kind of worried because I was ejaculating at that point and was quite worried about the possibility of pregnancy, which sounds strange.

"At one point, he forced us into a room and locked us in and told us we couldn't come out of the room until we had had sex. And we sort of lay there and looked at each other and went—you know, 'We'll just lay here. We won't do anything.' He came in and he forcibly took off her clothes and then he popped out. And we still didn't do anything. So he threatened us with bodily harm.

"He came in with his belt off and sort of wild-eyed and said, 'If you don't get it on in a set period of time, I'm going to beat you.' What happened at that point was that my mother came into the house and so everything cooled down.

"But later he began having sexual relations with Mary, who was sexually active. I mean I learned she had gone through similar circumstances in other foster homes. So had John, the first boy. That was how he gained his keep at the home he was in before ours and the one after ours.

"And Mary too. It was for special favors. Sort of earning her keep and for special favors.

"But as to how I coped with the incest, I guess I compartmentalized it, if we want to use that word. I was able to carry on my everyday life with my mom and dad and occupy a family position and go on with life. A minimal amount of guilt showing. And yet it was very obvious when dad was in his playing-around mood. It was—you could pick it up by the vibrations.

"In a short time, you could expect a call to the basement. Unless my mother was out of the house. Then it took place all over the house. But otherwise—there was the call to the basement. 'Here, help me square up these picture frames.'

"And sometimes, you know—'I can't do it right now. I'm doing my homework,' or, 'I'm doing something. Why don't you ask mom?'

"And the other times, my mom, not knowing what was going on, would say, 'Go help your father.' And you would sort of put your head down and march, hands in pockets, to the basement, knowing that he would be waiting down the basement steps and around the corner with his zipper down and his penis hanging out for a blow job. And it was like, 'Oh my god. I don't want to do this. I wish I could jump out the window.'

"And sometimes I hated it. But sometimes—there was a different side of my dad that I normally didn't see. There was a seductive quality to it. A total relaxation. He was not as gruff. He was not as stern. There would be some caressing from him which, I guess, I can look at it now and say—there were times and there are times—I know myself well enough now to know that there are definitely times when I want to be caressed. And I want to be touched. And I want to be spoken to gently. And I guess even as a kid, the same moments were there. There were times when it was OK to do that because it sort of fulfilled the need I had, at the same time as getting him off.

"And he got quite brazen there for a while. It was out in cars. We would be going down the road and down would come the zipper. And it was like, 'Hey, how about playing with this for a while?'

"But we couldn't tell my mother. Because we had been threatened by my dad. He told us that our mother would kill us if she ever found out because it was evil and dirty and because we were taking part in it. She would punish us, not him.

"But I'm the one that finally, ultimately, told my mother what was going on. Because I saw that it was hurting my sister very much, that she had almost committed suicide. My mom took it much better than I would have hoped for. She urged my father to get counseling or therapy and did not leave him, did not divorce him, stood by him.

"It was one of the times when my mom was out of the house. And my father had gone in to have intercourse with my sister, which he hadn't done before. He had done other things. But he had never attempted full intercourse with her. And she would not let him do that. And he got very angry with her. Called her a whore and a slut and so on and so forth. And I heard all this.

"I was extremely angry. And the next thing I remember, he slammed off and went to the recreation room downstairs. Sara was just hysterical and beside herself and went in to the bathroom and stayed there for a long time. And then came out. She was crying and all, so I went in to her and talked to her and she said she had gone to the medicine cabinet and taken aspirin—a whole bottle. So I went down to my dad and I started screaming at him and hollering at him. 'Look what you've done!' And with that he got up and left the house.

"He just stormed out of the house. So I took it upon myself to keep her on her feet and kept feeding her black coffee.

"At this point she was ten. I was fourteen.

"And right around then there was the night when my father drugged my mother—slipped some sleeping stuff or some sleeping tablets on her. And he called me into her room and had her totally nude on the bed. Doesn't this get hairy?

"And he was going to instruct me on the finer points of sex. He called me. I walked into the room, took one look around, and ran screaming out of the room. Then he had not only her to handle but me to handle. I was filled with disgust. With anger. It's coming back to me now that I think of it. 'It's bad enough that you are involving me and my sister—and now this. I mean, my god, you know, what is left? Who else is left? My grandmother?' It was a great deal of anger, and I can drop back into that feeling. It was— hatred.

"I remember he said something which—I was going to say, which I don't want to repeat, but it wasn't that embarrassing. It was, 'How do you like this?'—or something. And I just turned around and ran out of the house and kept right on going. So then he had to find me and calm me down.

"And it was a couple of days after the stuff with my sister. And I was extremely nervous, very apprehensive. I remember I said to my mother, 'I think you had better sit down. I have something to tell you that you're not going to believe. And I don't want to get anybody in trouble. I don't want to get dad in trouble or anything like that. But he's been making Sara and me—fool around.'

"And she didn't know what fool around meant. And she said, 'Well, what do you mean fool around?'

"I said, 'Making us expose ourselves to each other.'

"And she said, 'Well, is that all?'

"I said, 'No. He made us feel each other up.'

"And—'Well, is that all?'

"And I said, 'No.'

" 'Well, how long has this been going on? Has it just started?'

"I guess she was looking for a tie-in with his drinking, which he'd started to do right around then and which was becoming a little problem.

"And I said, 'No. This has been going on for years.'

"She said, 'Why—.' She was really hurt that I hadn't come and told her. 'When does this happen?'

"I described that it had happened when she was out of the house, at class or at our PTA or different times.

" 'Well, what did he make you do? And why didn't you tell me?' She was really hurt.

"I repeated that he told us that she'd skin us alive and that, you know—he'd said she would kill us and all this. She said, 'Do you really think I would have done that?' And I said no.

" 'Well, why didn't you tell me?'

"You know, sort of a double bind. But after I told her, she was very protective. And—she lashed into him. She grew quite hysterical. Started yelling and screaming at him and he sat down and cried. And said he was really sorry. And that he knew it was wrong. And he couldn't help himself. But he also threatened me at that point, too. He said that if he ever got ahold of me alone, he was going to kill me.

"And I believed him."

"See, when I was four and so," Sara said, "it didn't bother me. Until my brother told my mother about it. And my mother confronted my father with me present.

"And then all of a sudden I knew it was nasty. It was a no-no. And then—after that point, it repulsed me. Or at least that episode changed my thinking about it.

"When he told, I was a little kid still. I'm not sure of the age. I just remember I was four when it all started. But I remember my father and I came back from some place, and my mother was sitting on the couch with my brother. And mom said, 'Sara, I want to ask you a question. Herb, don't go away'—that was my father. 'Don't leave the room.' So I was standing there and mom said, 'Has daddy been doing anything to you?' And I knew exactly what she meant. Exactly.

"And I said yes. And so my mother—she didn't divorce him.

She stood by him. She thought that was the end of it. Like she and I have talked about it since then. And she thought that was the end of it. At that point. Right then.

"But it wasn't. It continued.

"I really don't know why David told. I really don't remember why David told. I know that dad introduced it to all the foster kids we had, too, which is not too cool.

"But as for how I felt—I hated it as soon as I found out it was a no-no. From the time David told.

"And you see, my father believed in informing us kids about the things that would occur in our lifetime as far as sex goes. He gave me many a lesson. Like—I think I was around twelve years old when he told me about prophylactics and how to use them. He didn't demonstrate on himself. He used his son as a thing. And he said, 'Make sure there's about this much at the top so that, you know, when the man ejaculates, that doesn't split the prophylactic.'

"He also gave me instructions on how to kiss.

"He also said that if he ever found out that I—like I was twelve years old, like I'm really going to go out and find some guy and have intercourse—but he said that if he ever found out that I did have intercourse, he was going to be the next in line.

"That scared me to death.

"I remember specific scenes like the time he tackled me. When I was home one day and he was on night work. And I remember him tackling me and wrestling around the floor with me in between the living room and the hallway leading to the bedrooms.

"I remember locations where we were talking about different things: In the kitchen he told me about David being so accepted by mother.

"I was very young and he told me that because my brother was born rather sickly my mother took him right to her bosom. When my sister—the one who died—was born, that was the apple of his eye. His daughter, his shining light. His blond-haired, blue-eyed baby. And then I came along. And I was just either/or. And when my sister died, it was a whole big chunk of his life that had died. She died at three. I was one.

"And he said that he took me as being his favorite then. And you know—throughout my whole life I felt like a substitute.

"I remember when he was drunk and he was slovenly like. And he scared us to death with his driving. Every Saturday we'd go to the grocery store. But he'd drink himself out the front door. And drink on the way. A weekend drinker. And by that time he was two sheets to the wind anyway. And we almost had a lot of serious accidents. That scared me to death."

"I believed he could kill me," David said. "I went driving with him one time, and at the speeds we were traveling, he didn't care whether he killed me and him both. He was traveling through our development at like 55 or 60 mph, which is rather tricky. And even later, when he was teaching me how to drive—it got to the point where things had sort of settled down—his technique would be to take me out on the interstate highway. And I would be learning how to drive, and he would just reach over the hump on the floor and press my foot to the floor—behind the wheel of this large American car. And he would hit speeds of 100 and 110."

"And then on top of this," Sara said, "when I was fifteen I was raped. I didn't tell either of my parents. Because I was afraid my father would carry through with his threat—about being next in line.

"There were three guys and I was walking my dog like I usually did. And I cut through the park. And these three guys approached and were—real cool to the dog. And this dog would greet and lick any stranger's hand. And two guys took the dog and the one guy pulled me into the woods and proceeded to rape me. And the other two—well, the first guy scared me so badly that I really didn't have time to think. And the second two—I guess the dog was carrying on so bad, they finally took off. But I did look at the license plates. They were out-of-state tags. But I had no—I just cleaned myself off. Nobody was home at the time. So I just brushed myself off, got myself back together, and shakily walked home, where I felt really scrungy, dirty, everything else.

"After that, sex. Oh, I was concerned about my reputation at school, but that didn't stop me. This is not pretty widely known—but I did have sexual intercourse many times in high school. Didn't think anything of it. All I felt was I was a substitute or I was being used. I knew I was. The only reason these guys were doing it was because I would do it. And I—I felt terribly guilty every time. I mean I was just shrouded in guilt. I felt guilty as hell every time I did it.

"And right now, you know, like I try to have oral sex with my husband and I just can't. It gags me. And I just sit there the whole time just rigid.

"And so we just don't do it. I'm sure it all goes back to that. I'm sure if I could get rid of those hang-ups—I mean I'm sure I'm not as experimental as my husband would love me to be.

"I feel so guilty. I feel like I'm shortchanging him. I'm sure there's other ways to enjoy sex or love-making. I just feel horrible. I just can't do it. I've got all these inhibitions and I'm—to a certain extent I'm a prude now. You know, I went from being very free with my body to being almost prudish."

"I can remember the first time I tried to make it with a girl," David said. "And it was like I froze. Because the image of the locked bedroom came back. It was like, 'You better perform or else.' And that was scary. I'm not sure I could definitely say that isn't why I'm more into the homosexual realm of sexual behavior than the heterosexual at the moment. If I were to be really psychological, I would say it would be a way to be close with my father again.

"I became sort of sexually inactive for all of junior high school. I didn't date or do anything sexually. And in high school the same way. My only date for all of high school was my senior prom. And I stayed out till all of twelve o'clock. A real hot night. I became very sexually inactive and not interested in either male or female. As a matter of fact, I had no sex life until my junior year in college. And then that happened to be gay.

"It was more like an experimentation that I should have gone through at eleven or twelve. It was, 'If you'll let me see yours, then I'll let you see mine.' Very immature. Then I went from that to several female relationships in which I was engaged—twice. And then finally into a very heavy relationship with a girl that I went with for three years and was all set to get married and settle down and raise a family. And my dad died at that point.

"And see, when I was in college, he started to back up again. He wanted me to have sex with him for old time's sake and I refused. I said I didn't think it would be a good idea. It would open up a lot of old wounds and old feelings. Then, when he was dying of cancer, it became very important to him to have sex with me again. And I said, 'No. Absolutely not.'

"In a way, I was kind of guilty because it was very obvious that he was dying, and I thought, 'Hey, well, this is the last time anything can go on.' And it sort of tagged back into what I said earlier which was that it was a very close feeling between him and me—that way. There was a warmth that wasn't normally there. And yet I didn't really feel bad about saying, 'No. I don't want to do that. That's not where my head is.' "

"It wasn't until I was about twenty—well, twenty-two—that I went to a psychologist—and I realized that I was not a substitute in every person's life," Sara said.

"And that my mother really did love me.

"You know, a girl always wants to be close to her mother. My mother was good—don't get me wrong. She really was. She loved me. It just was—I was more of the extrovert, so it seemed like I got in more trouble.

"And it wasn't that she ever put me aside. She always had time for me. She always played with me. I'm still pulling things out of my past that my mother did with me that I can use to guide me in raising my own children. Games she played. And how she took time to draw me pictures and things like that. So I mean she really didn't push me aside. It was just my feeling of insecurity. And my father's comments to me that made me feel like I was the outcast.

"And I went through a period of hating him. Not him so much, because he was a good person. He did work hard. And he was good. I hated what he did. But then I—well, I thought I understood why he did it. Because he had such a screwed-up life as a kid. And he told me one time, too, when he was drunk, that he had slept with his mother.

"My mother and I talked quite a bit when I was going through all my mental changes, emotional changes, during the period I was going to my psychologist when I felt rejected, depressed. I could never hurt anybody else and I guess that's another part of suppressing anger. I couldn't take my anger out on the people that really hurt me the most. So instead I did bodily harm to myself.

I've got scars all over my body—well, not all over my body, but my arms in particular from burning myself with an iron when I was mad. From just taking a knife when I was angry and slicing my finger or my hand. Because I was mad at somebody else and yet I couldn't do them any damage. I couldn't even yell at them. I had to do it to myself.

"Like once with my husband. We were having a very heated discussion. We were both yelling at each other. And somebody drove up—a friend of my husband's. And this was the incident when I cut myself. He drove up in front and instead of my husband going out there and saying, 'Listen, can you come back later?' he invited the guy in, sat down, and they very coolly started discussing things like the weather, how are you doing, and all. And he just dropped me in the middle of that. Like in the middle of a big fight. He just turned me off.

"And all I could think of doing was doing something to—vent my frustration and anger.

"So I slashed my hand.

"He didn't know about it at the time. I didn't tell him. I told him later.

"And the other time. This dispute we were having about going someplace. And he made me so mad because he wouldn't go. And—I think it was a high school reunion or something. Because he was afraid of my meeting—he didn't want me to see my old boyfriends and all. So to vent my anger I burned myself with the iron.

"And the suicide thing was just that type of thing. A whole mess of things. Everything was just coming down too quickly and I couldn't handle it.

"And it was like—bleed the evil out or something. I must have been a whole lot angrier as a kid than I could ever express. But I'm still not really connected up with that. When I was going through the therapy bit—I was there for several months—I expressed a lot of anger I had bottled up inside me from my childhood. You know, 'Dad, I don't like it. I don't want to do it anymore. I'm tired of you doing that touchy-feelie bit. Stop bringing the other kids into it, the foster kids.'

"But the suicide business started when I went off to college. I was—one time I was really into the Moody Blues. It was a Friday or Saturday night. Everybody in the dorm had left. And I'd gone around to everybody's room to get all the downs I could find—tranquilizers, Seconals, Tuinals, whatever I could find. And I took a whole mess of pills. And I was into drinking grain alcohol at the time because it was really the best buy for the money. So I washed it all down with grain alcohol. And I was getting really noddy. I was really getting lower. I mean really just laying back and listening to the Moody Blues. My candles were burning. My incense was burning. Oh, it was such a mellow scene.

"And it was around ten or eleven o'clock. And nobody would be back until about two in the morning. And this girl—we apparently were so attuned to each other's wavelength—that she came running into my room. She was all the way across campus and all of a sudden she got this feeling. Bad flash. Something was wrong. And she kept me drinking coffee and walking around all night long. I was miserable—but I think that was one of the most serious attempts at the time.

"Then—in 1972. My father died in 1972. In 1972—that, I think, was another attempt at suicide. I wouldn't swear to it, but I know I didn't really have enough energy to be driving. I'd been up in the mountains and partying all weekend. And I was really into drugs. And my father had died. And I'd never been able to accept the fact that he was going to die. That really played a very heavy thing on my head.

"Anyway, that weekend I went to the mountains. And I was doing all sorts of things like speed, doing LSD—the whole bit. It was five o'clock Saturday morning, and I was up all day Saturday, all night, all day Sunday. Then I drove home. And as soon as I got home, I turned around and drove back to the mountains. And partied until about four A.M. Monday morning. So I'd had no sleep all that time. Then I got a little sleep and drove home Monday night. That's when I had the car accident.

"It was bad. If I hadn't been asleep at the wheel, I would've killed myself—it was that bad. But I had been asleep so I kind of bounced around but completely totaled my car. It was the best car I'd had, too. Anyway. . . .

"Two weeks in the hospital. Mom came. We talked. I couldn't do anything and I had to depend on her. But we talked. But that didn't really straighten my head out either.

"We talked about how dad's death had affected me. It wasn't so much the past but how dad's illness and his death had affected me and gotten me into drugs. And I was giving up drugs and all this stuff. Soul-searching, but really superficial soul-searching.

"But when I started with the psychologist in 1974—that's when we really did talk.

"We went back and covered everything. And I guess what I was trying to do was make my mother feel guilty. For not knowing what was going on. And I wanted her to know that dad had done those things. And we'd talk about how he was, how he was to her. How he had accused her of being the cause of his death. How my sister—the one who died—all that stuff he'd told me about him needing a substitute, someone to fill in for her. She said that the pediatrician at the time had thought dad was the worst man in the world.

"Because he didn't care. He didn't—I guess he was just more or less trying to make him seem better to himself. Like you tell yourself a lie for so long that you finally believe it. He wanted to put himself up as a good father. That he was the loving, giving father. But all those years. All the damage he did for so many years.

"And mom felt so guilty. She was horrified. And like—she doesn't cry too often. But she broke down and cried. It was something she didn't know about. And she really felt terrible that it had gone on. She said, 'Well, why didn't you tell me?' And I said, 'Mom, you're a lovely lady. I love you. But you're just kind of hard to talk to. At that time, anyway, you were.'

"But I was really angry at her for not knowing. For not seeing it. She knew the alcoholism didn't stop. She—never asked about it.

"I don't think really she knew the extent of it. I think—she told me she thought it had just started when David blew the whistle. She didn't know it had been going on for years. She had no idea, no way of knowing. And she said she didn't know it continued after that. She figured if anything was going on, we would volunteer the information."

"I think," David said, "when I went into homosexuality, it was right after my dad had died. I think I was looking for a father figure—a warm, caring male person. Because my dad and I at that point were getting very close. There was a lot of caring. A lot of support. We would sit down and talk. 'Well, what do you plan to do?' 'Hey, I really think you're going to be a good person.' 'I think you're going to be OK with kids. You have more patience than I ever had.' And—'I really feel sorry about that.'

"And he apologized several times for what he had done. He said, you know, he was very sorry. It was very, very sad. Because he was saying, 'Hey, I'm really sorry that happened. I wish I had the rest of my life to make it up to you.' And I would say, like, 'You don't have to make it up to me.'

"It was a relief, his apologizing. It was also—it was like coming out of a big, big shell. It was like he was in a different light. He was no longer this tormented—he did not appear to be tormented and he was not a tormentor, meaning that he didn't seem like this big, bad bogeyman who inflicted pain.

"I think after he died and finally having had this warm, caring person that I hadn't had for so many years, except in a sexual context, I think that threw me for a big loop. So I immediately went back to the first mode that I knew which was a sexual, warm person, which pushed me over into the homosexual realm.

"And you know—the body scent was the same. Otherwise there was no similarity between him and my father. I think that was part of the attraction.

"But I would say there is a good deal of anger that I haven't resolved. The question of 'why me?' Was it something my mother was doing? Why did my dad turn to the kids? Why me, as a male child, as opposed to my—. Even though there is a side to me that says I wish it were totally me, and that he'd left my sister alone. But there is a wondering, a questioning—was there something in me that triggered something in him?

"Was it something I did or said. Or should I not have asked my father—I'm taking it to extremes—should I not have asked my father about sex. Should I have been able to pick up on cues that said he was not capable of answering questions of a sexual nature? Should I have asked my mother, my uncle, my grandfather, you know, anybody else?"

"I don't think he was ever sorry," Sara said. "We never talked about it. I was—you just don't talk about things like that in the family. But I don't think he was ever sorry for it because he figured—in his mind, I'm sure—it was alright. You know, he was teaching us about sex. And that was his way of teaching us. Now I'm going to have a little different approach with my kids, I'll have you know.

"But, you know, right until his death I found I was more sympathetic toward dad. I could understand how all this was going on. All these psychology courses and everything in college—I could justify his doing it because of his lousy childhood and because of the death of my sister and how much he felt about it.

"And I blamed my mother for cutting out sex. As far as I knew he wasn't getting any from her. I couldn't swear to that. But that's what he told us. And I guess I believed my father. I would've believed anything he told me.

"Because he was the only one that really told me that I was loved. You know, my mother would say, 'Yes, I love you, Sara . . .'

"But he showed me love. As far as sex goes—I'm not saying he showed me love. But you could kind of think of it in terms of that. Instead of turning it into a mystery. It was my childish way of thinking he was expressing love for me. He felt more for me than he did for a mistress. He saw me as a mistress, probably.

"And you know, I can—I have a few perverted tendencies toward my son. This makes me feel like I'm sick. When he was an infant and I was changing his diapers, I'd think, 'Wow, that's a cute little thing he's got.'

"But my husband would go over to change the diaper and the baby would kick his feet in the air and he'd play with him. And I'd say, 'Stop. Leave the penis alone.' And my husband actually thinks I have a penis fascination or something. He says, 'Sara, you're making too big an issue of it.' And I think he's overreacting to my reaction. Because he knows about my past. And I have a feeling he thinks I might do the same thing to my kids that was done to me. But I am so scared that I am going to make a false move—oh, I'm petrified.

"And I've joined a very conservative church. Because that way they'll lead sheltered lives. The people in the church are not—street-wise, like I was. They're so immature as far as street knowledge goes. And I was so worldly wise.

"I think—I condemned my father. I was thinking of having him baptized by proxy, but I decided against that. Because—he did me wrong. He cheated me out of a normal childhood. And I feel I hate him for that. And I guess it's why I feel guilt—guilty. Because I hated him. I never loved him.

"He really was—as far as a lousy father goes, he would take the cake. And yet he was such a good father as far as doing things, trips.

"When we did things—they loved each other. You couldn't have asked for two nicer parents. I remember going camping and all four of us in our little pup camper laughing for about three or four hours just playing a game like Password."

"He sort of threw me a curve in there," David said. "Because at the end of his life he was incredibly warm and we were incredibly close. I have those memories now. And I didn't come through with the same set as I should have. He was warm and he was close and he did accept me as a person in my own right toward the end of his life.

"And that helped a whole lot. I can remember feeling when he died—it was like a friend had died. And I can remember—I don't think I have told anybody this—it was like when I fully realized he was going to die, it was like I wanted him to die just to end his suffering because he was suffering incredibly. And I can remember crying very, very bad the day he died. It was the finality.

"Obviously, I wish it had not happened. But I can also see some benefits from it, which sounds very strange. It opened up a counseling side of me—a very sympathetic side. Able to handle people that have troubles in their background.

"It was very painful. It made me feel like a complete isolate—dealing with a handicap and dealing with this going on.

"I look back now and I don't understand how all those years I operated on two different levels. It was very warm and close—and yet I was holding that secret. I look at it now and I don't understand how I could have led such a dual life. It was like bedtime stories and kisses good-night and being tucked in at night. But I was operating out of fear. Only how could I operate on those two wavelengths? I don't understand.

"It does do damage. It makes people feel isolated. It makes them feel different. It makes them wonder, 'Hey, is there something about me that is causing this? Is there something I'm doing to cause it?' In other words, take the blame on themselves.

"Kids aren't ready. It pushes them. I mean with my sister, she was very knowledgeable about things she should not have known about at that point. Or even been thinking about. At that age, you want to feel safe and in control and intact. She had been violated.

"I really think she took it worst."

"I really think David too it worst," Sara said. "Because—I can accept homosexuality, but I can't condone it. For some odd reason, I think I'm the strongest. This is my own personal opinion. I think I am the stronger person emotionally. Physically, I know I'm stronger.

"I'm no longer living in the past. I'm no longer saying, 'Well, my dad did this to me.' I don't live with what happened to me then. I can plan a future without dwelling on the past.

"As for why David blew the whistle—I'm sure there are parts of it that I blotted out. Or have just conveniently forgotten. But I don't remember that at all. I really don't. That's the truth. To this day, it's a real puzzle for me. Why did he blow the whistle? What had dad done to him?

"I'm sure we both have different memories about the whole experience. Because—I was younger. So some things might stand out differently in my mind.

"But I feel like I'm worth something now. I've got kids who need me. I'm living for something. I don't have to feel that I'm a substitute. Because I'm not a substitute for at least my kids in this world. Not a substitute mama.

"And the things that would trigger the suicide attempts were things that would happen in the present to remind me of feeling I was a substitute.

"First a substitute for my sister.

"And then a substitute for my mother. In the sexual sense.

"But you know—David and I both have gone different ways but neither one of us committed suicide. And I have a feeling it's because there were good times too. And we couldn't exactly hate the man. That's why I think I try to justify a lot of this.

"Emotions are so hard, so funny to deal with. You can have one strong emotion one way and just keep it that way—like hate. But then something stirs other memories. And he could be so good. And then so awful. And the pillar of the community.

"It's kind of funny, isn't it? He was just one mass of contradictions."

Another Grisly Detail

"Hey, Jenny. Good work."

"Really? You liked it?"

"Phooey. But thanks."

"It felt really strange doing it."

"You don't feel better?"

"I wouldn't say—particularly. You know, I was remembering—those times—when he'd come into my room . . ."

"Yeah ? . ."

"Well, see, at that time, during those years, my mother would always go have a long bath, a reading bath—after us kids went to bed."

"So you figure he—."

"Yeah, I figure he'd sort of—get done with me, get stirred up or so—and then go back and go to bed with her."

"Good grief."

"Yeah. Really. Strange."

Shampoos, Yet

Implicitly and explicitly, we give men permission in this society to exploit others to soothe their sexuality. Can we be very surprised, then, when that permission is extended to include their own children? Or *are* we surprised? Are we, as a society, in *collusion* (as we've accused mothers of being)?

Sexual abuse depends on secrecy, on furtiveness. Is it simple (or simpleminded) to think that if the rules and regulations and their reasons were sounded loud and clear, if mothers and fathers and kids were engaged in an open societal awareness—poof. We'd have blown the game.

And what a silly game it sometimes is.

Eleanor is twenty-five, bright, quick to smile. Her husband, Brian, has driven her up to see me. As he goes off for a walk with my family, we sit down—and she jumps right in.

"My situation with my father, I can remember, started when I was around seven. Before that, I really remember very little. And then what I remember was—the first time—my father—I woke up in the middle of the night and my father was in bed with me. OK. And do you want graphic detail or whatever?"

"As much as you're comfortable with."

"OK. So I was in bed and my father had put me on top of him.

He had—I had pajamas on, but he had put his penis right next to my vagina, OK? And I remember waking up and being extremely surprised and upset. And my whole thing was that I was trying to pull away, and he said something about that he really loved me and that didn't I like him to be really close to me. You know. I didn't. And then I just remember really pulling away from him.

"From then on there would be incidents where my mother would be gone and it would be at night. I don't know where she went. But it would be at night and he would want me to come downstairs after I had gotten ready for bed. And it was things where he would hug me and squeeze me but he would come, OK? And then I would have great fears that I would be pregnant. This was when I was like nine. But I had just enough knowledge to know there was some connection.

"So there was this fear that started building up with that.

"Then there was—every time I wanted to go somewhere, to go on a date, later, to go out with friends, I had to give a certain amount of hugs. Or whenever my father ever touched me, it was always just very suggestive. And whether it was just that he was squeezing me or touching my breasts or whatever, there were always a lot of problems with that for me.

"Then—one of his ways to get me alone was that I was supposed to give him shampoos in the basement.

"Shampoos. And I remember that it was something that I absolutely detested doing. I mean I just hated doing it at all.

"And it was like if I refused to give the shampoos then you know, that made him upset. And consequently the whole family got upset. So there was this pressure.

"See, they kind of used me to keep things together for the whole family. I'm one of four, the oldest daughter and the second oldest—I have an older brother. I was an extremely good child. And my father and my mom didn't really get along that well, so she would kind of use me to buffer things. In other words, if my dad came home and he was in a bad mood, it was my responsibility or my job to kind of put him into a better mood.

"Just my presence could get my father out of a bad temper. My mom and dad would have a fight and my father wouldn't eat dinner. And I could get my father to eat dinner. And by my giving into my father sexually, that made him happy. And my mom knew that—I think she sort of knew."

"You think she shoved you in her place?"

"I think so, to an extent. I think that was better for her than anything else. I don't find her a strong enough person to say, 'I'm going to take the four children and leave you.' I can't ever imagine her doing that. And see—my father started making money and I think she liked that. She liked the social life and the business trips. I don't think she wanted to risk that. It's hard for me to believe she didn't know. It really is.

"I never—never told my mom at all about my father until I guess I was twenty-two. I had come home to see my sister. And my sister was really afraid of my father. On Saturday mornings he would come up and get in bed with us. That always used to bother both of us and we used to scream. It was just a big thing. We just hated it. And my mom would just say, 'Well, that's what fathers do. And my father did it. And your father really loves you.' And on and on.

"So at twenty-two, I told my mom. My mom's reaction was that she thought it was a dream. That I just—maybe it was all just not true. Then from there she wanted me to talk to someone. Well, my parents are very much into the Catholic religion. And my mother wanted me to talk to this priest.

"So I said OK. I mean. 'That's all right with me.' When I was in high school, one of the factors that helped me was that I had a counselor that I really talked to a lot, at least once a week. And his approach to the whole situation with my father was that— 'well, it really is too bad and there are a lot of things you can do while you're staying there.' You know, 'One thing is don't go near him in your pajamas'—or whatever. And you know, 'Don't be alone with him in the house.' But it was one of those things where you're a teenager and you're starting to go through the time when you're rebellious against your parents anyway, so I was more so. And there was just a real lot of friction. But yet this was really a good outlet for me, talking, because I did what he suggested—as far as not going near him and not giving him a lot of hassle.

"Then I got into being very distant. I was still saving myself, you know? So when mom suggested it, I went to the priest.

"Well, this priest wanted to know everything. He wanted me to make it very vivid. And I said, 'I really don't feel that's necessary.' But his whole thing was that, my father—in each one of the instances, did my father pull away? Did he come away, rather than was he forced away? And I said, 'Well, if you're asking me if somebody came into the room and had to pull him away from me, no, that never happened.'

" 'There was never anybody around.'

"Well, then he said, 'Well, see? Your father, you know, eventually pulled away from you. So it's like his love kind of got off a little bit on the wrong track, but not really—not anything.'

"So that was pretty hard to take."

"Was there any suggestion you'd brought it on yourself?"

"From him? No. More the thing that your father really loves you and that his love just kind of went down the wrong path a little bit. But there was really nothing for me to worry about at all. And for me not to be concerned about it. If it was something where someone had to pull him away from me, then he would be more concerned.

"So then I went and told my mother that I did not want to talk to him again. And I told her I did not want my sister to talk to him, absolutely not. I think in some respects I was more concerned about her than myself—because she was so afraid. There were never any instances other than him touching her and her not liking it. And also—he's really perverse in the sense that we'd be sitting at the dinner table and we would have gone out on a date and he would start getting into that guy you're going out with— 'All he's interested in is. . . .' "

"Is what *I'm* interested in?"

"Yeah. Right. And you'd better be careful and on and on. It was just very upsetting to both of us. Especially to her, though.

"And that was the first time I told my mom."

"What would he do while you were giving him shampoos?"

"OK. We would go into the basement and I would give him a shampoo. And then after the shampoo, it was the same kind of thing as that night when my mom was gone. He would just hold me and tell me how much he loved me and he would just start rocking against me. And he would come. And that was like once a week on Saturday. Or once every two Saturdays. But it was frequent enough. It was always on Saturday. That I remember.

"What happened, as I said, was I would kind of forget about it. And I'd kind of—wake up in the middle of the night and know something was not right with my relationship with my father.

But—I struggled so hard to be a good child, you know, that that was kind of working in there too. How could anything be wrong? Because it was really important for me to have perfect parents. Really important to me. And my standards of perfect parents were very rigid.

"I don't think it's easy for my parents to love or to really know what love is all about. So for me this was one way of getting love, OK? For me to be really good and for me then to think that I had perfect parents and for me to give in to my father and the whole thing.

"It was one way of getting love. And I was very close to my mom. Through all of that—until I went to college.

"I remember I wanted to tell her. But I didn't want to cause a lot of problems. And I didn't want to have my mom hate me. I think the reason why I thought she would hate me was because of the fact that I would be causing a hassle in the family, between my parents. My parents' relationship was just on-again, off-again.

"But she and I were really close in the sense that—when I was five or six—we were still in the other house. It was before we moved. And my father and mother would not talk for like a month at a time. My dad would not talk to anybody. He just would not talk in the house at all. And at that point my mom was sleeping in my bed. And she would break down to me a lot. Just tears. And she didn't know how she would make it because she wouldn't have enough money. The whole thing. At that point they were in bad money straits. It was before he started to make a lot of money.

"And see we were preschool children. I can't imagine exposing all that to such a young child even if I felt like I wanted the comfort. Sure, five- or six-year-olds can be very comforting. But my mom had a problem too.

"She—I don't remember what the technical name for it is—but she is a compulsive spender. What she does is she uses up all their money. I have no idea what she uses it up on. And that's why they had fights. That's what happened all those times—she cannot handle money at all. There are people like that. At first I used to think it was just her. But then I went and talked to a social worker about it, because it was just getting ridiculous. It was happening so many times and the whole pattern was repeating itself. My father would get very upset and feel victimized. But it's just something people have, like alcoholics. It's the same kind of thing. With her, she would just use up all the money they had and go on credit. And then my dad would have to start all over again. And he started as a construction worker and wound up vice-president of a construction firm. And did very well. And then I guess it was two or three years ago he got out of that and then recently he's been ordained a deacon in the Catholic church.

"Yes. It's really something. But it's been kind of good for me, because it really brought up a lot. I couldn't go to the ordination, no way. I mean I'm not a professed Catholic anymore by any means but—."

"A number of women I've talked to came from Catholic homes. What *is* it?"

"I wonder if it's that—like when I was a child, divorce was such a horrible thing in the Catholic church—."

"And adultery?"

"Such a horrible sin. It was so bad."

"So you turn to a seven-year-old."

"I know. You gotta be hard up.

"But see, my father really stuck to Catholicism and to go outside of the family would've been so bad. The counselor I went to in school brought that up a lot. How I had to realize that it—would've been a lot better if he went outside the family. But this made it a lot easier. And caused a lot fewer problems.

"But after I did tell my mother and she had me talk to the priest, it was just denial. Like it never happened. So now I'm in an uncomfortable position. Can I go home? And play along with the farce?

"What happened was I didn't go home for about six months. I just completely stayed away. And then I started realizing I really wanted a family. That was really important to me. So maybe I should just accept them the way they are. That lasted for a while. Then—well, then mom and dad had another bad time—with her spending money. So my mom came to me and she said she felt I should just tell my dad about everything. That he needed to be told. Kind of to mix me up in the battle or something."

"You never did feel like mentioning it to him?"

"Um. That was never—oh at different times it would come up as far as my sister and I talking to him about how we really didn't like the way he treated us. But then we got it for being lippy. 'You respect your father'—and the whole bit. 'You don't talk to him like that. Back talk.' And you see I was so consumed with obeying anyhow that it was something I just never spilled out. I just wasn't that kind of a child. Unfortunately. And so it's something that, in my mind, just goes away and then comes back and goes away and comes back again.

"I never really dealt with it until—I guess I was fifteen. And I had been going out for a while, and I met Brian. And I really cared about him. He was my high school sweetheart. And one night we were parked in our driveway and it was something about the way he touched me and I—just started screaming that I didn't ever want him to touch me again. And I just got really upset. And then I just kind of broke and screamed the whole situation to him.

"Before that, I can remember with girl friends wanting to talk to them about my dad, but just never being able to get it out. It just couldn't get past that first—my-dad's-a-shit kind of thing. It just never got past that. I just couldn't do it.

"And at the time it was more a kind of thing that I would act like it didn't happen. I think there was a lot of guilt going on. As far as with my mom. I was enough aware so that I was getting confused about whether my father cared about me or my mom. And I felt guilty because I really cared about mom a lot. So I think then I started putting more energy into her. Because my impression of mom has changed dramatically recently—from the way I used to think of her. I always thought of her as being a strong person and somebody I could talk to about anything and somebody who would always be there for me and in support of me."

"All direct personal evidence to the contrary."

"Yeah. And now I see that's not the way she is at all. And I don't think she ever was that way. She's a really weak person, a really weak person. And it just amazes me that I saw her completely differently. Just out of need. Just out of need.

"But this—the abuse—would just be something that would kind of come up for me and then I would deal with it and then I wouldn't think about it for a while. After the incidents stopped. Which I would say was when I was about thirteen.

"We fought a lot then. I really did start putting up more fuss. I do remember one scene where I refused to give him a shampoo.

"But I got into so much trouble—it was just too hard for me.

My mom just really got down on me and then what happened was I talked to my older brother and told him about the whole situation. He couldn't deal with it at all. It just went in one ear and out the other. And even to this day it's still like that. He does not understand the way I feel about my parents at all."

"Well—that's the way it seems. Incest isn't the taboo. Talking about it is."

"Yeah. I—always knew something wasn't right about it. Because I felt uncomfortable about it. It wasn't something I could put my finger on and know why this was bothering me. I've really been thinking that maybe it's important for me to go to my father and talk to him about it. But I never have. Because my mother's denial was really hard for me to deal with. And then when he got ordained—this was one of the hardest things for me to stomach. To me it just seemed horrible.

"And what was happening, too, was that in the last six months to a year, every time I saw my father I'd have these nightmares after I'd seen him.

"Nightmares where we were fighting—he had a really bad temper—or reliving the times when we would be together whether it was shampooing or whatever. I remember when I was in college, I was afraid he was going to come up and visit me. That was a real fear of mine. The first year I was there he used to call me and talk to me like I was his long-lost girl friend. About how much he missed me.

"But this last year I'd wake up in the middle of the night and be afraid I was going to beat Brian up. I would just get so upset and so confused. For a while I wanted to sleep alone because I was afraid I was going to wake up and hit him. But he said not to worry about it. And I remember one time coming back from my parents' and just being half hysterical. Because at the dinner table, there'd been my mother talking about child abuse and how it was really good that none of her children were abused in any way and all this. So that really upset me. And the not going to the ordination—they don't understand how I could do that. And yet—I really wanted to be there. I wanted to be part of the family and yet—I'm really not a part in a way.

"So it's a little bit unsolved for me still. Just from the standpoint that it's hard to be around my parents and pretend—that nothing ever happened.

"I don't think those incidents were really OK in my mind at all. And I still don't think I'm totally resolved about what to do with all that. Because it is really important to me to have a family, to have ties. And yet every time I see them—all that pretending. It's very upsetting. So maybe it's better for me not to.

"There's still that part of me that wants to be the good daughter. And by my refusing them, I'm not the good daughter.

"I guess I feel I had to take a certain amount of responsibility for the whole thing, because otherwise, I fall into a great thing where I feel like the big victim. See, I needed love from my parents so much. And I really didn't get it. Maybe if I wasn't that kind of a child, he couldn't have manipulated me in the same way."

"How much responsibility do you think a seven-year-old should have to take for being dependent on and needful of her parents' love for godsake?"

"I guess when I say responsibility, I mean there's a way of feeling that you were the victim and you were just totally abused. You know, this whole thing happened to you and you just sort of start wallowing in self-pity. That really isn't very productive.

"So now when I look at the whole situation, OK, I feel that I was abused and yet when I say responsibility, I can see how this whole thing evolved because I was the kind of person I was. Sure, I mean, my father has problems. Still does. And see when I've told people, their reaction has been—how could I live through something like that?

"And that's really hard for me. It's important for me, for people to understand that it's something that—just happens. It certainly wasn't very good. But they act—like I should be a saint or something.

"So that's where I am. And also just recently there was a radio program, a special report on incest, three days in a row in the morning for ten minutes. And they brought up the whole thing about the child being very seductive and growing up and turning to prostitution and drug addiction and that the mom is a weak person."

"Nothing about the dad."

"No. But that the girls are just—damaged."

"Victims."

"And I don't want to be seen like that."

"No. Neither do I. Neither do I."

She Tempted Me and I Fell

"Listen," I said to the voice on the phone, "you sound marvelous. Tough. Sturdy. Clearheaded. Sorted-out. Come over and tell me *your* terrible tale and cheer me up."

There is a story about how I almost didn't get into some fancy prenursery school. They asked me why a ball and an orange were alike.

I said they weren't.

I'll stick with that. Surface similarities still don't strike me as much as functional dissimilarities.

What fascinated me on this journey was not how alike our experiences were and their effects. But how different. And yet how solid the common ground was—to allow us to stand on it, talking intimately, late into the night.

Sturdy. She clumps up the stairs to my apartment, totally at home in her body. And in my house.

"Where do I put my coat? Where do we sit? Another flight of stairs? Jesus. I wouldn't go through this for anything but incest."

Sit. Drink?

"If you want a name to disguise me, I'd like you to call me Frances, because I always wanted to be called Frances."

"OK, Frances. Shoot."

"Well, you know, I grew up in a small town—kind of middle class. My father was a self-taught engineer and my mother was raised in a very religious family. She was raised to be a wife and a mother. They would both have been extremely horrified if she had wanted to have a job. Both parents were extremely intelligent people who would have certainly done well at college if they'd been able to go. That may, I think, have had something to do with some of my mother's frustrations.

"But one of the concepts my mother grew up with was that a woman was totally responsible for the success or failure of marriage and family life. And this was a generally accepted concept in the community.

"In the sense that if your husband was playing around it had to be your fault. You weren't a good wife, you see. If your children turned out to be juvenile delinquents, it was your fault. You didn't bring them up properly, right?

"Now, my older brother was mother's pet. I was three years younger and I was a girl and that was it. Forget it. I mention that to kind of explain why I grew up really hating my mother. I really did. See, I did so much better than my brother in athletics and in school subjects—and every time I did well she'd say, 'Well, we mustn't make a fuss about this because it will upset your brother.'

"And she nagged me. And I can understand, looking back, what her intentions were. But the thing is when you're a little child you don't know about that. So all I could see was that she made a lot of fuss over this male person three years older than myself who was not very healthy, who was whining and sniveling, and who got pushed about by the boys in the neighborhood. Whereas I could beat up everybody, male and female. And I wasn't getting credit for anything I did.

"And my father was a remote kind of person—but the decider. His background—first of all, he was the only boy. He had five sisters. And his mother brought him up to be the prince in the family. Everything he wanted he had. He would give my mother X amount of money a week to run the house and the rest of it was his. So we might be—this was during the 1930s, the depression years—we might be a little tight for food and clothing. But father was always beautifully dressed. He looked very nice.

"I can give my mother credit for one thing, though. And that was when I wanted to go on in high school, in college, she was very keen that I do so. Because her own ambitions had been thwarted. Her father's attitude was that a woman doesn't need a high school or college education because she's just going to get married. But on the other hand, once in a while—although my father really detached himself from us because we were my mother's problem—once in a while when I was growing up, when she was really nagging at me, he would intervene and tell her to leave me alone. So I'd get a feeling of—there is somebody that occasionally is on my side. Right?

"So what happened by the time I was thirteen years old and already fully developed as a woman and menstruating—when he started just asking me to sit on his knee, he'd hold and kiss me. I remember saying to him, 'We're together. Because mother doesn't love either of us.'

"I'd overheard a number of family fights, you see.

"So initially it was just that kind of thing which didn't seem to be that big of a deal. Sitting on your father's knee and having your father kiss you wasn't—that's just, he's your father and he loves you.

"Now I really don't remember how long it was after that before he started wanting to play around with me sexually—wanted to play with my genitals. But when that happened, I had an immediate feeling of being trapped. Like, 'I don't want this to happen.' I was thirteen. My father was thirty-nine. He was a very young-looking, handsome thirty-nine. If we'd had a relationship as human beings, I think I could have been sexually attracted to him.

"But he used to say to me, 'You have to let me do what I want to you because I made you and you belong to me.' And I got very trapped. Because somehow even when I was thirteen, I had a feeling that if I told my mother she would see me as the other woman. Or maybe nobody would believe me and maybe he would beat up on me. And I couldn't risk either of those things, so I didn't say anything to her—and there wasn't anybody else I could talk to.

"And he wanted to have intercourse with me, but he never did. The closest we got to sexual intimacy was that he got into oral-genital sex with me, which I thought was kind of nice. I'd been masturbating since I was eight. And I figured, 'Well, if I'm stuck in this situation, you know—at least as a bonus.' And I masturbated him.

"And he would try to get me to agree to go to bed with him. But my big thing was always, 'I'm not going to get pregnant. I'm not going to have an illegitimate baby.'

"And you know, when I think about this now, I think, 'Why did he never say to me, "Well, it's OK. I'll take precautions"?' He never said that. And I think now that this goes along with the whole male bit. Because in their marriage, I knew my mother took precautions. She had the book hidden under the underwear in the bottom drawer, and I found it when I was eleven. Marie Stopes's *Radiant Motherhood*. It was all about birth control.

"So I knew my mother practiced some kind of birth control. There were only the two of us kids and everybody else on the street had six or seven children. But I guess it was part of his male thing that he wasn't going to use a condom or anything. It would interfere with his masculine pleasure.

"And yet the thing is—and this was a man who had a very strong sex drive—he never tried to rape me. Isn't it weird, when you're living in a negative situation, you have to give somebody credit for something negative? Like—he didn't do that.

"I guess, maybe, he wanted me to be a willing partner.

"Now the thing was, about a year later, we were on a camping holiday. Theoretically, I was taking an afternoon nap in the tent. And my mother stopped by and saw my father—we were both fully clothed. My father was lying on top of me. So she said, 'What's going on?'

"And he went off and told her his own story. I found out later that the story he sold her, which she bought because she needed to believe it, was that he could see I was very sexual. I've always been a fairly healthy animal. And he had decided that if he didn't take care of me, I would be running around with all the boys in the neighborhood. And maybe I'd come home with an unwanted child.

"Well she needed to believe that so she bought it. But she asked him to leave me alone. She said, 'No. She'll grow up to be a prostitute.' So between the ages of fourteen and seventeen, when I left to go to college, it was an off-and-on pattern. He would stay away from me and even treat me in a very negative manner. He'd nag me, 'You've got to help your mother.' 'What kind of a person are you?' to sort of impress my mother with the fact that he wasn't bothering me.

"And then he'd start trying to get back into things again. He'd follow me upstairs when I went to take a bath and come in and dry me with a towel. In a very small house, three rooms downstairs, three rooms upstairs, my mother had to know what was happening.

"I think there was a kind of rhythm during those three years. He would abstain and then he would start trying to get closer to me again. Then finally she would realize he was doing that and she would take him to task about it. He would get very contrite and cry and say he was sorry. He would confess. He was never going to do it again.

"And I heard these conversations. Sometimes they'd take place in front of me. He'd go off and have a few beers to get his courage up and then he'd come home and cry. But you see—the pattern was, she'd forgive him. Now once he was forgiven, then he was free to start all over again. The past sins had been forgiven.

"The thing is my mother was not prepared to go out and break with this man to support herself financially, economically. But also I think she probably really believed that if things weren't working out, it had to be her fault. So it was easier to believe that it was my fault. That the woman tempted him and he fell.

"And she tends to believe this to this day, which is why I don't see her.

"My mother is the kind—we all keep up appearances, we all tell social lies—but the trouble is that after my mother has told her lies a certain number of times, she starts to believe them.

"And she knew that she couldn't support herself. She knew that if anything about this came out, that society's reproach would be against her. She will tell me now that the reason she kept the marriage together was because she wanted to see me finish school and go on and become independent. She was always—I was one woman who was brought up, 'Don't get married. Have a career.'

"And I turned around and got married.

"But I really was a very bright kid. And my mother felt herself trapped in this marriage because she hadn't been able to get a higher education. And my mother felt she couldn't get out of it because she wasn't trained to do anything. She could scrub floors. So her story is that she kept the marriage together for this reason. And I can challenge her with this. My father died fourteen years ago. And I say, 'Look—by the time you were forty-one I was eighteen years old and away at college. My brother was twenty-one and supporting himself. You could have left him then and gotten yourself a job. Why didn't you?' And she has no answer. She stayed with this man. And this was during the war when almost anybody could get a job because people needed the men to go away and get killed.

"But—if you get divorced it's a shame. Divorced people can't remarry. It was basically fear.

"But for me—school was someplace that was out of the house and I did well there. And when it wasn't school, I'd be out in the woods and the hills and the fields. And it hurt while it was happening, but when I look back, I realize that I'm really lucky that my mother didn't love me. She left me alone. So I could go off and I could do what I wanted to do.

"Well, you could say how do you define love? I'm sure she thinks she loved me. I'm sure she thinks she was a very good mother. That she did what she could for both of us within the background she was brought up in. But she had a lot of hostility toward me because—this was a story I heard over and over.

"Once I'd become a teenager and my mother found out about this relationship with my father, she made me her confidante. It was almost as if I became the mother and she became the child. And then she'd tell me all about her married life.

"Now the one thing she never told me was one thing my father did tell me. And that was that my mother was pregnant when they got married. She didn't tell me that. But she did tell me that when she was pregnant with me and she went off to her mother-in-law's house to have me and to have my brother taken care of meanwhile—well, my father wasn't the kind of man who was going to be sexually deprived because his wife was pregnant. She was in labor with me for about two days and during the first day of my life sometime, my father came to her and confessed he'd been out with another woman.

"Before I was twenty-four hours old. 'Please forgive me. I have sinned. While you were getting ready to have my child I was—a woman tempted me and I fell. And I'm telling you because if I don't she's going to make trouble for me.' And my mother did the forgiving bit. She wanted to leave him. She was very upset. But again—she had stern parents. And their attitude was—'You've made your bed, and you must lie in it.'

"There really wasn't anybody she could go to. If her parents had been willing to take her in, she probably would have left him.

"By the time I was six months old, she did write to her mother about all this and that was the response she got from both parents. They must have considered her very immoral, you see, that she got pregnant before she was married.

"But you know—oh, I have to tell you this. The capacity of human beings for self-deception. Remember I said how my mother turned me into a confidante and came to me for advice because I'd read the books? By the time I was fifteen, I had read the books, you see. Your own homegrown psychologist. Well, it's really weird. One of the things about my mother was that she was a penny pincher, and she would only buy kind of bare minimum of clothing. All the time I was a teenager, I had three bras—one on, one in the wash, one clean. So a couple of weeks went by and all we could find were two bras. And eventually, my mother found the other one, crumpled up and stained under my brother's bed.

"And she watched him give it back to me. And she said, 'What do you think he was doing with it?'

"And I thought, 'Jesus Christ, if she doesn't know he was jerking off in my bra, I'm not going to tell her.'

"I had this thing, 'Is she really dumb? Or does she need, really need, to deny her son is sexual? Does she really need to deny these things happen?'

"So what occurred to me if I thought of telling anybody was that nobody's going to believe me—a child against a parent. People are going to say the child was making it up. These are respectable people. Why would they do a thing like that?

"And I certainly didn't think it had happened ever to anyone else. This was the strange feeling I had when it was going on. I think maybe most women do. I thought I was the only person in the world this was happening to. And I must be a very terrible person—otherwise this wouldn't be happening to me, see? That was it."

"How did you know it was wrong?"

"My problem, Louise, is that I don't think incest in its broadest definition—is wrong. If people want to do it."

"Yeah. It's occurred to me that by the time we're adult, most of us don't like our relatives well enough to sleep with them."

"Right. I think what's wrong is that my father was exerting parental authority to get me to do something that I didn't want to do.

"I mean, he was the main man. He was very, very handsome. It's funny. I was terrified of my father when I was a kid because he was remote. Because he had very little to do with us children. He was somebody with a gruff voice who came in and administered punishment. But I recognized because of my mother favoring my brother that if anybody was going to stand up for me it would be my father who would do it.

"What turned me off about what was going on between us was the fact that what developed was a situation in which in order to get some kind of sexual contact with me, he would try to bribe me. So, for example, I wanted a bicycle for my sixteenth birthday. And he wouldn't let me have one because he knew if he let me have my own bicycle, he wouldn't be able to come to me later on and say, 'I'll let you borrow my bicycle over the weekend for a trip if you'll let me play with you.' And by that point, I had decided I was in a situation I couldn't get out of at that time. And therefore I would get out of it whatever I could get out of it, you see. This is where a bit of the prostitute business comes in.

"So to the extent that I participated, I kind of said to myself in the back of my head, 'OK. I've got this situation. I'll get out one day. I don't know how. But this guy wants to fool around with me. And he's prepared to do certain things for me to get what he wants.' So he'd say, 'I want to play with your pussy.' And I'd say, 'Well, OK. But if you do that I want to borrow your bike on Sunday because I want to go for a trip with the girls.' Or, 'I don't have any pocket money. I want some extra money to buy books.' "

"Did you have any sort of sense of power in this?"

"Yeah.

"You know I'm glad you brought that up. You should be a

psychoanalyst. To this day, in any sexual relationship I have with anybody, I get more pleasure out of giving pleasure to someone else than I do out of what I receive from them. I have a real power trip on how I can orchestrate on somebody else's body and have them whimper and sobbing and crying into a sexual climax. It's a real power trip. And the power trip on my side is that I don't let anybody do that to me unless I decide I want that to happen. So that's a big power trip. You really called me out there.

"But see, even at fourteen I was pretty tough, pretty independent for my age. If he'd beaten me up or raped me, I would've run away from home. I just had this very strong survival instinct.

"So I guess I don't think it *has* to be always badly destructive. But I think that maybe a minority of us were not destroyed by it for varied reasons. Either we had our own resources or we found resources or we figured out for ourselves this wasn't the way things had to be. That we weren't guilty. That we weren't being punished by God. But I think people who don't have those resources need resources the way battered wives need a place to go. I think a young teenage girl—never mind an eight-year-old—feels very cut off and isolated in this situation.

"And trapped. I felt so trapped. That's the thing I keep coming back to. I was reacting to the power a lot. And you see that's what I reacted to when I was married. It looked like we were going to have a good marriage. We both went to the same college. We were both liberal politically. We talked a lot about sexual equality and whatnot. But what I found most difficult to bear in marriage was the fact that, theoretically, we would discuss everything and agree on it. But it was funny how we would always agree upon what my husband wanted. And not what I wanted, you know.

"I didn't like, as a kid, the feeling that I had to let this man do this to me because he was my father. And I had no choice. And that came up again in marriage when my husband wanted to have sex with me and I didn't want sex. And one of the things that my husband did to me after the second child was say, 'I pay the bills around here. You're supposed to give me sex.' I said, 'Great. You're making me into a prostitute.'

"Now that was a repetition in a sense of the same situation. The man is in the position of power. Whether or not you like it, you're going to do it. And I kept saying, 'If you don't have the freedom to say no, then it doesn't mean anything when you say yes.' Right?

"And when I look back on it, that's what it did to me. I was in this situation with my own husband—who was really in many ways a sweet person. He's a great person to have as a friend. But he's not a good person to have as a husband because the minute he marries, he gets into this kind of framework. You know. Men do this, and women do that.

"And there was in me this element of no matter what was happening to me, nobody else would believe me. I could be in the right but nobody would believe me. In fact, when my mother later realized that there was this coming near/moving away thing with my father, she said to me, 'If you ever go to the police and say anything about this, they'll just send you to reform school.' So she was interested in shutting me up too.

"And that carried over into the marriage. When I felt I had a correct opinion about something or my interpretation of what was going on was right, somewhere inside myself I still didn't believe it. And I became a complete doormat. My husband was the kind of man who can't admit he's ever made a mistake about something. He was trained as a lawyer, so he's a cool, unemotional arguer. He doesn't blow his stack.

"So even when deep inside myself I knew I was right, I was convinced I was wrong.

"And one time he sexually overreacted to one of our daughter's school friends. And this embarrassed him a lot. And he got very angry with me. And I said, 'What's going on?'

"And he said—by this time the marriage was going downhill because of his totalitarian attitudes—he said, 'Well, if you were taking care of me properly in bed, I wouldn't have felt turned on by our daughter's friend.'

"And then he said, 'It was your mother's fault that your father messed around with you. Because if she'd been taking care of him he wouldn't have messed around with you either.' And then he said, 'But I can't go to bed with somebody who is young enough to be my daughter.' And of course that meant to me that he really wanted to.

"But he never did. But 'it was your mother's fault that your father messed around with you' is this whole business of men blaming women for what men do.

"As for survival, I think a lot depends on the kind of resources people have inside themselves as well as what they find outside. For example, I don't like to be described as a loner. I would say I'm an individualist. Well, I was like that when I was seven years old. I never felt I had to go along and do something just because the crowd was doing it. If it wasn't something I wanted to do. If it was something I didn't see any sense in doing. I had a strong sense of what I wanted and a sense of survival. It may have gone along with being physically very healthy and reasonably bright. And the fact that the one way that I could get out of the situation I was in was doing well in school, winning a scholarship, going to college. That was what made me financially independent at the age of seventeen.

" 'I'm going to live. No matter what anybody does to me, I'm going to live. Nobody's going to kill me.'

"And I figured it out. The guilt thing.

"To some extent, I took pleasure in it and felt guilty about taking pleasure in it, yes. And I even realized before I got away from home that if my father's approach had been different, if he'd seen me as a person who was not only sexually mature, but as a woman who was interesting to talk to, good to know—well, he was a good-looking guy. Why not?

"So I think—never mind incest—take any sexual relationship. Husband and wife. Lovers. I think if there's ever an element of force, physical force, economic power, emotional blackmail— that's what makes it wrong.

"Let me put it this way. I watched my own sons growing up. And the older boy is tremendously physically attractive. The younger one is charming, too, and hasn't got any problem getting girl friends. But the older boy is a classic, a beautiful person to look at.

"And I could look at him and say, 'That is an absolutely gorgeous person. And yes. He's sexually attractive.' But I couldn't seduce him. Because he was dependent on me, right? It would have been a power thing. I could see where he was sexually attractive. But either because of what had happened to me or because I recognized that—obviously he would have responded, because the young adolescent male has a very healthy sexual appetite—but I would've been laying a power trip on him. 'I'm your mother. You've loved me all your life. This is just another way we're going to love each other. And besides, you need me. You're dependent on me.' That would've been so wrong. A power play.

"And you know, of course, I confronted my father before he died.

"He just laughed at me. So I went away and never came back.

"And she wrote to me when he died, and so I duly turned up and looked at him in the coffin to make sure he was dead. And mentally put a stake through his heart. And then I saw her going through this whole hypocritical trip with the neighbors after he was buried as if everything had been peachy-creamy. I thought, 'I should have stayed away and sent her a telegram saying, "Congratulations." I really should have.'

"She needed this fantasy. And I'm angry with her for a lot of reasons. Because she still has this—the wife and the mother is responsible for the success of a marriage and the success of the children. And if anything goes wrong, it's her fault.

"I have no guilt about being angry with people for what they did to me. I guess if I was to put a label on my father, I'd say he was a psychopath insofar as he always believed that whatever he wanted was OK and was right. Everything was OK. He didn't feel that he was doing anything wrong. He couldn't have a sense of guilt. He couldn't see, you know, what he was doing to me. And that's what made me angry with him. My ex-husband had that in common with my father—a similar sense that he wasn't guilty or responsible for anything. Except my ex-husband doesn't have that psychopathic quality.

"My father laughed at me. He didn't know what I was making a fuss about. I was being very silly. It was OK. He was my father. He could do whatever he wanted with me.

"My ex-husband was different. Brought up in a kind of religious sin system where if he made any kind of mistake when he was a little boy, he'd be reminded about it forever. And that's a pretty destructive thing to do to a kid. He was never able to admit that he ever made a mistake.

"And let's be honest. When you're raising sons, you begin to see the kind of trip society lays on boys, what I used to call the hairy-chested, red-blooded-male syndrome. And I mention this because I feel like I've gone on quite a lot about the father-daughter thing. It seems to be kind of easy for men to get away with because of the way that society has always relegated women to be men's property. The wife is his property. The daughter is his property. But men get these trips laid on them too.

"But what I really think you should get across is that I went through this experience when I was a teenager. That I did not let it stop me from getting married and having children. That what I disliked in my marriage was exactly what I disliked in my relationship with my father, which was any kind of an economic or emotional power play laid on me to get into sex. As I said before, if you can't say no, then it doesn't mean anything when you say yes.

"But I reached a point where I felt stifled as a human being. And I felt I had to move out of this situation. So I went out and I finished my education. And I am now an independent person who supports herself as a counselor.

"You might say that my development was retarded. I didn't run away from home until I was forty-one. OK?"

Bad Thoughts

"Hey, Jenny. How are you?"

"Ohhh. Not so good."

"What's up?"

"Ohhhh. Just a lot of bad thoughts. Tell me something?"

"What?"

"How do you survive? How did you survive?"

"Funny. One of the hardest moments I remember was when one psychiatrist said to me, 'It's amazing you survived.' Until that moment, it had never—ever—occurred to me I might not have. Might not yet. Poor man. I'm sure he meant it as a compliment. Instead it was like a pointy missile that made a considerable crack in my—not confidence, but sort of gut innocence."

The conversation continued in my head:

How did you survive? (she said).

You're repeating yourself, kiddo. (I said).

I know.

Initially? By total immersion. I spent five hours a day practicing piano. I knew, really, I was deeply unmusical. But it was—as math might have been, as Latin sometimes was—a *whole* world, an away world. Orderly. The enigmas were rational. The rules mostly held. The exceptions could be learned. If you worked hard, behaved right, the piano did not betray you. You wouldn't get mugged by it.

Then?

A couple of months after my seventeenth birthday, I graduated from high school and went to Paris to study music. Ostensibly. I didn't need to go to Paris to study music. It was a case of this town ain't big enough for both of us.

I was holding him at bay. But some visits were unavoidable without spilling the beans. Total rejection would have looked fishy. And I was still reeling. I wasn't conscious enough to even think of total rejection. Except for the piano, life was a series of motions.

I learned to dissemble. I learned to avoid. Emotionally, I learned to be light on my feet.

"Come here."

"What?"

"I just want to hug you."

"Got to go. Got to practice."

"Surely you have time for a hug."

"Nope."

Out. I could feel his disappointment follow me. Bad lesson. I had learned how to use the power to reject. You know, I don't think he knew I'd been hurt. I know I didn't know then how badly. I was running—and I *was* running—on automatic pilot. I think in that hotel I had tried so hard not to be present consciously that I'd left my—I would almost say soul, but I suppose I must say unconscious—without any defense. The impact was profound.

Do you suppose men think sex can't hurt?

I think they believe two things. That it can't hurt and that it can destroy. As in rape. Whichever is convenient. I think, like your father, he would have said I was overreacting. That would have been convenient.

So you just went away?

Kind of. He wanted me to see the hotel doctor before I left for Paris. He wanted me to have "protection." I didn't want "protection." 'You never know,' he said. Indeed. That seemed true enough. He bought me a diaphragm.

One stuffed leopard. A few clothes. A small suitcase for my eleventh birthday. And a diaphragm. Some provider.

The second night out I threw the diaphragm overboard. Drama. Gesture.

Then—I did not menstruate for twelve months. Then. In Paris, I became engaged to an American Catholic composer. A virgin— and so we would both be, he said, until nuptial vows. Safe. Except he spoke endlessly of the eleven children he wanted us to have. Guilt found a home. I knew/worried/knew I was incapable of having one.

And then?

And then and then and then. It was hard to be terrified for a whole year. It was negative. It was exile. In the end the year did what years do. It got itself over. I went home. I moved out. I failed. I went back. I moved out. I pushed toward a career.

And men?

I didn't seem to be easily discouraged. I seemed to be sure there was somebody out there one could turn into a serviceable daddy.

Was there?

No.

Flashbacks?

Oh yes. I'd wake up feeling I was being gagged. A funny pressure on my jaws. But I didn't make the connection at the time. Not for years. See for a long time I could say, "My father chased me around a hotel room." But without remembering exactly how he caught me. It was too blinding to look at. I was in my twenties, and married, before one night I got up and wrote it all out, all of it—tersely though. To conceal, rather than reveal. Then filed it away. Forgot I'd done it. Like I planted a second land mine for myself. It was a real jolt when I found it later.

And?

Kept moving. Kept working. Tried crying. Didn't suit me. Tried laughing. Liked it better.

One day, I'd gotten it half together by then—copywriting job, apartment—I was twenty-one or so. I was visiting my mother. We were in the kitchen. She had a kiddie bridge table and chairs. Red. I was sitting. She was cooking.

"Dear?" Brightly. "Guess what. Your father has asked me to marry him again. What do you think?"

WAAAAGH.

He married someone else. I cut him off, cut him out. Saw him

226 | Kiss Daddy Goodnight

once after. From a half-block away I saw him on the corner of 59th and Madison. The light changed. He crossed. I didn't call, didn't run after.

He died.

Grew up a little. Lucked out a little. Got married. Had kids. Kept working. Chose the cheerful.

Hmmmm. No recipe?

No recipe.

How do you feel about it now?

Talking about it? Sad. Very sad.

So it doesn't go away?

It recedes.

I don't like that.

You don't have to like it. You just have to live with it. Like a small, nasty pet you've had for years.

Recipe. Getting on with It

Funny thought. You can get so wrapped up in incest you neglect your own family. Time to get on with it.

Cheesecake. Combine four well-beaten eggs, one and a half pounds farmer cheese, one cup sugar, one teaspoon vanilla, one teaspoon salt. . . .

"I think," said my mother, stopping by the kitchen on her way out, "you know, I think maybe he was trying to tell me. During that time, I remember him talking about how highly sexed he was. How he had trouble controlling himself.

"But at that time, I found him so physically—nothing, uninteresting—I just didn't listen."

"Yeah."

"And now I go from, 'I'm so mad she didn't tell me. Why didn't she tell me—at the time?' to, 'I'm glad, really, she *didn't* tell me.' "

"I know."

"And as far as the book went—I'd go, 'Why does she have to tell all this?' And then—when you seemed so discouraged, as though you wanted to scrap it—I'd think, 'Oh, she has to do it. I want her to do it.' But I was afraid to say anything."

We fell silent beneath the whir of the blender.

"Well, I'm off to Altman's. Do you want anything?"

"Nuh-unh. See you later."

As I started to sponge the counter, I noticed she had left two typed pages, folded. "L:" they said on the outside, "For whatever it's worth." Was this my flow chart?

"The truth came like a blow," she'd written. "I felt an anger I cannot describe. I wished I could kill her father. Although he was dead, I wanted to kill him. I was incoherent with rage. I was heartbroken. I shed tears.

"How could such a thing happen to *me*? What had I done that was wrong? What had I ever done that was right? This anger and self-pity was followed by a sense of betrayal. Of shame.

"For years after she'd had this experience, I went on—as I always had—to praise him to her. I wanted her to think well of her father, to admire him. I told her he was an intelligent man; he was liberal in his thinking; never spoke ill of anybody; and would never hurt anyone (I believed all that). And what ability he had!

"I kept a memo from his editor praising a story he wrote and saying that 'anyone who can write like that should be making $50,000 a year.' As a theatrical press agent, Brock Pemberton said, he would rather have him work two days a week than anyone else five. Dick Maney, a dean of theatrical press agents, said he considered him his only potential rival. These pathetic bits and scraps I treasured against the facts I didn't want to remember—his unreliability, his inability to keep a job, even a job he wanted.

"The bitterness piled up. And the worst, it seemed to me, was the exposure Louise would subject herself to—to write about such a thing in a book.

"Remember, I was born into a period when people did not reveal their personal problems. Children who were not like other children, who were 'different,' were kept in the background, hidden away. Disease—another difference—was kept secret, a reflection on the family. As for the unfortunate girl who was raped, she often became an outcast, as though she were the criminal. Early conditioning. It's deeply rooted, very much a part of us.

"What would the world think of a girl who had an incest experience? Of me, the mother?

"But during these last months, my feelings changed. What triggered that? Maybe letters from among the many she received. Letters amazingly open, from all kinds of women, from everywhere. They wrote and telephoned and came or invited her to visit, to talk. Many of them were in very secure, conventional situations. They didn't need to come forward, had nothing to gain—and must have had at least a suspicion of risk.

"I came to realize that if it weren't for women who were willing to open up, to talk, we'd still be hiding our maimed children.

"My respect for these women is boundless. And for my daughter, whom I'd have been tempted to dissuade from writing this book (if she'd told me soon enough, the stinker), I have the utmost admiration."

Gee, mom.
Thanks.

Afterword

During my journey I spoke with 183 women. Some responded to ads that I ran primarily in the feminist press: in the N.O.W. national newsletter (then called *Do It NOW*, currently called *National N.O.W. Times*), in *Majority Report*, in *Off Our Backs*, in the *Houston Breakthrough*. I advertised also, once, in *Psychology Today*, twice in the *New York Review of Books*, twice in the *Columbia Spectator*, and several times in the *Daily Tarheel* in Chapel Hill, North Carolina and the *Maine Times*.

Some women were referred to me by friends or acquaintances. Three women were referred by their psychiatrists or psychologists. I called one psychologist to thank him and, curious since he did not know me beyond my ad, asked what had prompted him. He replied that he hoped it would be of help to his patient to share her experience this way. I hope it did help. I think it did.

Some men with serious intentions also responded. Their stories ranged from the idyllic (the highly romantic and sensual initiation of an eighteen-year-old boy by his stunningly intelligent mother as he went off to college) to the paraphernaliac—a multigenerational inheritance through grandmother to mother and now to the son—of enema trauma (not at all unique, evidently; there's an enema society in California with 1,500 members). It was my decision that their stories were not within the scope of this book. The women's stories had the ring of the common. The men's seemed more extraordinary. I don't know, no one does know, how many women sexually abuse, have abused, their sons and daughters. If, as has been suggested, some men sexually abuse their daughters out of a sense of impotence that permeates the rest of their lives ("I can understand it," one man said to me. "If everything else in my life were shitty, if I were a failure on the job, if my wife saw me for the ineffectual bastard I was, who else would see me as the power- ful person I wanted to be other than my eight-year-old daugh- ter?") then it certainly stands to reason that a certain number of women, powerless along all other avenues, might abuse their parental power too. But, if we can continue to use reason without hard facts for another moment, it also stands to reason that more women, *even though powerless and desperately frustrated,* would experience a strong and constant involvement with the child-as- child, would have a strong sense of the child as a developing per- son rather than an object, would have a far stronger sense of themselves as parent. And the latter is a tremendously incest- inhibiting factor.

Consistent with the newly spoken-of fact that sexual abuse oc- curs at every level of society, the 183 women I talked with were from all classes, all races, all parts of the country. The majority of those who speak in this book seemed to me the most, or most ar- ticulately, representative of the variety of the impact-effects of sexual abuse *where some innate inner balance is present in the person.*

It was, for the most part, survivors that selected themselves out—by their ability to be clearer in talking and in relating the specific effects of the sexual abuse on their lives. Obviously, a great deal else has happened to each of us to help make us who we are.

I do concede some bias against playing into that need for melodrama, for "victims," which I sense in the world. With the exception of Carla all the women are white; for the most part they are people I felt the majority of readers might think of themselves as working next to, shopping alongside of, living in the neighbor- hood of (and ending sentences with prepositions with). They are not, in the main, what society would cast out as losers, for I quickly learned that most people have no difficulty believing that sexual abuse happens among the dimwitted, the poor, the morally obtuse, the overcrowded. Or that it has been inflicted on drug addicts, prostitutes, runaways, or the suicide prone. And the more I talked with people, the more I sensed a curious inflection: The innuendo I heard seemed to suggest that the fact that a woman is a prostitute somehow explains the sexual abuse, rather than the other way around. "Oh well, you know, a lot of *them* had incest."

Story.

A friend of mine recently went to the beauty parlor in her New York apartment-house building to have a manicure. Several of the women there had seen an incest program on television and were talking about it.

"Well, but you know," said one, "none of those women was from New York."

"Oh, no!" said another. "None of them was from New York."

There was a ruminative silence. Then:

"But," said a third, "you know? I hear there are a lot of *them* in New Jersey."

Melodrama is a definite pitfall for this subject. Already we have walking, talking incest victims silhouetted on our TV screens, their voices distorted, being asked whether they feel they were *scarred forever*. Making sexual abuse seem unearthly; making those of us who've experienced it seem "passed over," as though we were speaking to you from the other side. Or as though we were somehow doomed to a permanent lachrymose state. It is odd, this—that we are prone to look for retribution against the object of the broken "taboo," rather than looking for that retribution against the offender.

Eleanor did not want to be known as a victim. Neither would Frances or Maggie or Barbara or Jenny. Neither do I. Better, I think, to speak of the fathers as victims—of their own sexuality, their promiscuity with power. We were only incest objects. Chipped, maybe. Or chipped and mended. But still with value and integrity.

In some cases, too, selection was dictated by the fact that I was in no way equipped to, or inclined to, push where I sensed deep and threatening wounds. Several times women said they felt they had to cut out in mid-conversation—with apologies. "I'm sorry. I thought I could talk, but I guess I'm not ready. I can't." Tears. Several times, I cut out—I could feel too much sludge stirring.

And some stories seemed too damn much.

What is our commonality? First and foremost, that sharp sense of betrayal of trust, a *kind* of trust we can now never have. Certainly, some of us learn to trust again, but only appropriately, only in present reality. We have grown up (damn it). We will never have a loving, care-taking father. In an otherwise tantalizing article about the glories of *consensual* incest (which includes the tale of a son who crawled into his mother's bed for the first time when he was past fifty) I liked a statement by Willard Gaylin, a psychiatrist at Columbia Medical School as well as president of the Hastings Center, Institute of Society Ethics, and the Life Sciences. He said, "After all, a child will have plenty of intercourse in life, but he or she is going to have only one crack at a caring parent."*

Also, many women shared a sense of the loss of *both* parents. While it's true that many of the women I spoke to were angrier at their mothers than at their fathers, I feel that the very violence of our reactions against our mothers, our greater fury with them, shows not how much at fault they were, but rather how much *more* we needed from them, how much more we were conditioned to expect. *She must know* is the assumption a six-year-old makes, taking a screaming fall off her trike around the block. *She* knows everything. Where is she? Why doesn't she come?

What are the patterns of incest families? I have listened at length to many, many professionals struggling with this one, and I've struggled with it myself. I think the answer, mine, is not reassuring. I think the difference between millions of unhappy family units where sexual abuse takes place and millions of unhappy family units where sexual abuse does not take place is that in the former families the father commits abuse. Why does he do it? The abusive father must have a sense of paternalistic prerogative in order to even begin to rationalize what he's doing: playing doctor with his own kid. Weak or authoritarian in nature, he must have a perception of his children as possessions, as *ob-*

---

*Quoted in "Incest, the Last Taboo," *Penthouse*, December 1977.

jects. He must see his children as there to meet his needs—rather than the other way around. Sometimes there's a strong injunction against going outside the home for sex, but not always. Sometimes the marriage is sexually dysfunctional—but not always. "And anyway," said Lucy Berliner, "Masters and Johnson indicated that 50 percent of the marriages in this country are sexually dysfunctional. Does that mean that 50 percent of the families are incest families?"

"You have stopped being a wife and become a mother," my father used to say to my mother. Often, in listening, I heard that echo in the background of women's stories. The man stops seeing himself as a parent, and sees himself, instead, as an older child in the family. "Let's do this mischief and let's don't tell mommy."

In a paper entitled "The Family Constellation and Overt Incestuous Relations Between Father and Daughter" we find: "Incest usually began when the father and daughter felt the mother had abandoned them either by giving birth to a new *sibling* [italics mine], turning to the maternal grandmother, or developing some new interest outside the home." * Mother, it would seem, is everybody's mother. (In which case, psychologically, would all incest be sibling incest?)

From a paper entitled "Psychodynamics of Father Daughter Incest":

> What characterizes the incestuous father is that while fully exploiting his position as the authoritarian head of the home, he also acts in many ways like a caricature of an adolescent. Whether he uses threats, force, or blackmail, or offers rewards and bribes to gain his daughter, he behaves not so much as a grown man wooing a woman, but rather a maladroit adolescent attempting to win a young girl in his first love affair. The conduct of the incestuous father also resembles sexual play between brother and sister. He is like an older brother who forces his little sister to misbehave, threatens her with punishment if she tells the mother, and at the same time blackmails her by saying that if she complains

*I. Kaufman, M.D., Alice L. Peck, M.S.W., and C. K. Tagiuri, M.D., "The Family Constellation and Overt Incestuous Relations Between Father and Daughter," pp. 266–279.

about him, or the mother finds out, she, too, will be punished for wrongdoing. Mother will also be angry with her.

After incest has been discovered, there is almost invariably an invasion of deep guilt and remorse *about the wife* [italics mine]. It results from the realization of having injured her and substituted another in her place, with irreparable damage to the relationship, and a resulting anxiety that he can never return to his wife, and as a consequence may lose his family. There is a great need to be forgiven, *as if he were a child who must be reconciled to his mother* [italics mine].*

The very best solution to incest, it seems obvious to me, is prevention. And the main focus of incest prevention must be the father. Against my usual disinclination to categories that quickly render real human motives meaningless, I admire the progression of categories or levels of sexual involvement described by Dr. Roland Summit and JoAnn Kryso in their paper "Sexual Abuse of Children: A Clinical Spectrum."

The first they offer is "Incidental Sexual Contact" (a controlled and self-limiting coping with erotic attraction or dependency needs toward their children).

Second, they cite "Ideological Sexual Contact"—"a situation where parents may encourage specifically sexual activity in the belief that increased sexual expression is beneficial for the child."

The third they call "Psychotic Intrusion"—"a situation where the adult has a psychotic level of confusion in reality testing and object choice, or where personal sexual impulses are projected to some kind of outside influence. The children become the object of a psychotic system."

Fourth, they cite "Rustic Environment"—which "depends on a cultural background where the taboos are markedly relaxed."

Fifth, they call "True Endogamous Incest"—which "develops as a surprisingly subtle distortion of normal relationships. Impulse control is decreased, ultimately, but the offenders are individuals who aren't notably impulsive and who may be quite well adjusted and quite well-functioning within other areas of their

*B. M. Cormier, M.D., M. Kennedy, and J. Sangowicz, M.D., "Psychodynamics of Father Daughter Incest," pp. 203–217.

lives. The breakdown occurs only when extraordinarily strong attractions develop as an outgrowth of role disturbances within the family, often limited to a specific point in time."

Sixth, they cite "Misogynous Incest"—"a variation of endogamous dynamics in which fear and hatred of women are relatively predominant."

Seventh, they call "Imperious Incest"—"a brittle fusion of elements from the ideological, rustic, and misogynous categories. These men set themselves up as emperors in their household domain."

Then, "Pedophilic Incest"—"Men especially have the proclivity to retreat from castration fears and discomfort with peer relationships in search of a sex object they consider more innocent and less threatening."

"Child Rape" follows—"The child rapist confuses masculinity with power and can feel sexually adequate only by frightening and overpowering his victims."

They then list what they call "Perverse Incest" or "Pornographic Incest"—"in the absence of any better superlatives to describe kinky, unfettered lechery. These cases become more bizarre, more frankly erotic, more flagrantly manipulative and destructive than those in earlier categories. Many of them have a kind of self-conscious, sex-scene quality in which the individual seems to be trying to set up rituals to fulfill a variety of forbidden fantasies. . . .

"This group is called pornographic because of an apparent need to go beyond limits of socially acceptable sexual practice to explore whatever is most forbidden. Furthermore, the participants may want to record their achievements and to see themselves putting the fantasies into action: diaries, secret confessions and Polaroid photographs seem to heighten their excitement. . . .

"Previous categories involved predominantly one-to-one relationships, however disturbed or transient they might be. Multiple partners are more the rule here. . . . There may be organizing and advertising, as with a Los Angeles group organized for the advancement of incest. . . .

"Here the activity with children is contrived to gratify perverse needs and the rationalization evolves as a denial of guilt. Here the child is an accessory of the adult. Rather than preparing a child for eventual adult sexuality, the child is drafted and trained to enact lurid parodies of adult sexual function. . . ."*

As was the case, of course, with Annabelle.

When I spoke with Dr. Summit, he described several cases of pornographic incest that he had encountered. And he expressed the hope that it was, nationally, relatively rare. I certainly hope so too.

It seems apparent, both by its incidence and by the noticeable absence of any sincere, widespread dread of retribution, that incest is not truly a taboo. Just a very, very long-lived, well-suppressed secret. The most reassuring thought I have is that, as long as society refuses to sanction it, breaking open the secret may very well break down the incidence.

Generation after generation, women have learned that you don't say things like that. You don't talk about things like that. Because *they*, the men that you need now and those you will need in order to survive later, will turn against you. Will call you liar first and, if that doesn't work, whore. Will make you an outcast. Convenient. A learned and continued cover-up for a collective unconscious conspiracy that has permitted sexual abuse to continue as a mute, "just-don't-get-caught," patriarchal prerogative for century after century.

Incest programs are rapidly being developed across the country (a list of the main programs is appended). As the subject continues to surface, no doubt there'll be many more. The goal of most new programs is, wherever possible, to keep the family intact. Given the mess that jail/foster care/stigma/welfare can be, given the havoc incest-discovery creates, I can't really quarrel with that goal just so long as the primary concern is that the girl is protected *not just through the treatment program but into the future.* I was told of one family that had been through a program; they then moved out of the state. The abuse resumed. The girl's sister reported it. But the girl herself refused to talk with the social worker. She'd been that route, been through all the emotional family uproar. She'd had that line. She didn't trust it, wouldn't buy it, a second time. And who can blame her.

Some percentage of failure, in any program, is inevitable

*R. Summit, M.D., and J. Kryso, M.S.W., "Sexual Abuse of Children: A Clinical Spectrum."

Women and men, we're not all nice guys, not all fixable. I just hope that, in their zeal to succeed (and by proving success, get funding), the treatment programs do not evolve into a kind of institutionalized sorry-saying, a kind of cleansing ritual, for the father.

"Why are people so anxious to place the onus on everyone *except* the offender?" Lucy Berliner asked. Why, indeed. In her work she sees mainly middle-class families. About the men, she said, "These guys just don't see they've done anything wrong. They say, 'What's so terrible about it?' The main purpose of treatment at first is to get them to see what they've done as wrong. It's different from the battering parent. The battering parent feels guilty."

Other social workers suggest that the men do feel guilty. It would seem to me, though, that even where guilt is expressed, the guy, on the carpet, knows very well that this is what's expected of him. "I strayed and I'm sorry, forgive me," is well within the male/female tradition. That guy knows that saying he felt guilty is the path to the Band-Aids: to understanding and forgiveness.

The fathers of the women in this book that did not get caught certainly showed no signs of guilt. And Sandy's father? Who did get caught? He said, "I know that didn't have any effect on you, Sandy. Because if it had, Sandy, you'd be deathly afraid of men."

I hope that great care and thought is given to telling the mothers the ways in which what happened was *not* their fault as well. *All* wives and mothers have received a binding double message. As wives, we have been told our primary responsibility is to support our husband. To stick with him, to endorse his behavior, his decisions, through thick and thin. As mothers, we have been told our primary responsibility is to support our children. Can we blame women who, in crisis, are unable to decode this double message?

There are additional reasons to use care in formulating attitudes toward the mothers (not the least of which would seem to be that they are not exactly going to come running forward for help if they know what they can expect is blame).

One mother I spoke with who'd been, with her family, through an incest program, told me (as she'd learned it) that it was her *job* that had been the problem. She'd had to travel, had to be away sometimes. Now she had given up that job.

Murder. We can't do that. We can't tell women that while it's good to be strong, to be assertive, to have careers as well as families (and we obviously can't tell women who *have* to work)—doing so makes them responsible for incest. That, really, if mother is out of the house, the oldest child in her family is going to get into mischief with her daughter.

If men are *expected* to be children, women should *adopt* them, not marry them.

Another reason.

Adrienne Rich writes:

> Many daughters live in rage at their mothers for having accepted too readily and passively "whatever comes." A mother's victimization does not merely humiliate her, it mutilates the daughter who is watching her for clues as to what it means to be a woman. Like the traditional foot-bound Chinese woman, she passes on her own affliction. The mother's self-hatred and low expectations are the binding-rags for the psyche of the daughter. As one psychologist has observed:
>
> "When a female child is passed from lap to lap so that all the males in the room (father, brother, acquaintances) can get a hard-on, it is the helpless mother standing there and looking on that creates the sense of shame and guilt in the child. One woman at the recent rape conference in New York City testified that her father put a series of watermelon rinds in her vagina when she was a child to open it up to his liking, and beat her if she tried to remove them. Yet what that woman focuses her rage on today is that her mother told her, 'Never say a word about it to anyone.' "*

If a mother is perceived as acquiescing to guilt where the father has been sexually abusive, two things, it would seem, might happen. Either the child will be confirmed in her notion that mother is indeed responsible for all things. Or the child will see her as willing to accept any blame in order to keep the family together. In which case the child may very well feel rage at her mother for what she sees as a real and continuing guilt: helplessness. That

*Of Woman Born, pp. 246–247.

child, then, is getting a definite and scary message about her own future as woman/wife/mother. She may very well angrily reject it and prefer to identify with the aggressor.

Perhaps rather than looking for patterns of incest families, it might be more profitable ultimately to look for patterns of nonincest families. To look to clues for prevention.

Incest can only happen in secret. If parents, preferably *both* parents, sit down with a child at the age of four or five or whenever they tell her about not getting into cars with strangers and so forth—and at the same time tell the child that no one has a right to touch her in certain ways, *not even if it's someone she knows and loves*—that child is being given a power she needs.

And if parents intrude when anyone—grandfather, uncle, cousin, family friend—touches a child, handles a child, in any way that the child objects to, that child is getting another message she needs: Her body belongs to her. She's allowed to say no. She's permitted to object. She's effective. She's in control.

This book's hoped-for place is as a human document, a bridge to understanding. Other books will be done, are no doubt now being done, that will be more informed by the traditional methodologies: by samplings, charts, graphs, pieces of pie. To make real the life experiences that are the meaning behind *victims* of *sexual molestation* (or *inappropriate behavior*) by *male caretakers* was my goal. To define incest in people's minds as sexual abuse of children (in defiance of attempts to murk it up by including fifty-year-old men and their mothers). To attempt to rescue the subject from both hysteria and denial.

A great deal of the background work I did for the book—the reading and speaking with authorities and experts—has deliberately been left out. It got in the way of that goal.

I have been warned many times of the things I will be accused of in doing the book, and in doing it as I have—personally, without distance, and with minimum reliance on expert interpretation.

"They will examine your pathology."

Really? Free? And all these years I've been paying for it.

"You'll be accused of being flip. Why, for instance, do you insist on 'diddling?' "

Well. Consider *fondling.* That's not what happened to Maggie. Consider *molesting.* That's not what happened to Frances. Consider *seducing*. That's not what happened to Wendy, to Sandy. *Diddling* connotes an act that is gratuitous, unnecessary. And repeated sexual abuse of a child by a needed and trusted parent or stepparent is the most purely gratuitous form of abuse there is. It requires thought. It does not arise out of anything as uncontrollable as rage (or else a man with an erection is in a socially menacing pathological state). It does not stem from physical addiction. Rather, it arises out of an assumed prerogative, superstructured with rationale, protected by traditions of silence, and, even more than in rape, an assurance of the object's continuing fear, shame, powerlessness and, therefore, silent acquiescence.

Will I be taken seriously?

I can only hope so. The women in this book are saying important and serious things. I believe we are raising serious questions. I hope they will lead to further serious discussion.

Wendy sent me her graduation picture. Maggie has a new job she likes. Barbara is sounding much sturdier. Jenny is out on her own, happily involved in her college routine. I cannot ever thank enough all the women who spoke with me and helped me realize this book.

Appendix

It is a sign of how far we have yet to go in the area of sexual abuse that most of the social workers I have talked with around the country suggested that a mother seeking help first make a phone call to a local child protective services agency or a family counseling center—*without giving her name*—and find out as completely as possible how the incest situation would be dealt with. Find out what the law is in that particular state. What is the most frequent disposition? (Is the father often arrested? Is the daughter often removed? If so, is it only temporary?) What factors affect the disposition? (For example, if the mother is willing to do everything in her power to support and protect her child, will that give her greater control of the outcome?) What measures can be taken to insure confidentiality? What are the next steps to take?

Laws do vary from state to state. In all but eight states certain people—doctors, social workers, nurses, psychologists, among others—are required to report the abuse. In most cases, these reports must be made to the department of social services. In other cases, like Maryland, the report can be made either to the department of social services or the police. In some states, like California, it is mandatory that the report be made to the police.

Nationwide, social service efforts are mainly to help the family and to keep it intact *wherever possible*. However, in different areas, the attitudes of individual case workers (and police departments) are different.

Rape crisis centers and shelters, as well as local Parents Anonymous groups are also good places to seek information. Hot lines particularly allow you initial anonymity.

FACILITIES WITH INCEST TREATMENT PROGRAMS

ARIZONA
Tucson Center for Women and Children
419 South Stone Avenue, Tucson, 85701
(602) 792-1929

Center Against Sexual Assault
137 West McDowell Road, Phoenix, 85003
(602) 257-8095

ARKANSAS
Ms. Sharon Pallone
S.C.A.N. (Suspected Child Abuse and Neglect)
Hendrix Hall
4313 West Markham, Little Rock, 72201
(501) 371-2777

(S.C.A.N. services are mainly for sexually abused children under twelve years of age and their families, but they will offer referrals.)

There are S.C.A.N. services available in eleven counties in Arkansas, all listed in local directories.

CALIFORNIA
Henry Giarretto, Director
Child Sexual Abuse Treatment Program/Parents United
840 Guadelupe Parkway, San Jose, 95110
(408) 299-2475

COLORADO
Robert Schrant
National Center for Prevention and Treatment of Child Abuse
1205 Oneida Street, Denver, 80220
(303) 321-3963

CONNECTICUT
Ms. Norma Toteh, Director
Suzanne Sgroi, M.D.
Sexual Trauma Treatment Pilot Program
94 Branford Street, Hartford, 06112
(203) 566–3040

DISTRICT OF COLUMBIA
Children's Hospital National Medical Center, Child Protection Center
111 Michigan Avenue, N.W., Washington, 20010
(202) 745–4100

FLORIDA
Dr. Dorothy Hicks, Director
The Rape Treatment Center, Jackson Memorial Hospital
1700 N.W. Tenth Avenue, Miami, 33136
(305) 225–7273

GEORGIA
Rape Crisis Center, Grady Memorial Hospital
80 Butler Street, S.E., Atlanta, 30303
(404) 659–7273

IOWA
Department of Pediatrics
or Adolescent Clinic University Hospital, Iowa City, 52242
(319) 356–1616

MICHIGAN
Bennie Stovall, Coordinator
Child Sexual Abuse Division, Children's Aid Society
71 West Warren Street, Detroit, 48201
(313) 831–3300

MINNESOTA
Deborah Anderson, Coordinator
Sexual Assault Services, Hennepin County Attorney's Office
2000 C Government Center, Minneapolis, 55487
(612) 348–5397

Child Adolescent Services
Ramsey County Mental Health Center
529 Jackson Street, St. Paul, 55101
(612) 298-5681

Child Protection Intake Unit, Ramsey County Welfare Department
160 E. Kellogg Boulevard, St. Paul, 55101
(612) 298-5655

Face to Face Health and Counseling Service
730 Mendota, St. Paul, 55106
(612) 772-2557

(primarily for adolescents and their mothers and young adults)

Sexual Abuse Counseling Team, Wilder Child Guidance Clinic
919 Lafond Avenue, St. Paul, 55104
(612) 645-6661

NEW JERSEY
Mary Wells, Codirector
Family Service of Burlington County, Meadow Health Center
Woodlane Road, Mount Holly, 08060
(609) 267-5928

NEW MEXICO
Family Resource Center
8016 Zuni S.E., Albuquerque, 87108
(505) 262-1911

NEW YORK
Brooklyn Society for the Prevention
of Cruelty to Children
P.O. Box 423
Times Plaza Station
Brooklyn 11217
(212) 875-7600

James Walsh, Director
Victims' Information Bureau of Suffolk (VIBS)
501 Route 111, Hauppague, 11787
(516) 360-3606

Diane Meier-Erne Alliance
1654 West Onondaga Street, Syracuse, 13204
(315) 424–1880

OHIO
Rape Prevention Program
Consultation and Education Department
Columbus Area Community Mental Health Center
1515 East Broad Street
Columbus, 43205
(614) 252–0711

Community Relations Department
Franklin County Children Services
1951 Gantz Road, Grove City, 43123
(614) 276–9061

OKLAHOMA
C. Eugene Walker, Ph.D., Director
Pediatric Psychology Service, Oklahoma Children Memorial Hospital
Box 26901
900 N.E. 13th, Oklahoma City, 73104
(405) 271-4415

Parents Assistance Center
2720 Classen Boulevard, Oklahoma City, 73106
24-hour, 7-day-a-week hotline: (405) 525-7339

At-Risk Parent-Child Program
Hillcrest Medical Center and the University of
Oklahoma College of Medicine
Utica on the Park, Tulsa, 74104
(918) 584-1351

PENNSYLVANIA
Maddi-Jane Stern, Director of Social Services
Center for Rape Concern
112 South 16th Street, Philadelpia, 19102
(215) 568–6627

TENNESSEE
Child and Family Service
114 Dameron Avenue
Knoxville, 37917
(615) 524-7483

(This is a demonstration project. There is a sex abuse teletape message and help line for adolescents as well.)(615) 573-2222

TEXAS
Sherry Tayne, Project Director
Project S.E.Y. (Sexually Exploited Youth)
510 S. Congress, Suite 312
Austin, 78704
(512) 476-6015

24-hour Austin hotline: 512-472-2411

WASHINGTON
Lucy Berliner
Sexual Assault Center
Harborview Medical Center
Seattle, 98104
(206) 223-3047

Peter Coleman, Coordinator
Child Protective Services Incest Program
Department of Social and Health Services
1301 Tacoma Avenue South, Tacoma, 98402
(206) 223-3000

Bibliography

American Humane Association. *National Study on Child Neglect and Abuse Reporting, Highlight of 1974 and 1975 Data.* American Humane Association, Childrens Division, Denver.

Armstrong, L. "The Crime Nobody Talks About." *Woman's Day,* March 1978.

Bender, L., and Blau, A. "The Reaction of Children to Sexual Relations with Adults." *American Journal of Orthopsychiatry* 7 (1937):500–518.

Benward, J., and Densen-Gerber, J. *Incest as a Causative Factor in Anti-Social Behavior: An Exploratory Study.* New York: Odyssey Institute, 1975.

Breuer, J., and Freud, S. "Studies on Hysteria (1893–1895)." *The Complete Works of Sigmund Freud,* Vol. II. Edited by J. Strachey. London: Hogarth Press, 1955.

Browning, D., and Boatman, B. "Incest: Children at Risk." *American Journal of Psychiatry* 134 (1977) 1:69–72.

Center for Women's Policy Studies, *Response to Intrafamily Violence and Sexual Assault.* (All issues have information of ongoing interest.)

Connell, N., and Wilson, C., eds. *Rape: The First Sourcebook for Women.* New York: New American Library, 1974.

Cormier, B. M., M.D., Kennedy, M., and Sangowicz, J., M.D. "Psychodynamics of Father Daughter Incest." *Canadian Psychiatric Association Journal* 7 (1962):203–217.

Corpus Juris Secundum. "Incest." American Law Book and West Publishing Company 42 (1977):503–519.

Cory, D., and Masters, R. E. L. *Violation of Taboo: Incest in the Great Literature of the Past and Present.* New York: Julian Press, 1963.

DeFrancis, V. *Child Abuse Legislation in the 1970's.* American Humane Association, Childrens Division (1970), Denver.

Durkheim, E. *Incest: The Nature and Origin of the Taboo.* Translated by Edward Sagarin. New York: Lyle Stuart, 1963.

Ellis, A. *The Origins and the Development of the Incest Taboo.* New York: Lyle Stuart, 1963.

Finkelhor, D. *Psychological, Structural and Cultural Factors in Incest and Family Sexual Abuse.* Master's thesis, University of New Hampshire. Unpublished.

Freud, S. *The Complete Works of Sigmund Freud,* Vol. III. Edited by J. Strachey. London: Hogarth Press, 1955.

Freud, S. *The Origins of Psychoanalysis; Letters to Wilhelm Fleiss, Drafts and Notes, 1887–1902.* Edited by Marie Bonaparte, Anna Freud, and Ernst Kris. Translated by Eric Mosbacher and James Strachey. New York: Basic Books, 1954.

Gebhard, P., et. al. *Sex Offenders: An Analysis of Types.* New York: Harper and Row, 1965.

Giaretto, H. "In His Own Words." *People.* May 1977.

Greene, N. "A View of Family Pathology Involving Child Molest From a Juvenile Probation Perspective." *Juvenile Justice.* February 1977, pp. 29–34.

Helfer, R., and Kempe, C. eds. *Child Abuse and Neglect: The Family and the Community.* Cambridge, Mass.: Ballinger Publishing, 1976.

Helfer, R., and Kempe, C. eds. *The Battered Child,* 2nd ed. Chicago: University of Chicago Press, 1974.

Henderson, D. "Incest: A Synthesis of Data." *Canadian Psychiatric Association Journal* 17 (1972):299–313.

Herman, J. and Hirshman, L. "Father-Daughter Incest: A Feminist Theoretical Perspective." *Signs, Journal of Women in Culture and Society,* June 1977.

Herman, J., and Hirshman, L. "Sexual Abuse of Children." *Sister Courage,* May 1976.

Hunt, M. *Sexual Behavior in the 1970's.* Chicago: Playboy Press, 1974.

Kahn, M. *The Privacy of the Self: Papers on Psychoanalytic Theory and Technique.* New York: International Universities Press, 1974.

Kaufman, I., M.D., Peck, Alice L., M.S.W., and Tagiuri, C. K., M.D. "The Family Constellation and Overt Incestuous Relations Between

Father and Daughter." *American Journal of Orthopsychiatry* 24 (1954):266–279.

Maisch, H. *Incest.* Translated by Colin Bearne. New York: Stein and Day, 1972.

Mano, D. "Incest." *Oui,* December 1975.

Masters, R. E. L. *Patterns of Incest,* New York: Julian Press, 1963.

Masters W., and Johnson, V. "Incest: The Ultimate Sexual Taboo." *Redbook,* April 1976.

Mead, M. "Incest." *International Encyclopedia of the Social Sciences.* New York: Crowell, Collier and Macmillan, 1968.

Miles, H. *Forbidden Fruit: A Study of the Incest Theme in Erotic Literature.* London: Luxor Press, 1973.

Nobile, P. "Incest, the Last Taboo." *Penthouse,* December 1977.

Peters, J. J. "Children Who Are Victims of Sexual Assault and the Psychology of Offenders." *American Journal of Psychotherapy* 30 (1976) 3:398–421.

Peters, J. J., et. al. *Social and Psychiatric Data on Philadelphia Rape Victims (April–October 1973).* Center for Rape Concern, Philadelphia, 1975.

Pittman, F. "Counseling Incestuous Families." *Medical Aspects of Human Sexuality.* April 1976, pp. 57–58.

Pomeroy, W. "A New Look at Incest." *Forum.* November 1976.

Ramsey, J. "My Husband Broke the Ultimate Taboo." *Family Circle.* March 1977.

Renshaw, D. C. "Healing the Incest Wound." *Sexual Medicine Today.* October 1977.

Rich, A. *Of Woman Born, Motherhood as Experience and Institution,* New York: Bantam Books, 1977.

Saline, C. "The Family Secret." *Philadelphia,* August 1977.

Sgroi, S. M. "Sexual Molestation of Children, the Last Frontier of Child Abuse." *Children Today,* May/June 1975.

Shengold, L. "The Effects of Overstimulation: Rat People." *International Journal of Psychoanalysis* 48 (1967) 3:403–415.

Shengold, L. "More About Rats and Rat People." *International Journal of Psychoanalysis* 52 (1971) 3:277–288.

Shengold, L. "The Parents as Sphinx." *Journal of the American Psychoanalytic Association* 11 (1963) 4:725–751.

Sloane, P., and Karpinski, E. "Effect of Incest on the Participants." *American Journal of Orthopsychiatry* 12 (1942):666–673.

Strouse, J., ed. *Women and Analysis: Dialogues on Psychoanalytic Views of Femininity.* New York: Grossman Publishers, 1974.

Summit, R., M.D., and Kryso, J., M. S. W. "Sexual Abuse of Children: A

Clinical Spectrum." *American Journal of Orthopsychiatry.* Scheduled to appear in April 1978.

Swanson D. "Adult Sexual Abuse of Children (The Man and Circumstances)." *Diseases of the Nervous System.* October, 1968, pp. 677–683.

Weber, E. "Sexual Abuse Begins At Home." *Ms*, April 1977.

Weeks, R. "Counseling Parents of Sexually Abused Children." *Medical Aspects of Human Sexuality*, August 1976.

Weiner, I. "Father-Daughter Incest: A Clinical Report." *Psychiatric Quarterly* 36 (1962):1132–1138.

Yorukoglu, A., and Kemph, J. P. "Children Not Severely Damaged by Incest with a Parent." *Journal of the American Academy of Child Psychiatry* 5 (1966) 1:111–124.

Index